MW01234886

Foreword by

JAMES ADAM RICHLIANO

## How to Access the Lyrics on the CD

In addition to the 12 guitar instrumentals, the included disc contains printable PDF lyric sheets for all the songs in the book—perfect for merrymaking! To access these sheets, insert the disc into a computer, double-click on My Computer, right-click on the disc drive icon, and select Explore. (Mac users can simply double-click "The Christmas Songbook" disc icon that appears on the desktop.) The lyric sheets are located in the **"Lyrics"** folder, and can be printed on your computer's printer directly from the CD.

Produced by
Alfred Music
P.O. Box 10003
Van Nuys, CA 91410-0003
**alfred.com**

Printed in USA.



ISBN-10: 1-4706-1491-X (Book & CD)
ISBN-13: 978-1-4706-1491-1 (Book & CD)

Cover image from the Popular Graphic Arts collection, Prints & Photographs Online Catalog, Library of Congress, LC-DIG-pga-01599

Solo Arrangements: "Angels We Have Heard on High," "Away in a Manger," "Deck the Halls," "Joy to the World/It Came Upon a Midnight Clear," and "Silent Night" arranged and performed by Craig Dobbins.

"The First Noel," "O Come, All Ye Faithful (Adeste Fideles)," "O Holy Night," "We Three Kings of Orient Are/God Rest Ye Merry, Gentlemen," and "What Child Is This?" arranged and performed by Vincent Carrola.

"Jesu, Joy of Man's Desiring" and "Ukrainian Carol (Carol of the Bells)" arranged and performed by Aaron Stang.

# FOREWORD

*For hundreds of years* Christmas music has continuously inspired, healed, and united our hearts and voices in a way that no other musical genre can do, and the songs that have been chosen for this glorious and eclectic holiday songbook are a powerful representation of why the world returns to these cherished evergreens year after year, decade after decade, ad infinitum.

It is absolutely astounding to recognize that "Believe," popularized by Josh Groban and the film *The Polar Express* and included near the beginning of this collection, is one of only a handful of holiday hits written after the year 2000. As with many yuletide standards, its enormous popularity is indelibly linked to the timeless voice that sings it, and to the fact that it is well-written and extremely emotional, poetic, and melodic.

While "Believe" is one of the newest Christmas songs contained within these pages, "What Child Is This?" is almost a thousand years older, and its hauntingly beautiful melody can be traced all the way back to the 16th century. Not only did Shakespeare himself include the song in one of his plays, but Queen Elizabeth is said to have once danced to it when it was known by some as "My Lady Greensleeves." Like all of the songs here, it asks anyone who plays or sings it to consider the wonders of the season, and the endless possibilities and miracles that lie hidden within the depths of the human heart.

Bridged between the two millenniums represented here by "Believe" and "What Child Is This?" are dozens of other delightful sacred and secular songs that are instantly recognizable. Yet, if you are searching for a Christmas song you may never have heard about, this is the songbook for you, as it succeeds in including some lovely and delicious surprises along the way.

Among the newer surprises that you may actually instantly recognize is "Mary, Did You Know?" written by Mark Lowry and Buddy Greene and first recorded by Christian artist Michael English in 1991. The quiet mystery surrounding a poetically profound question contemplated in the song's religious lyrics is expertly conveyed by country superstars Kenny Rogers and Wynonna Judd, whose dynamic duet of it was included in Rogers's 1996 holiday disc *The Gift*. Since then, it has been recorded by many other artists, including Reba McEntire, Mary J. Blige, CeeLo Green, and Clay Aiken, and it looks like it's well on its way to becoming a rare post-modern poetic Christmas standard that dares to address the sacred birth in a way few songs have ever done.

Christian pop music artist Amy Grant, whose career has benefitted enormously from the release of close to a dozen holiday sets beginning in 1983, has herself co-written a song similar to "Mary, Did You Know?" in its stunning and daringly sweeping biblical references. That song, titled "Breath of Heaven (Mary's Song)," is also contained here, and makes a gorgeous companion piece to Lowry and Greene's song—especially for those searching for profound holiday themes that have more to do with favorite things other than Santa Claus, snowflakes, and mail-bound mall-bought brown paper packages tied up with packing tape.

Also, courtesy of Nashville, in the late '90s Janis Ian and Kye Fleming teamed to write the beautiful "Emmanuel," recorded by Janis, Kathy Mattea, and Dean Carter. This lesser-known song just may become one of your favorite things when you sing or play it for the first time.

One would be amiss to not mention the enormous impact Quebec native Celine Dion has had on Christmas music ever since she released 1998's *These Are Special Times*, her first seasonal set sung entirely in English. As you turn the pages here, you will find "Don't Save It All for Christmas Day," a song she co-wrote with pop songwriter Peter Zizzo and Rick Wake.

Some other wonderful secular post-1970 modern choices featured in these pages are Kenny Loggins's "Celebrate Me Home," Joni Mitchell's "River," Jackie DeShannon's, "Put a Little Love in Your Heart" (as performed in the final scene of Bill Murray's holiday film *Scrooged*), and "Christmas Vacation," a nugget written by Cynthia Weil and Barry Mann for the 1989 eponymous movie soundtrack.

While many of us are yearning to encounter newer Christmas songs that we may or may not have played or sung before, this songbook has thankfully given us many older ones, some comfortably familiar and others that are in need of instant discovery.

The Great American Christmas Songbook is alive and well within these pages and is represented by one of the greatest cherished musical evergreens ever written, "The Christmas Song (Chestnuts Roasting on an Open Fire)." Popularized and still very much associated with Nat King Cole, it was released in 1946 and written by Robert Wells along with big-band-era jazz crooner Mel Tormé, in the middle of an extremely hot July day in California, where the pair lived. In June of 1946, the King Cole Trio went into a New York studio to record a simple version of it without strings. Cole's wife, Maria, convinced him to go back into the studio two months later to re-record it with strings, along with a full orchestra, in order to make it more commercial. According to BMI, it has gone on to become the most performed Christmas standard of all time. In addition to "The Christmas Song," there are many other gems here, including "Blue Christmas," "The Little Drummer Boy," "Santa Claus Is Comin' to Town," "I'll Be Home for Christmas," "Have Yourself a Merry Little Christmas," "Jingle Bells," and three songs from the 1964 stop-motion animated children's television special *Rudolph the Red-Nosed Reindeer* written by Christmas songwriting legend Johnny Marks.

Also here are two other songs that Marks wrote, "I Heard the Bells on Christmas Day," and "Rockin' Around the Christmas Tree," a perennial favorite recorded by 13-year-old country crooner Brenda Lee back in 1958. When I interviewed Lee for my own Christmas book, it was clear that she felt the same way everyone else did regarding what the song has meant to people over the years. She stressed that no matter what time of the year it is, she will sing it for her audience and that even though 60 years have gone by, people are still letting her know that Christmas isn't Christmas until they hear her voice singing it.

One of the greatest things about this songbook is that it expertly allows Christmas music to be alive in the moment because it gives all of us the opportunity to sing it with our own voices and perform it with our own hearts in our own present time. Equally amazing is that in this book, you will encounter many older sacred songs that have rarely been recorded and may not have the instant-recognition status of "Silent Night." Among these are "Angels from the Realms of Glory," penned by a Scottish poet in the early 1800s, and "Good Christian Men, Rejoice," an old Latin hymn translated into English by American minister John Mason Neale in 1853. In 1851, Neale translated "O Come, O Come Emmanuel," a second Latin hymn that is also included here. Other less-heard yuletide songs presented here are "The Boar's Head Carol," from the 15th century; "Bring a Torch, Jeannette, Isabella," composed in France in 1553; "Star of the East," written by American composers in the late 1800s and recorded by Judy Garland in 1941; and "Hush, My Babe, Lie Still and Slumber," co-written by English hymnist Isaac Watts, who penned a second sacred song featured here, "Joy to the World."

After all of this, we are given what could be considered a glass of delicious comforting eggnog paired with the icing on our proverbial Christmas fruitcake. And that would be those sacred hymnal gems none of us will ever forget. So familiar are they that they need very little explanation. Some of them located within these pages are from the European sacred canon, which includes "Silent Night," "Angels We Have Heard on High," "God Rest Ye Merry, Gentlemen," "O Holy Night," "The First Noel," and "Hark! The Herald Angels Sing." Represented here as well are songs of the sacred American canon that have had a powerful international impact ever since the first one was written back in the 1800s. Those include "We Three Kings of Orient Are," "It Came Upon the Midnight Clear," the African-American spiritual "Go Tell It on the Mountain," "Away in a Manger," and "O Little Town of Bethlehem," co-written by Episcopalian minister Phillips Brooks, who was inspired to write it during a powerful spiritual awakening he experienced on an 1865 pilgrimage to the Holy Land.

This Christmas songbook will awaken you to the timelessness of all of the songs here, waiting to be performed individually and collectively in a way in which they may never have been performed before. What a deeply profound reminder of how they continue to unite us as one world in song and spirit. As Phillips Brooks so movingly wrote in "O Little Town of Bethlehem," faith certainly does "hold wide the door," and truly, "the dark night wakes, the glory breaks, and Christmas comes once more." It is my hope and wish that all of the songs here will somehow remind you of that glory and beauty.

Merry Christmas always,

James Adam Richliano
Christmas Music Historian

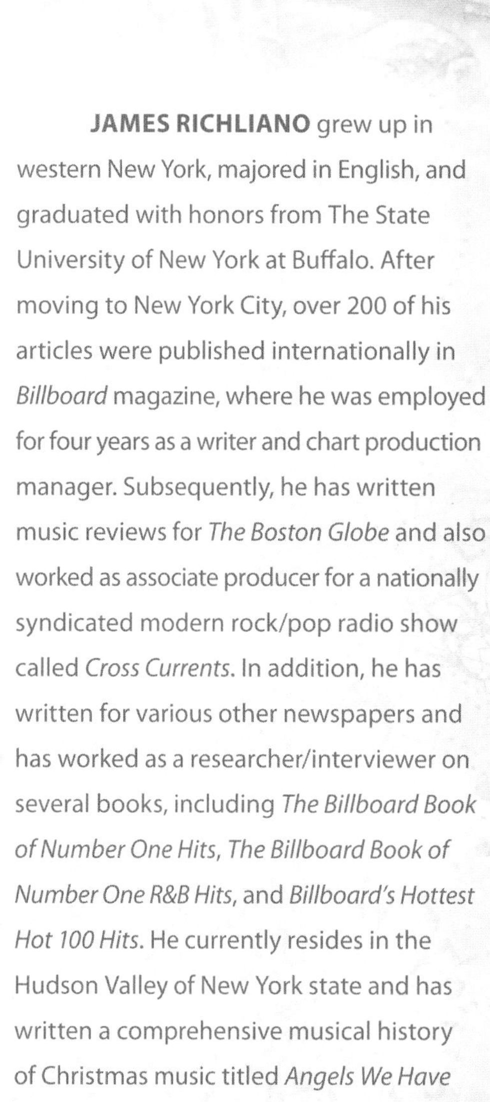

**JAMES RICHLIANO** grew up in western New York, majored in English, and graduated with honors from The State University of New York at Buffalo. After moving to New York City, over 200 of his articles were published internationally in *Billboard* magazine, where he was employed for four years as a writer and chart production manager. Subsequently, he has written music reviews for *The Boston Globe* and also worked as associate producer for a nationally syndicated modern rock/pop radio show called *Cross Currents*. In addition, he has written for various other newspapers and has worked as a researcher/interviewer on several books, including *The Billboard Book of Number One Hits*, *The Billboard Book of Number One R&B Hits*, and *Billboard's Hottest Hot 100 Hits*. He currently resides in the Hudson Valley of New York state and has written a comprehensive musical history of Christmas music titled *Angels We Have Heard: The Christmas Song Stories*.

## CONTENTS

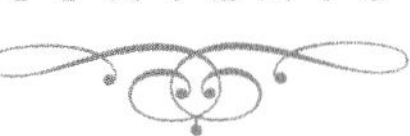

## SOLO GUITAR ARRANGEMENTS

# Angels from the Realms of Glory

Words by
JAMES MONTGOMERY

Music by
HENRY T. SMART

**Brightly**

*Verse:*

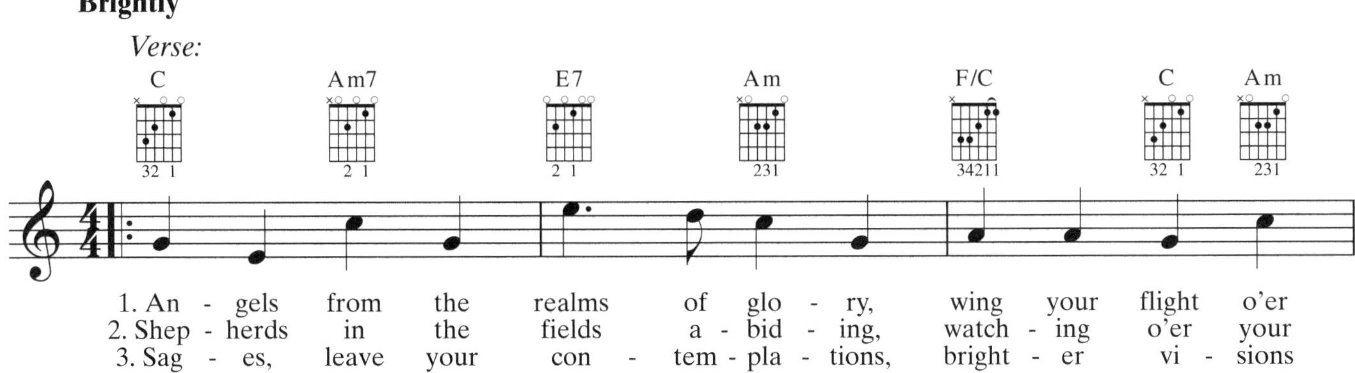


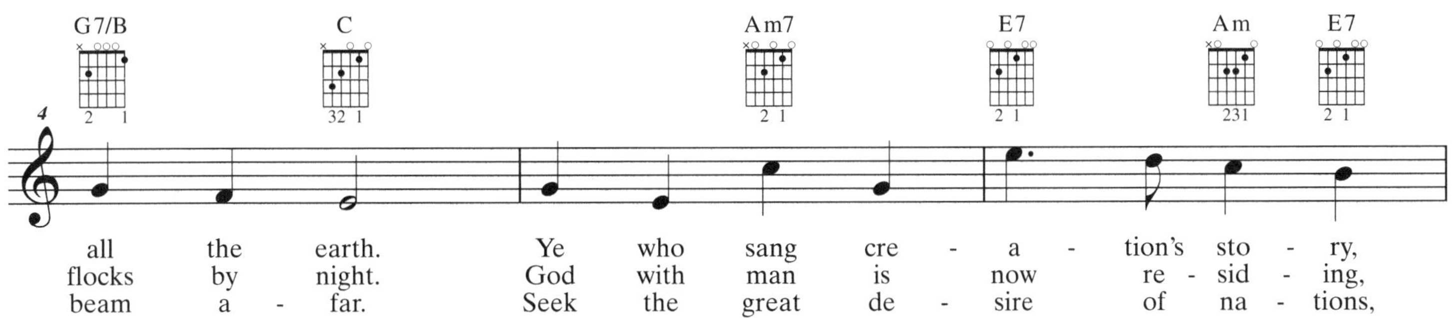


*Chorus:*

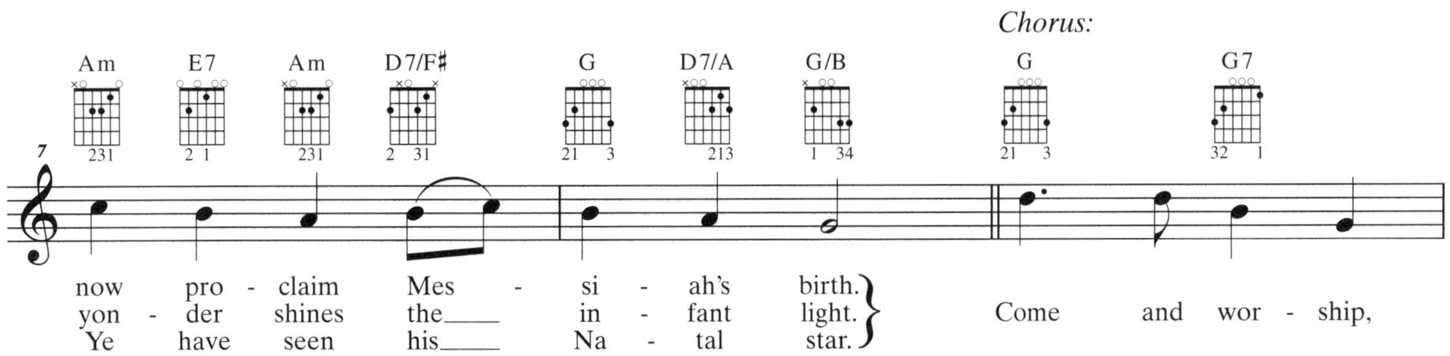


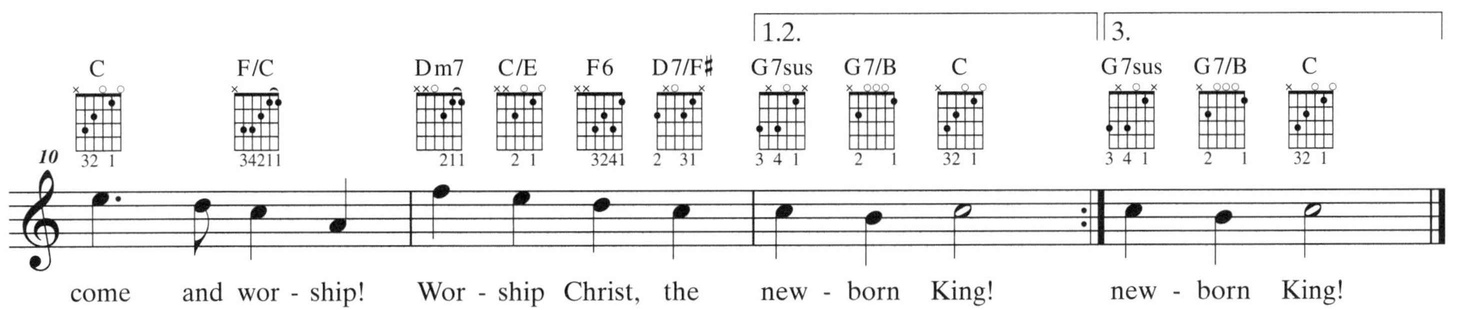

# Angels We Have Heard on High

# As Lately We Watched

Traditional Carol

*Verse 3:*
His throne is a manger, His court is a loft.
But troops of bright angels, in lay, sweet and soft.
Him they proclaim, our Christ by name.
And earth, sky and air, straight are filled with His fame.

*Verse 4:*
Then shepherds, be joyful, salute your liege King.
Let hills and dales ring to the song that ye sing.
Blest be the hour, welcome the morn.
For Christ our dear Savior on earth now is born.

# Auld Lang Syne

Words by
ROBERT BURNS

Traditional Carol

**Moderately**

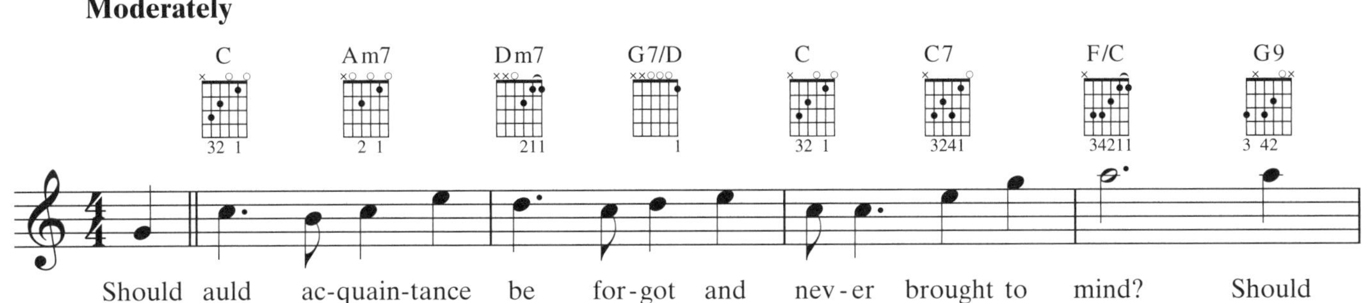


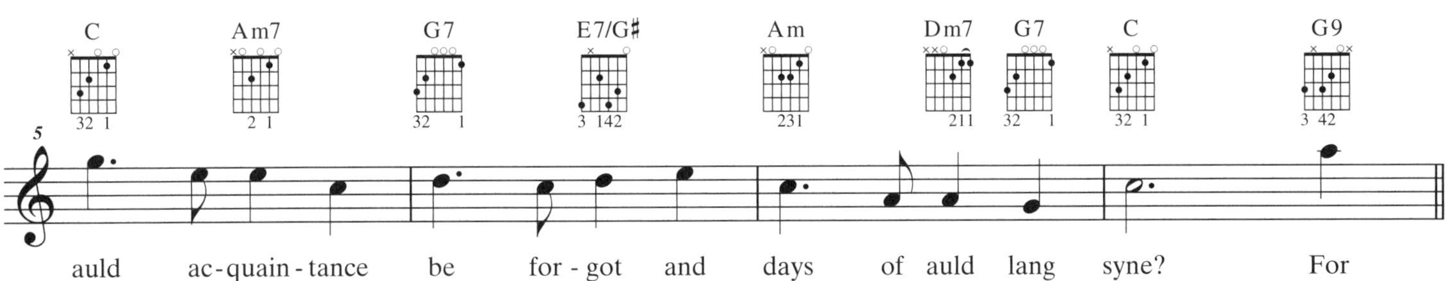


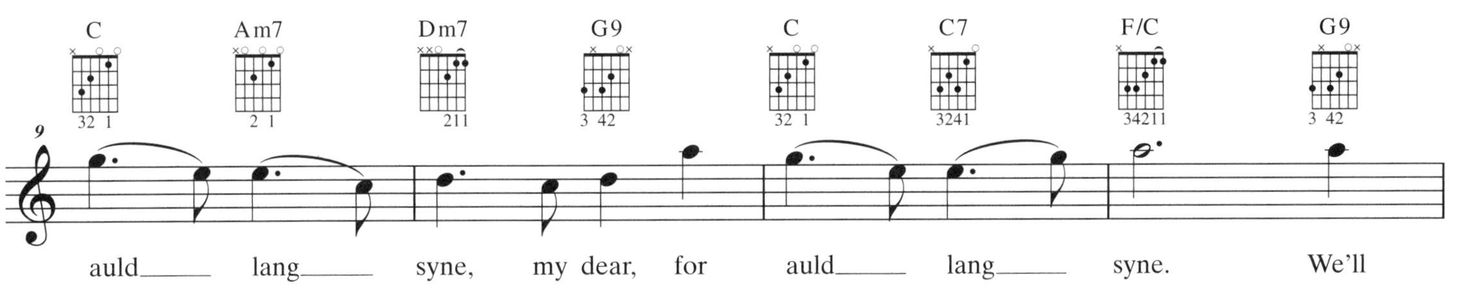


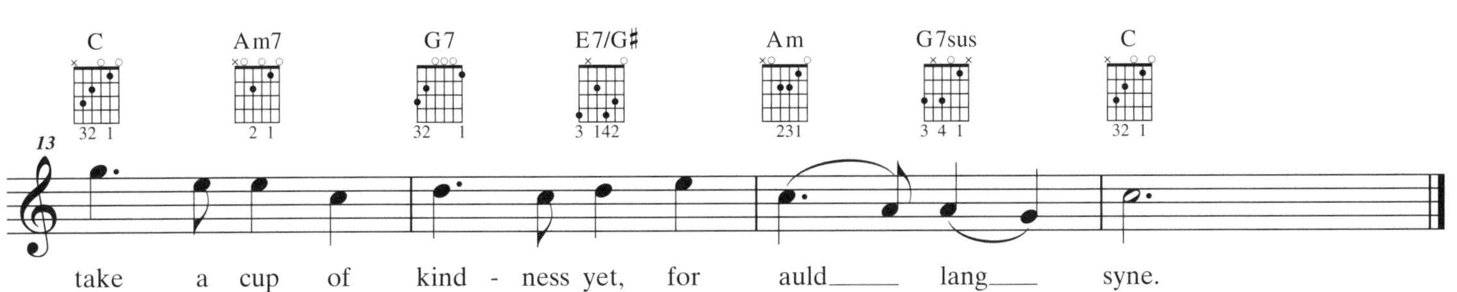

# Away in a Manger

Music by
JAMES R. MURRAY

# A Babe Is Born in Bethlehem

Traditional Carol

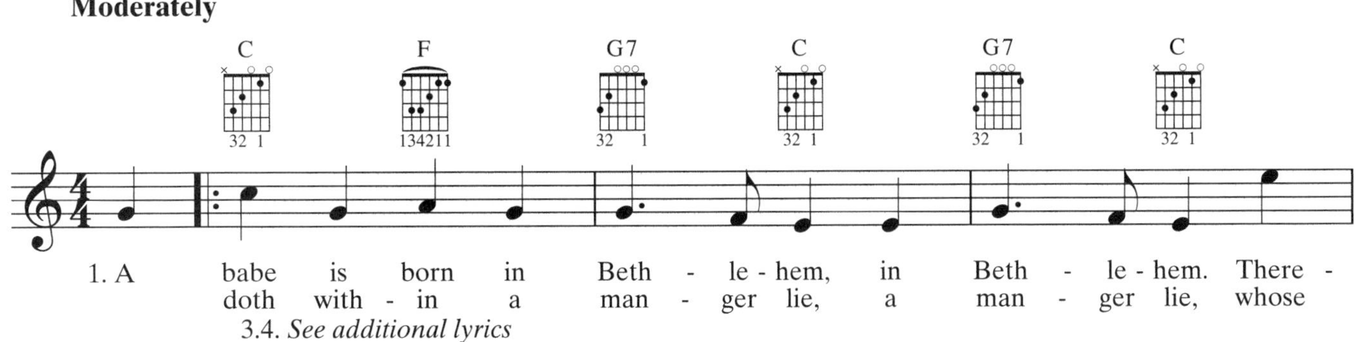


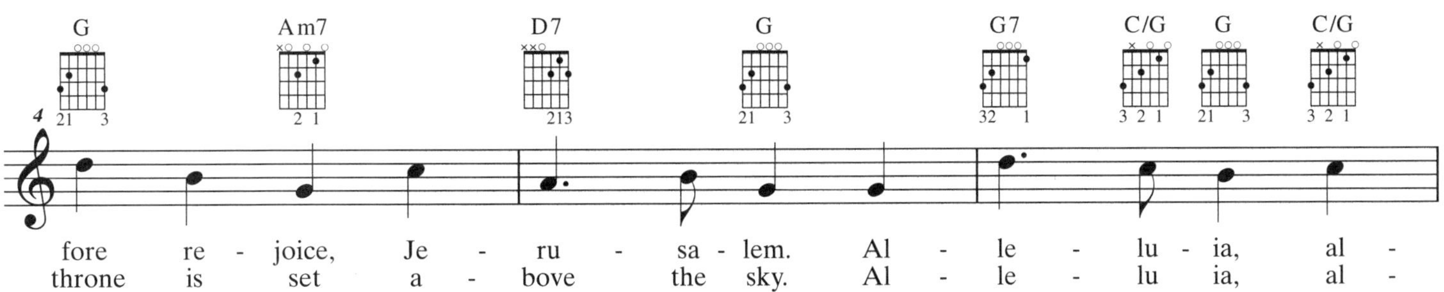


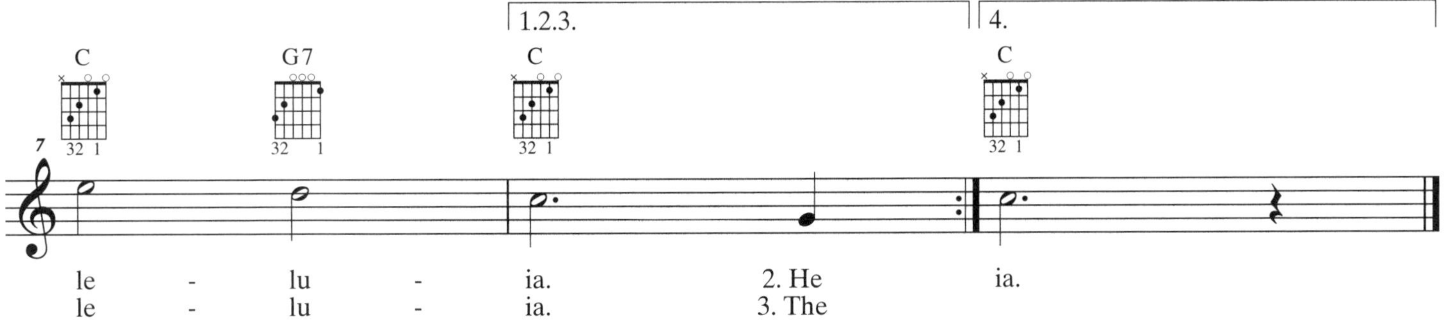


*Verse 3:*
The wise men came, led by the star,
Gold, myrrh, and incense brought from far.
Alleluia, alleluia.

*Verse 4:*
On this most blessed jubilee, blest jubilee,
All glory be, O God, to Thee.
Alleluia, alleluia.

# The Babe

Traditional Carol

**Brightly**

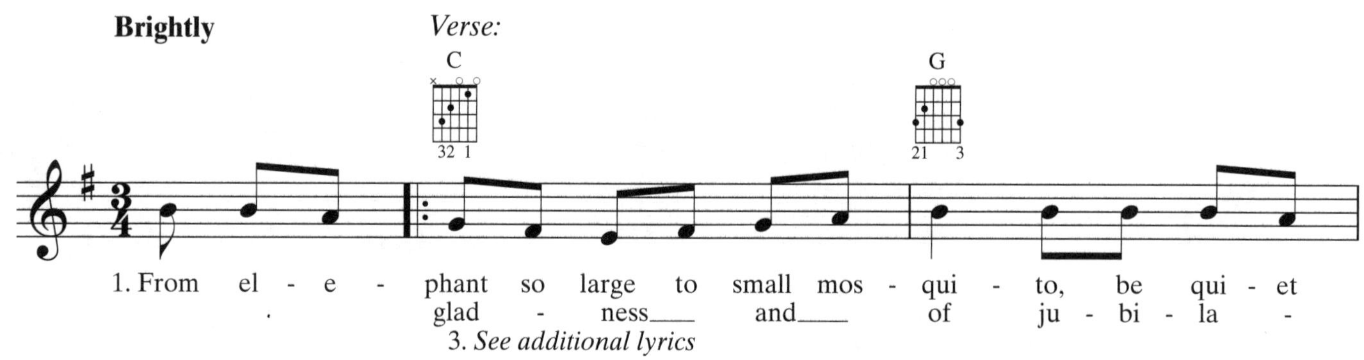


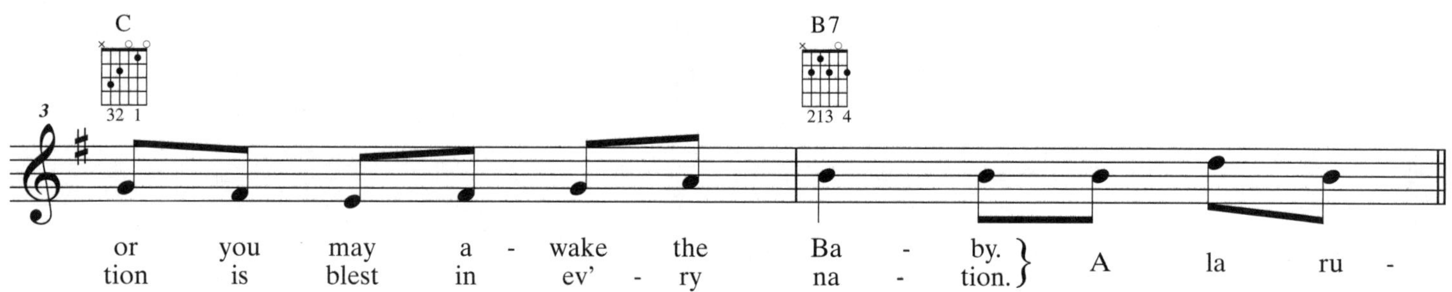


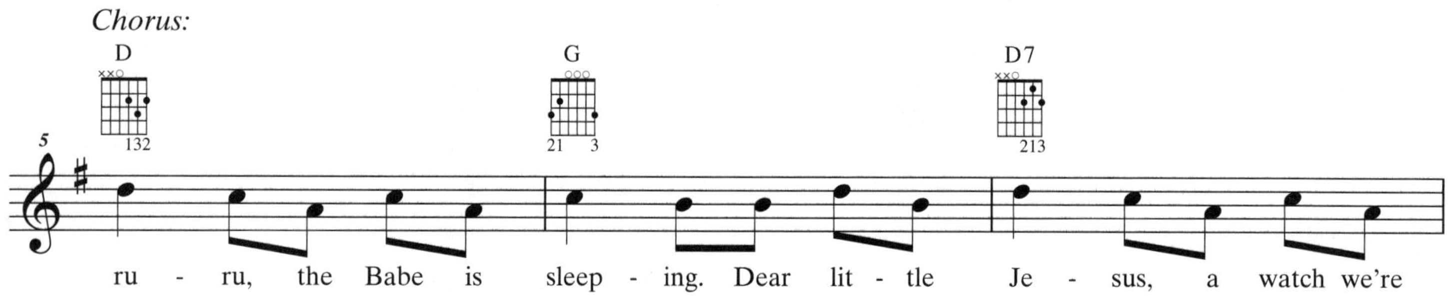

*Verse 3:*
Celestial voices, in sweet accents singing,
The wondrous tidings of His birth are bringing.
*(To Chorus:)*

# Believe

(from *The Polar Express*)

Words and Music by
ALAN SILVESTRI and GLEN BALLARD

G♯m
4fr.
134111
A
111
17
When it seems the mag - ic slipped a - way, we
When it seems that we have lost our way, we
D/F♯
1 23
1.
To Next Strain:
(To Chorus:)
Bsus
2fr.
1334
B
1333
19
find it all a - gain on Christ - mas Day. Be -
find our - selves a - gain on Christ - mas
2.
Chorus:
Bsus
2fr.
1334
B
1333
E
231
F♯m11
2 34
21
Day. Be - lieve in what your heart is say-ing,
E(9)/G♯
4fr.
1 234
A
111
E
231
B/D♯
4fr.
3111
24
3
hear the mel - o - dy that's play-ing. There's no time to waste, there's so
F♯m7
2 333
E/B
231
Bsus
2fr.
1334
E
231
F♯m11
2 34
26
much to cel - e - brate. Be - lieve in what you feel in - side and
E(9)/G♯
4fr.
1 234
G♯7(♯5)
4fr.
1 234
C♯m
4fr.
13421
F♯m7
2 333
28
give your dreams the wings to fly. You have ev - 'ry - thing you need

31
1.
B7sus
2fr.
13141
E
231
G♯m/D♯
4fr.
34111
if you just be - lieve.


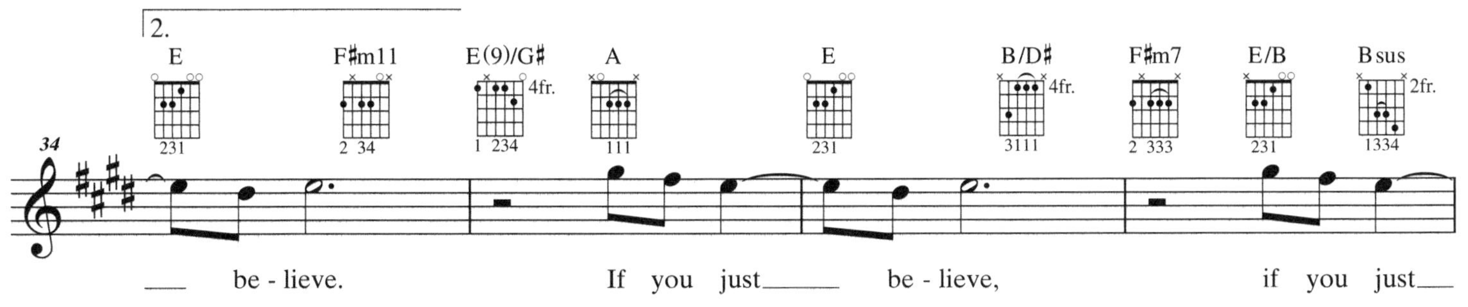

34
2.
E
231
F♯m11
2 34
E(9)/G♯
4fr.
1 234
A
111
E
231
B/D♯
4fr.
3111
F♯m7
2 333
E/B
231
Bsus
2fr.
1334
be - lieve. If you just be - lieve, if you just


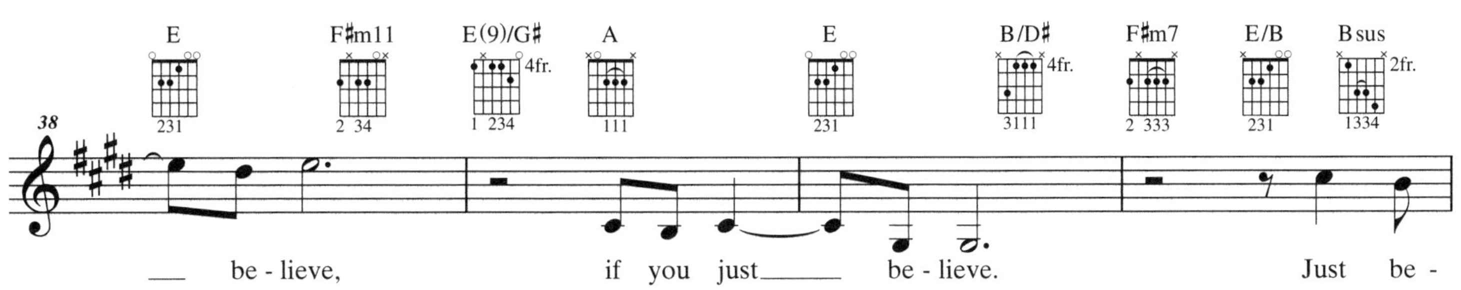

38
E
F♯m11
E(9)/G♯
A
E
B/D♯
F♯m7
E/B
Bsus
be - lieve, if you just be - lieve. Just be -


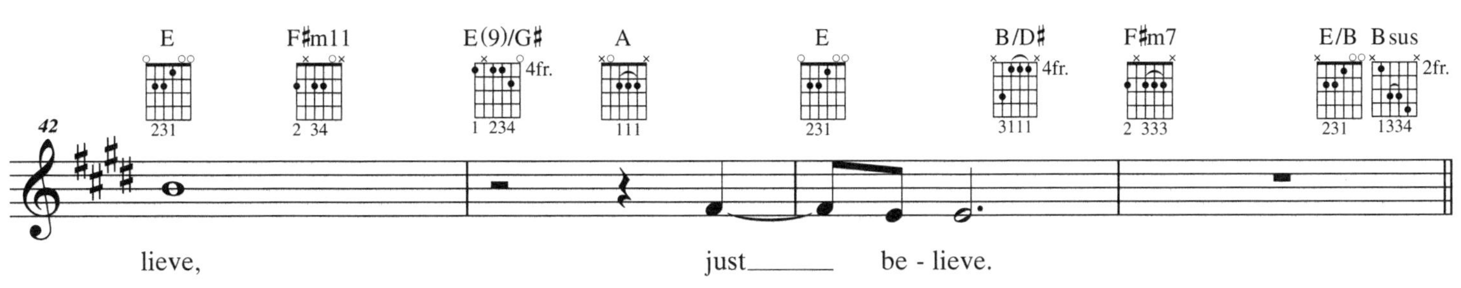

42
E
F♯m11
E(9)/G♯
A
E
B/D♯
F♯m7
E/B
Bsus
lieve, just be - lieve.


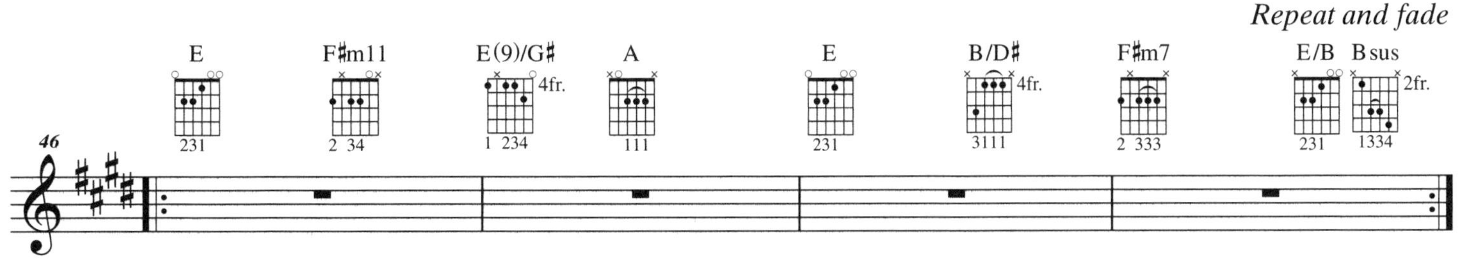

Repeat and fade
46
E
F♯m11
E(9)/G♯
A
E
B/D♯
F♯m7
E/B
Bsus

# Blue Christmas

Words and Music by
BILL HAYES and JAY JOHNSON

# The Bells of Christmas

17
Am7
2 1
D7
213
G
21 3
Em
23
Love was born to - day.
Peace was born to - day.
brought us love this day, and
21
Am
231
D
132
G
21 3
Em
23
Love was born to - day.
Peace was born to - day.
brought us peace this day.
25
G
21 3
1.2.
3.
D.C. al Coda
Coda
28
Am7
2 1
D7
213
G
21 3
Em
23
1. Love was born to - day.
2. Peace was born to - day.
32
Am7
2 1
D7
213
G
21 3
Em
23
Love and peace to - day.
36
Am7
2 1
D7
213
G
21 3
Love and peace this day.

# The Boar's Head Carol

Traditional English Carol

Moderately

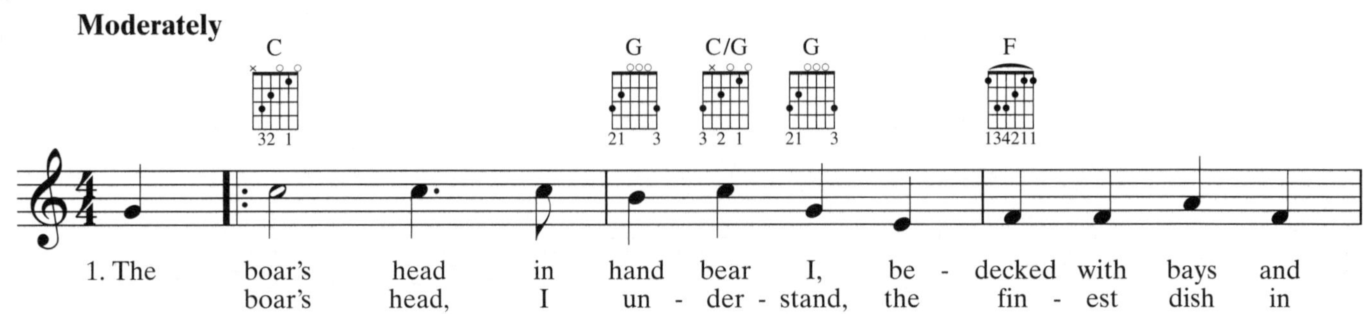


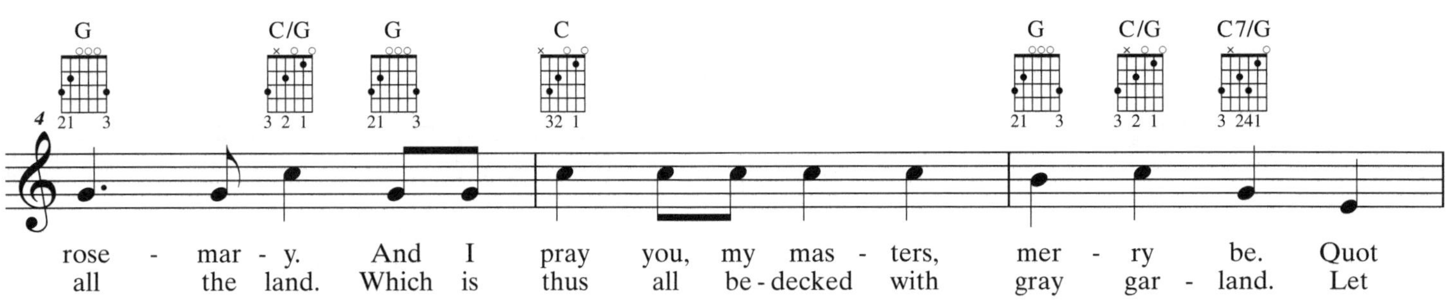


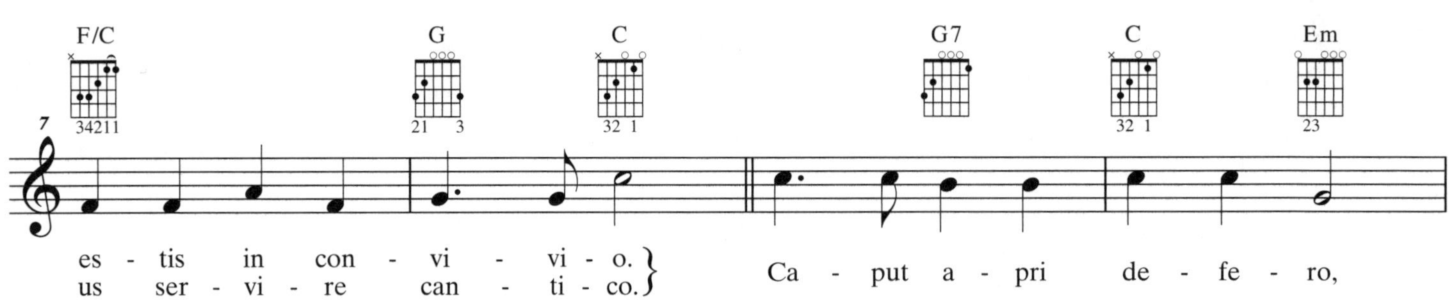


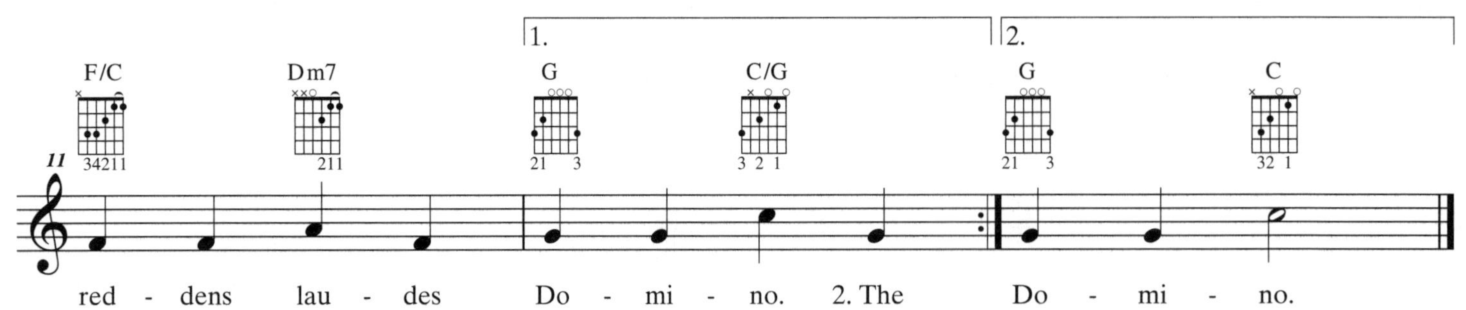

# Born Is He, This Holy Child

*Verse 3:*
Jesus, Thou all-powered Lord.
Now as Baby art Thou adored.
Jesus, Thou all-powered King.
All our hearts to Thee we bring.
(*To Chorus:*)

# Breath of Heaven

(Mary's Song)

Words and Music by
AMY GRANT and CHRIS EATON

G(9)
Bm
G6
Em9
Bm
Em/B
in a si - lent___ prayer,___ I am fright - ened________
Bm
A
D
Em9
___ by the load I________ bear.___ In a world as___
Bm9
G(9)
Em9
cold as___ stone, must I walk this___
Bm9
G(9)
G
A2
G(9)
path a - lone?___ Be______ with me now,___
Chorus:
A2
D2
D(9)
be______ with me now. Breath of
Em7/D
D(9)
Em7/D
F♯7/C♯
Heav - en, hold me to - geth - er, be for - ev - er___
Bm7(4)
G(9)
D(9)
Em7/D
near me, Breath of___ Heav - en. Breath of Heav - en, light-en my

D(9)
Em7/D
F♯7/C♯
Bm9
Bm
G(9)
To Coda
dark - ness, pour o - ver me Your Ho - li - ness, for You are
Em11
5fr.
Asus
Bm
Em/B
ho - ly, Breath of Heav - en.
Verse 3:
Bm
Em/B
Bm
Em/B
G(9)
Do You won - der as You
Bm
G6
Em9
5fr.
Bm
Em/B
G(9)
watch my face, if a wis - er one should have
Bm
A
D
Em9
5fr.
Bm9
had my place? But I of - fer all I
G(9)
D/F♯
Em9
5fr.
Bm9
am for the mer - cy of Your
G(9)
G
A2
G
A2
plan. Help me be strong, help me be,

G
A
D2
D.S. 𝄋 al Coda
78
help me.
𝄌 Coda
Em7(4)
A7
Chorus:
D
Em/D
82
ho - ly. Breath of Heav - en, hold me to -
D
Em/D
F♯/C♯
Bm
A/G
G
86
geth - er, be for - ev - er near me, Breath of
Dsus
D
Em/D
D
89
Heav - en. Breath of Heav - en, light - en my dark - ness,
Em/D
fingering?
F♯/C♯
Bm
A/G
G
Em11
93
pour o - ver me Your ho - li - ness, for You are ho - ly,
A7sus
D2
G(9)/B
D2
96
Breath of Heav - en. Breath of Heav - en.
G(9)/B
D2
G(9)/B
D
100
Breath of Heav - en.

# Bright and Joyful Is the Morn

Words by
JAMES MONTGOMERY

Music by
SAMUEL S. WESLEY

Lively

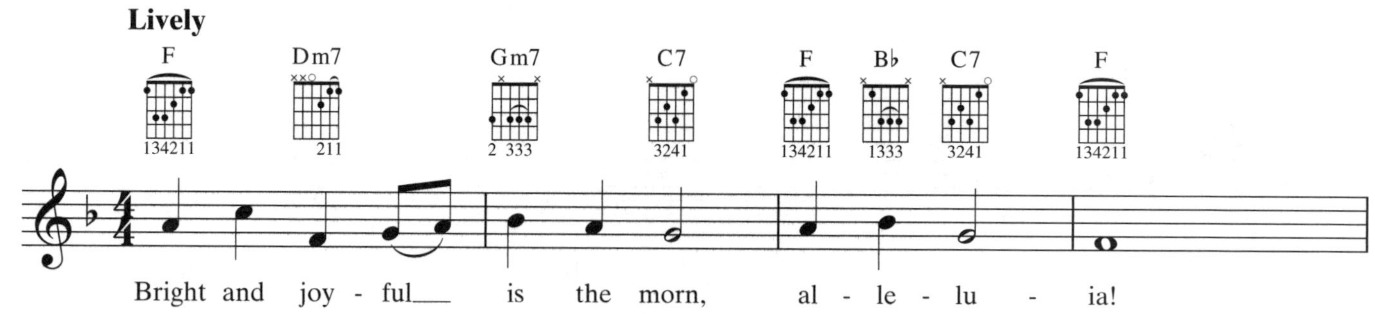


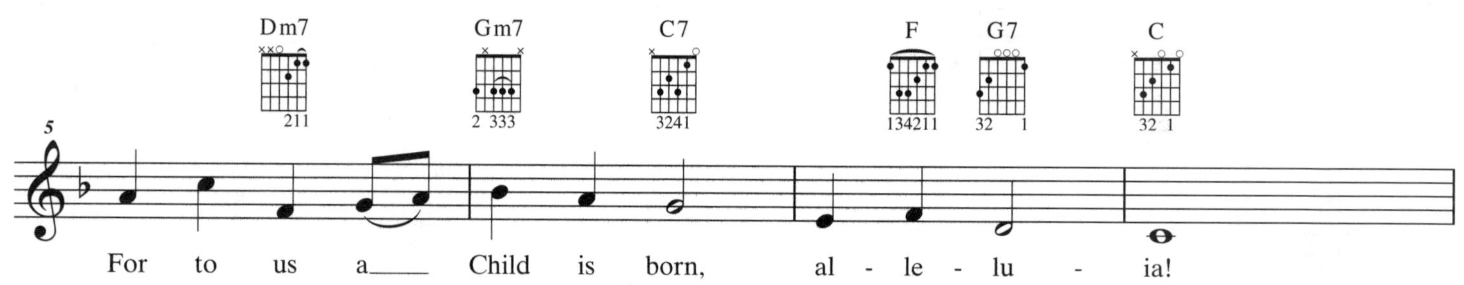


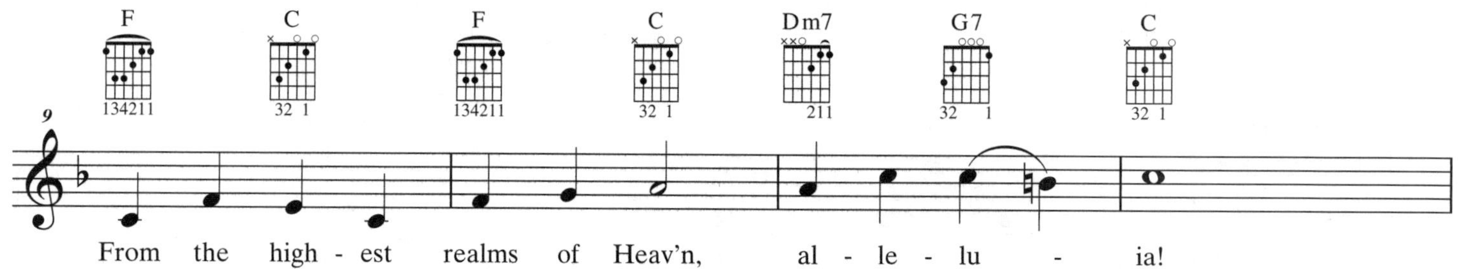


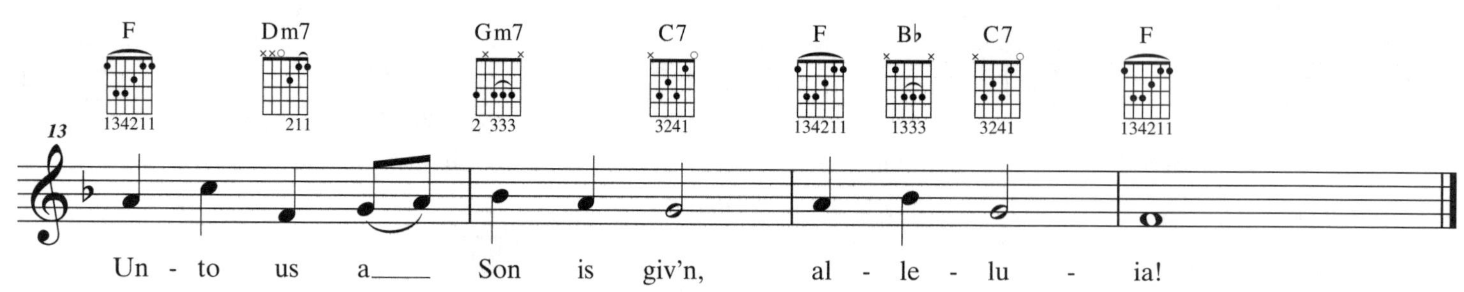

# Bring a Torch, Jeannette, Isabella

Traditional French Carol

# Buon Natale

(Means Merry Christmas to You)

Words and Music by
BOB SAFFER and FRANK LINALE

1. To Next Strain (To Verse:) | 2. Fine | Verse:

31 F 134211 | C7 3241

you. Far a - way, a - cross the

36 F 134211 | F♯dim7 2 131 | C7 3241

sea in sun - ny It - a - ly,

41 Gm7 2 333 | C7 3241 | Gm7 2 333 | C7 3241

there's a quaint lit - tle town; not a clock has been wound for

46 Gm7 2 333 | C7 3241 | F 134211

o - ver a cen - tu - ry. They don't know the

51 C7 3241 | F 134211 | F♯dim7 2 131

time or year, and no one seems to

56 C7 3241 | Gm7 2 333 | C7 3241 | Gm7 2 333

care. And this is the rea - son the Christ - mas

61 C7 3241 | Gm7 2 333 | C7 3241 | F 134211 | C7 3241 | D.C. al Fine

sea - son is cel - e - brat - ed all year, oh!

# Carol of the Birds

Traditional French Carol

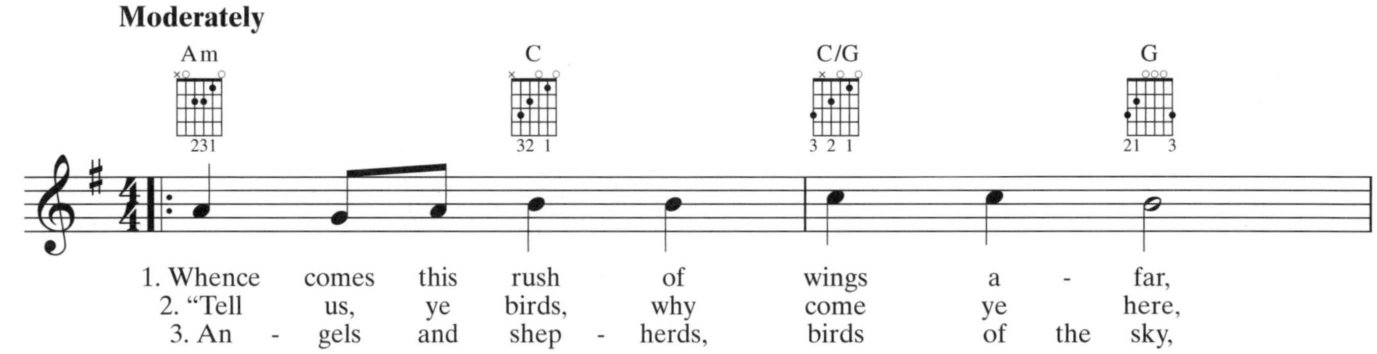


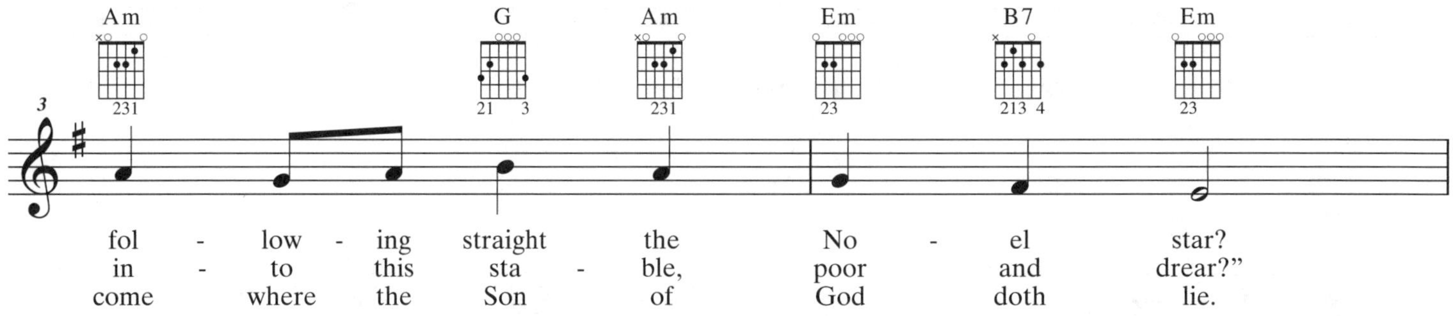


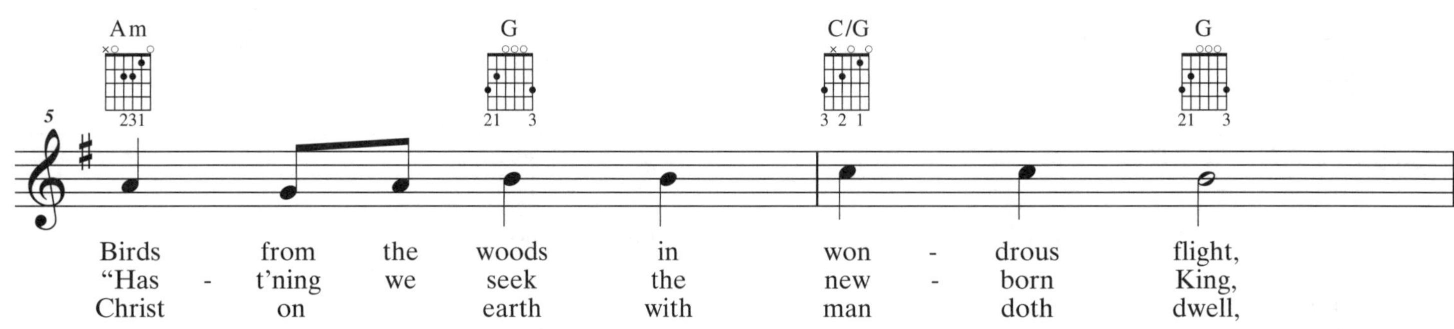


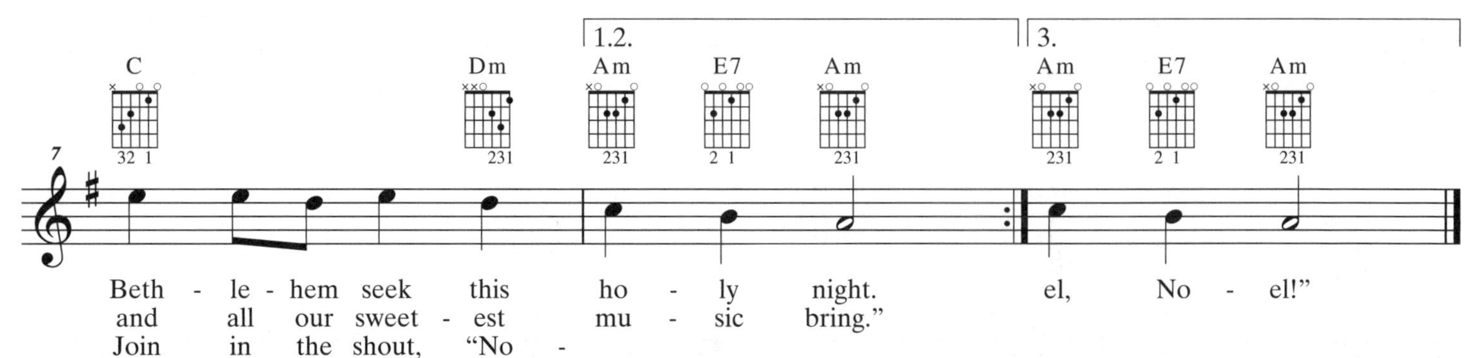

# Celebrate Me Home

C9sus C C9/E F F9sus B♭/F E♭9sus
find my - self too all a-lone, I can sing me home.
Verse 2:
F B♭/F C/E F B♭/F C/E
Un - eas - y high - way, trav - 'lin' where the west - er - ly winds can fly.
Dm7 G7sus C9sus C C9sus
Some-bod - y tried to tell me but the man for - got to tell me why.
F B♭/F C/E F E♭6
I got - ta count on be - ing gone. Come on, ma - ma. Come on, dad - dy. And,
Dm9 G7 E7 Am7 Cm7 F7(♯5 ♭9) B♭m7 Emaj7 D♭9sus
please, what you want from me? I'll be strong, I'll be
Chorus:
C9sus F Am7 Dm7
weak. Please, cel - e - brate me home.
Gm7 C C♯dim7 Dm7 Am7 Gm7 C Bm7(♭5)
Gim-me a num - ber. Please, cel - e - brate me home, play me one more

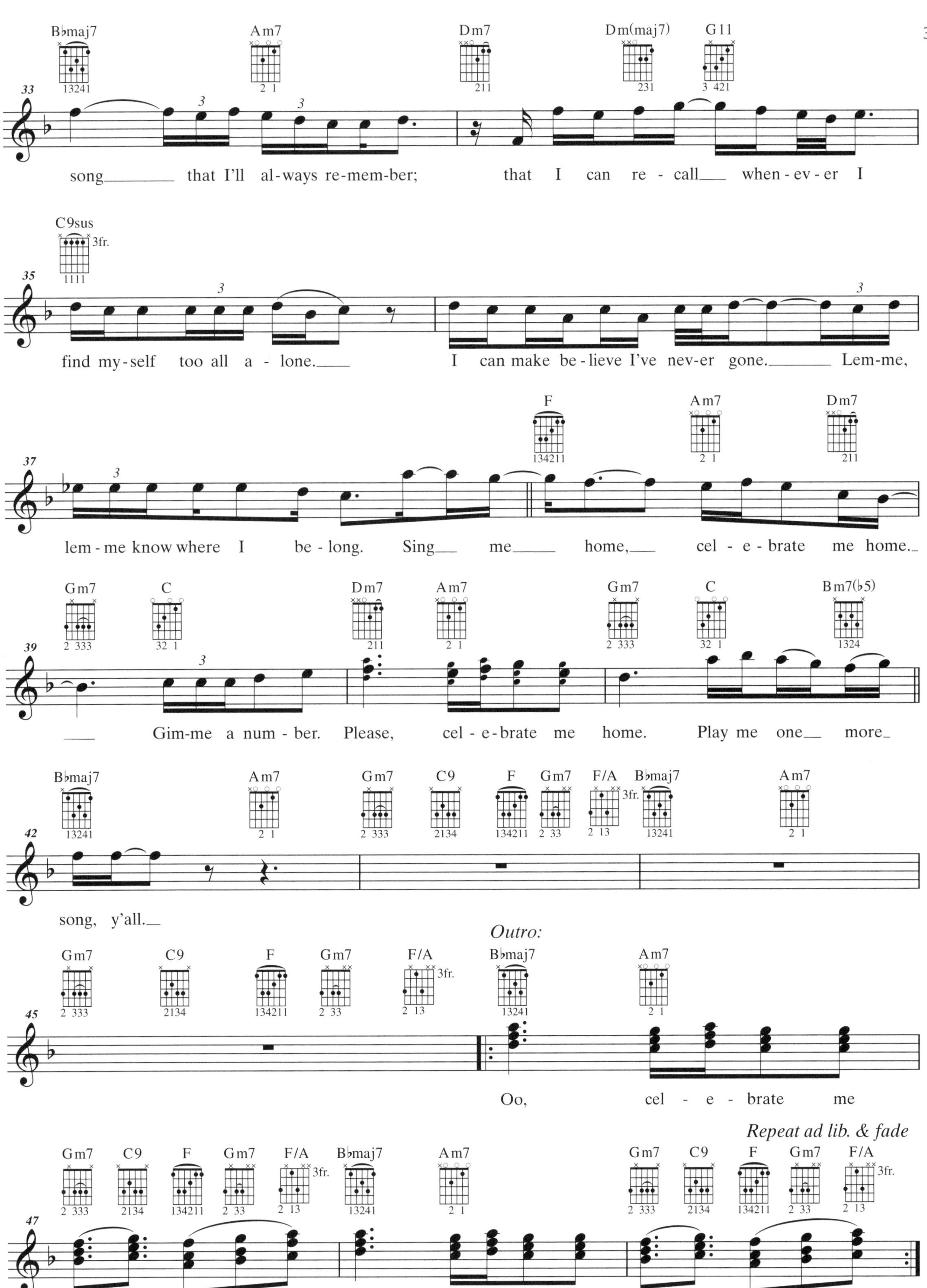
B♭maj7 Am7 Dm7 Dm(maj7) G11
song ___ that I'll al-ways re-mem-ber; that I can re - call ___ when-ev-er I
C9sus
find my-self too all a - lone. ___ I can make be-lieve I've nev-er gone. ___ Lem-me,
F Am7 Dm7
lem-me know where I be-long. Sing ___ me ___ home, ___ cel - e-brate me home. ___
Gm7 C Dm7 Am7 Gm7 C Bm7(♭5)
___ Gim-me a num-ber. Please, cel-e-brate me home. Play me one ___ more ___
B♭maj7 Am7 Gm7 C9 F Gm7 F/A B♭maj7 Am7
song, y'all. ___
Outro:
Gm7 C9 F Gm7 F/A B♭maj7 Am7
Oo, cel - e - brate me
Repeat ad lib. & fade
Gm7 C9 F Gm7 F/A B♭maj7 Am7 Gm7 C9 F Gm7 F/A
home. ___ Oh. ___ Oo, cel - e-brate me home. ___ Oh. ___

# A Child This Day Is Born

Words and Music by
WILLIAM SANDYS

*Verse 3:*
And as the angel told them,
So to them did appear.
They found the young Child, Jesus Christ,
With Mary, his Mother dear.
*(To Chorus:)*

# Christ Was Born on Christmas Day

Traditional Carol

# Christmas Comes Anew

Traditional French Carol

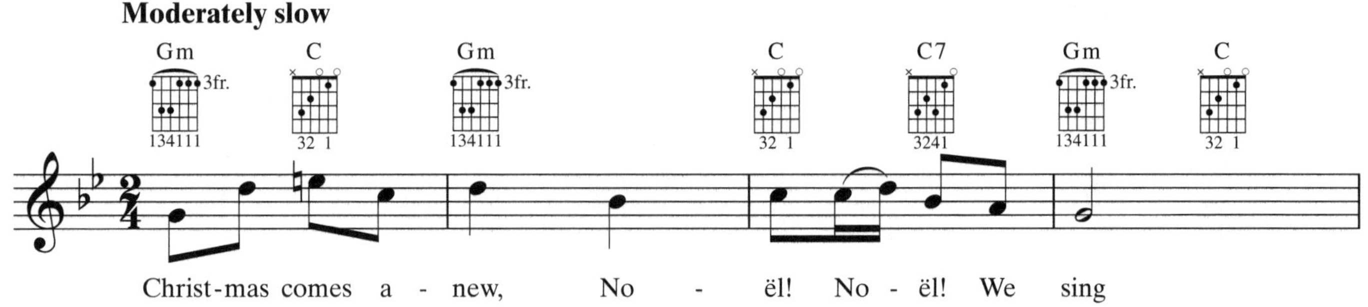


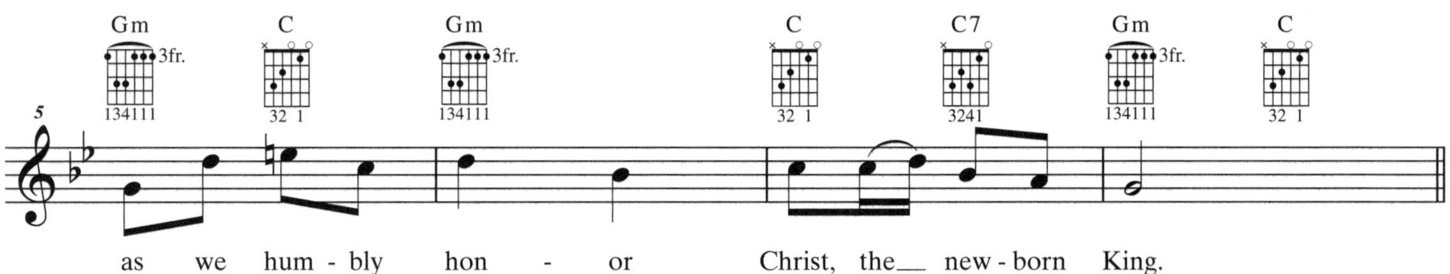


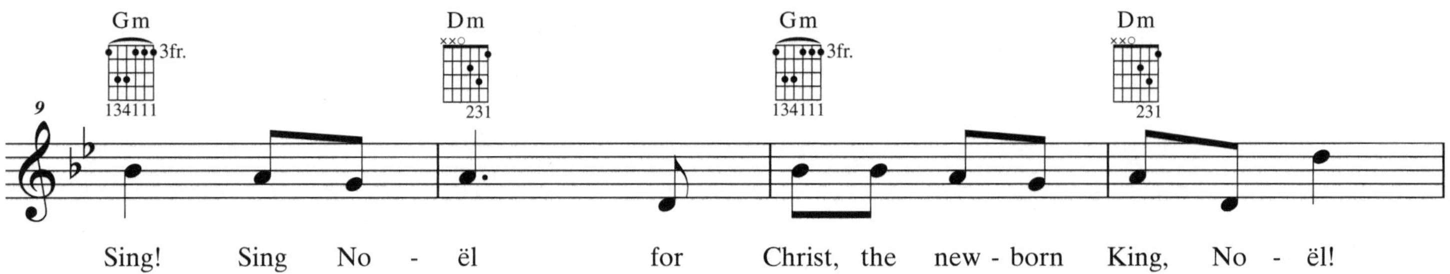


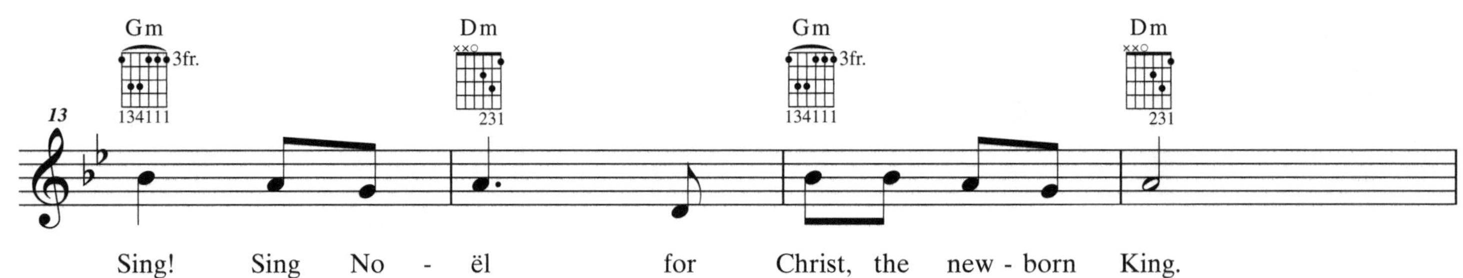


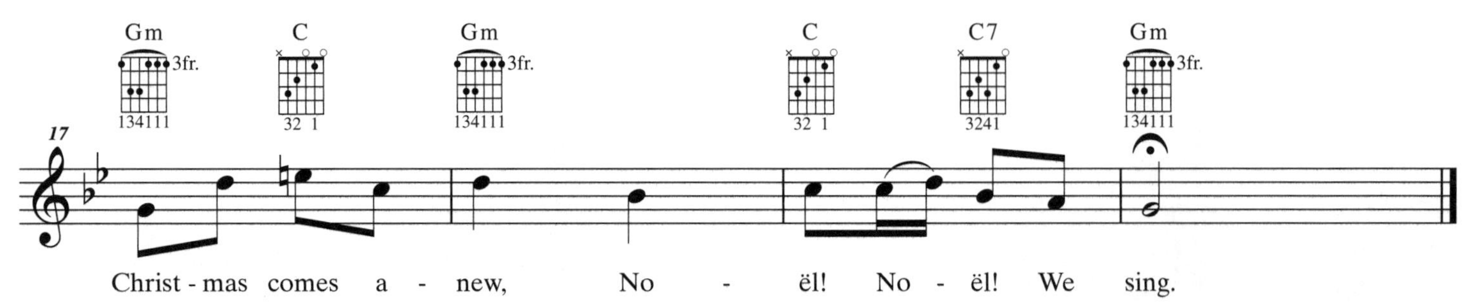

# Christmas Vacation

Words and Music by
BARRY MANN and CYNTHIA WEIL

F
Now it's get - ting clos - er; I can't wait.
Get a toast - y fire burn - ing bright.
Lang-a - lang - a - lang - a - lang-lang.)
Gm
Gon - na make this hol - i - day as per - fect as can be,
Give Saint Nick the warm - est wel - come that he's ev - er had.
1.
F
2.
F
Just wait and see this Christ - mas va - ca - tion.
We're so glad it's Christ - mas va - ca - tion.
Bridge:
F/A
Gm7
G♯m7
And when the nights are peace - ful and se - rene,
Am7
B♭/C
F
we can cud - dle up and do our Christ - mas dream - ing.
Gm
F
(Bkgd.) Jing - a - ling - a - ling - a - ling - ling.
Jang - a - lang - a - lang - a - lang - lang.
Gm
F
Christ - mas va - ca - tion.

Gm
B♭
Christ-mas va-ca-tion. Christ-mas va-ca-tion. Christ-mas va-ca-tion.
F/C
F
Gm
Christ-mas va-ca-tion. Christ-mas va-ca-tion. Christ-mas va-ca-tion.
F
We're so glad it's Christ-mas va-ca-tion.
Chorus 3 & 4:
Gm
3. Peace and joy and love are ev-'ry-where.
4. (etc.) La-la-la-la-la and ho ho ho.
(Bkgd. all times) Jing-a-ling-a-ling-a-ling-ling.
F
You can feel the mag-ic in the air.
Jin-gle, jan-gle, jin-gle as we go.
Jang-a-lang-a-lang-a-lang-lang.)
Gm
Let the spir-it of the sea-son car-ry us a-way.
F
Repeat ad lib. and fade
Hip, hip, hoo-ray for Christ-mas va-ca-tion.

# The Christmas Song

(Chestnuts Roasting on an Open Fire)

Words and Music by
MEL TORME and ROBERT WELLS

16
Dmaj7 Am7 D7 Am7 D7
night. They know that San - ta's on his way; He's load - ed
19
Am7 D7 Gmaj7 Gm7 C7
lots of toys and good - ies on his sleigh And ev - 'ry moth - er's child is gon - na
22
Fmaj7 Bm7 E7 Em7 A7
spy To see if rein - deer real - ly know how to fly. And
25
Dmaj7 G7(♯11) F♯m7 B7(♯9) Dmaj7 Am7(♭5) D7(♭9)
so, I'm of - fer - ing this sim - ple phrase To kids from one to nine - ty -
28
Gmaj7 C♯7(♭9) F♯7(♯5) Bm7 Gm6 Dmaj7 C♯7
two. Al - though it's been said man - y times, man - y ways; "Mer - ry
31
F♯m7 Bm7 Em7 A7 Dmaj7 Dmaj7
1. 2.
Christ - mas to you." you."

# Christmas Wrapping

Written by
CHRIS BUTLER

A
123
9
last year, ski shop, en - coun - ter, most in - t'rest-ing.
Did-n't, of course, 'till sum-mer - time, out to the beach to his boat, could I join him?

D
132
C2
3fr.
13411
B2
2fr.
13411
11
Had his num-ber but nev-er the time. Most of eight-y - one passed a-long those lines. So,
No, this time it was me, sun - burn in the third de - gree.

A
123
13
deck those halls, trim those trees, raise up cups of Christ-mas cheer.
Now the cal - en-dar's just one page, and of course, I am ex - cit - ed. To -

D
132
N.C.
15
I just need to catch my breath, Christ-mas by my - self this
night's the night, I've set my mind not to do too much a - bout

1.
A
year.
it.
2.
D
G
D
G
D
G
1.
D
G
D
2.
D
G
F♯m
Em
Dmaj7/E
Mer - ry
Chorus:
A
1.
Christ-mas! Mer - ry Christ-mas! But I think I'll miss this one this year. Mer-ry
2.
Verses 3 & 4:
A
think I'll miss this one this year.
3. Hard - ly dash - ing throughout the snow
4. A. and P. has pro-vid - ed me with the

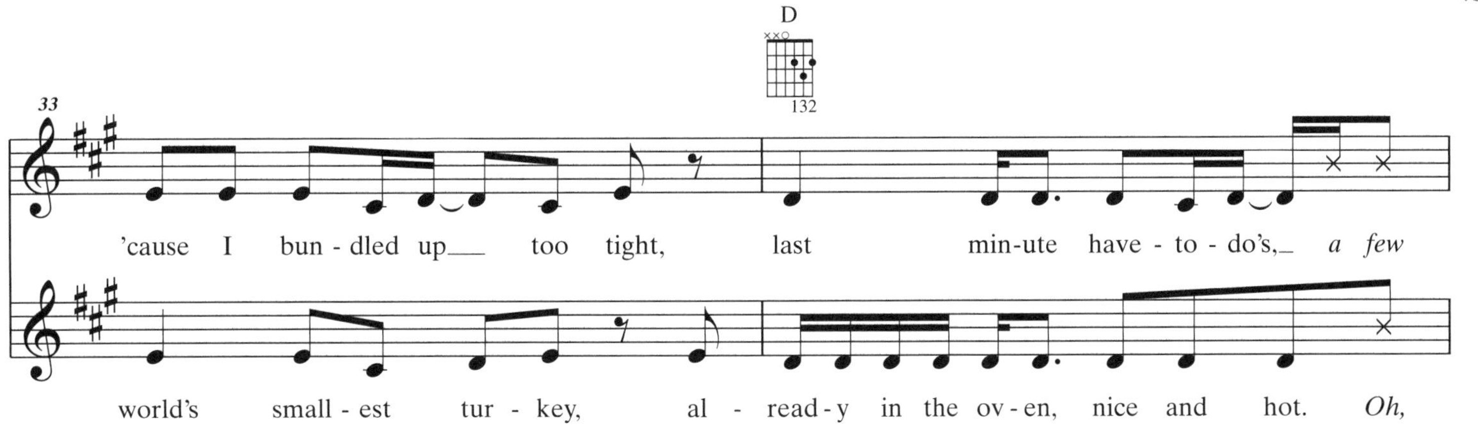
D
132
33
'cause I bun - dled up___ too tight, last min-ute have - to - do's,_ a few
world's small - est tur - key, al - read - y in the ov - en, nice and hot. Oh,

C2
3fr.
13411
B2
2fr.
13411
A
123
35
cards, a few calls be - cause it's R. S. V. P.
damn! Guess what I___ for - got?_ So on with the boots, back out in the snow to the

D
132
37
No thanks, no par - ty lights,_ it's Christ - mas Eve,_ gon-na re - lax,__
on - ly all-night gro - cer - y,___ when what to my won-der-ing eyes_ should ap-pear in the

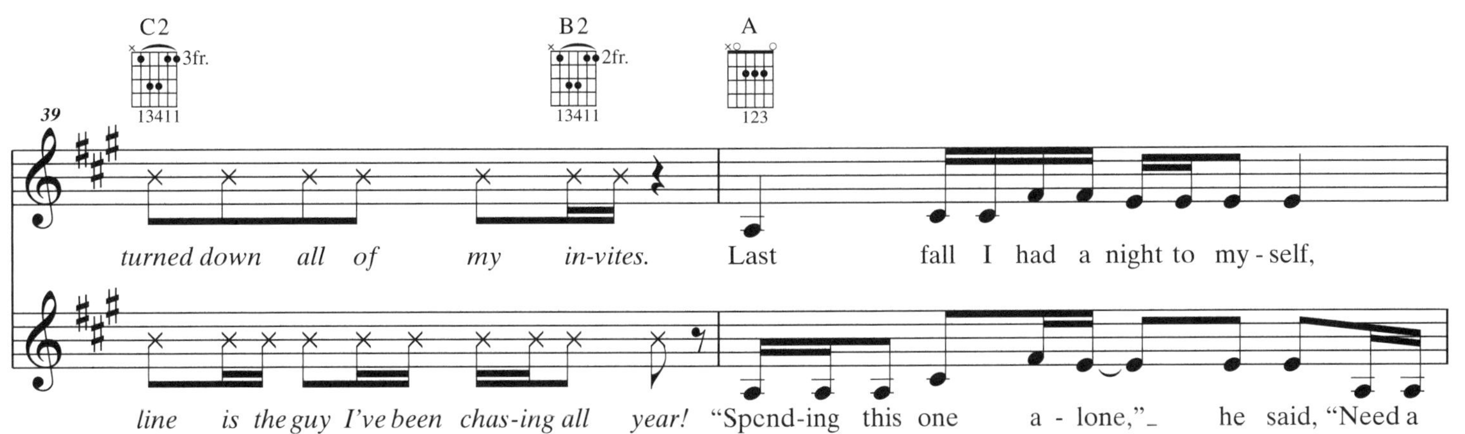
C2
3fr.
13411
B2
2fr.
13411
A
123
39
turned down all of my in-vites. Last fall I had a night to my - self,
line is the guy I've been chas-ing all year! "Spend-ing this one a - lone,"_ he said, "Need a

D/A
132
41
same guy called, Hal-low-een par - ty, wait-ed all night for him to show,
break, this year's been cra - zy." I said, "Me, too, but why are you... you mean
C2
3fr.
13411
B2
2fr.
13411
A
123
43
this time his car would-n't go. For-get it, it's cold, it's get-ting late,
you for-got cran-ber - ries too?" Then sud - den-ly we laughed and laughed, caught
D
132
45
trudge on home to cel - e - brate in a qui - et way, un - wind,
on to what was hap - pen - ing, that Christ-mas mag - ic's brought this tale to a
N.C.
A
123
47
do - ing Christ - mas right this time.
ver - y hap - py end - ing!
1.
2.
49

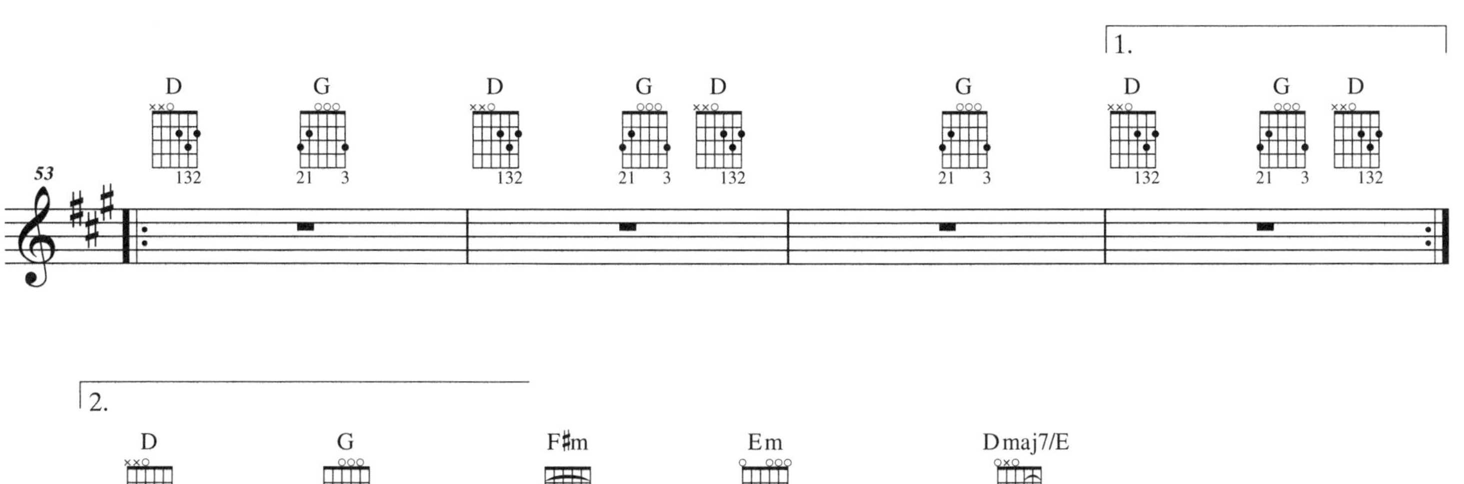


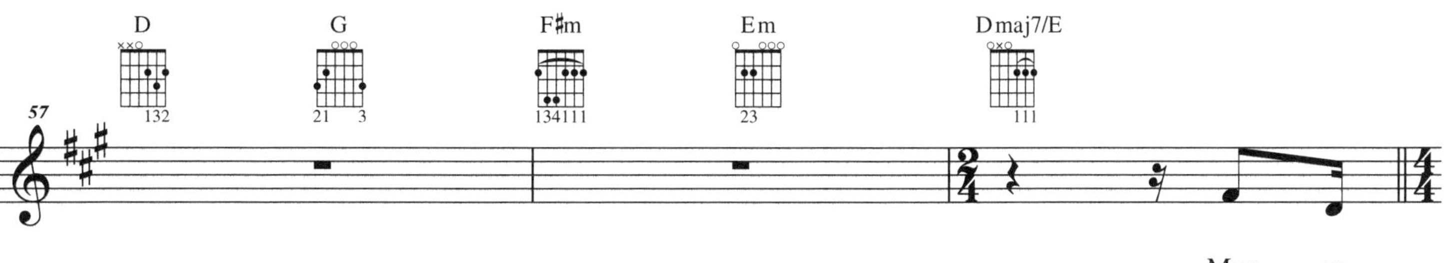


*Chorus:*

*Repeat and fade*

# The Coventry Carol

Traditional English Carol

*Verse 3:*
Herod the king in his raging,
Charged he hath this day.
His men of might, in his own sight,
All children young to slay.

*Verse 4:*
Then woe is me, poor Child, for thee,
And ever mourn and say.
For Thy parting nor say nor sing,
Bye, bye, lulloo, lullay.

# Dance of the Sugar Plum Fairy

Composed by
PETER ILYICH TCHAIKOVSKY

# December

Words and Music by
KENNY LOGGINS and PETER KATER

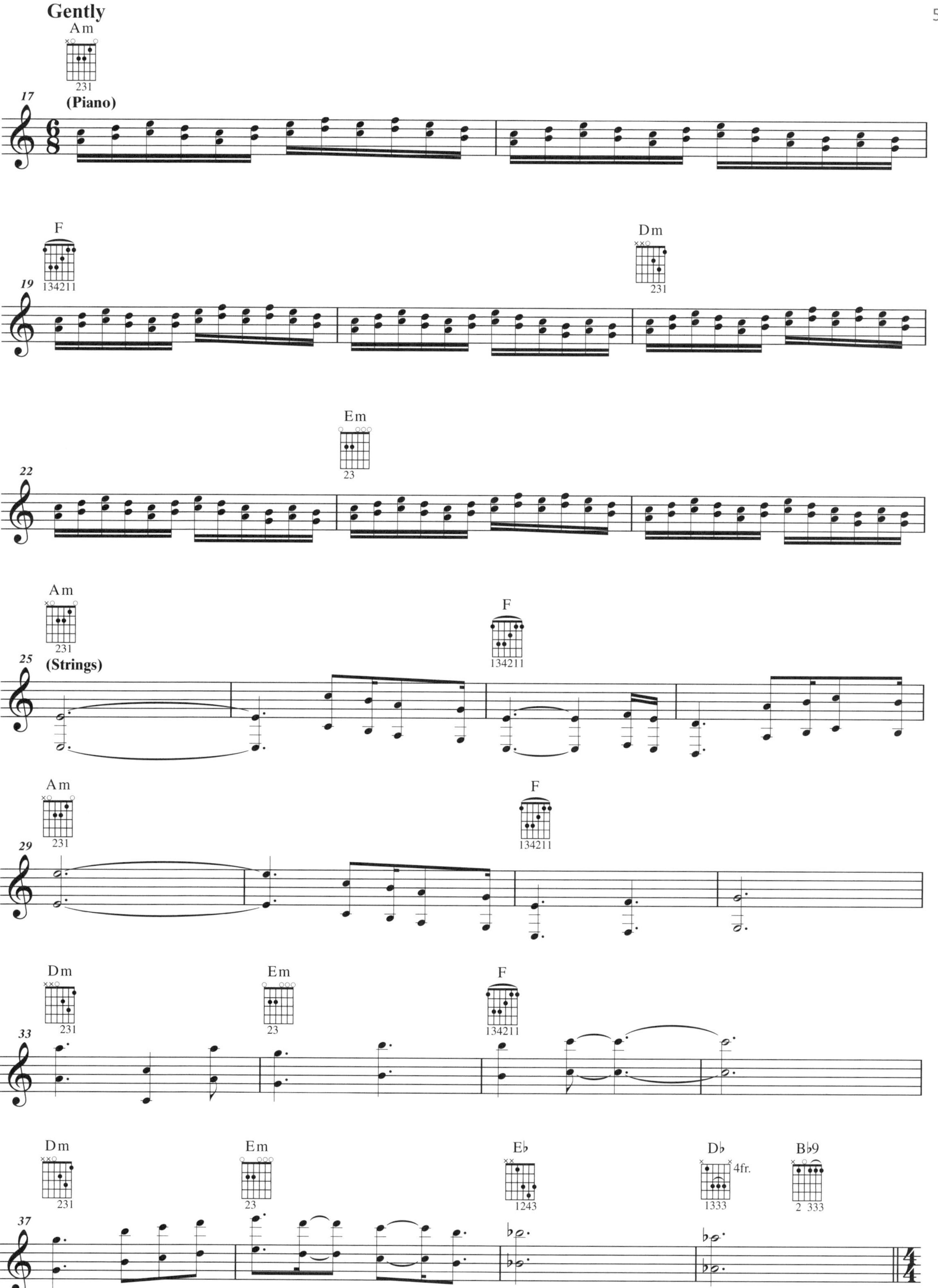
Gently
Am
231
17
(Piano)
F
134211
19
Dm
231
22
Em
23
Am
231
25
(Strings)
F
134211
Am
231
29
F
134211
Dm
231
33
Em
23
F
134211
Dm
231
37
Em
23
E♭
1243
D♭
4fr.
1333
B♭9
2 333

Tempo I
C
Am9
F
Dm7
F/G
Am(9)
Em
On - ly in De - cem - ber can the bro - ken heart
Abmaj9
Dm7
F/G
Am
Fmaj9
Dm7
Gm7
C9sus
feel so a-live. And the au - tumn ash - es be-come the sea-son's fire.
Fmaj7
Dm7
Bbsus2
Gm7
C9sus
Dm7
Am7
On - ly in De - cem - ber can I be in - side and
Dbmaj7
Gm7
C9sus
Dm(9)
Bbsus2
Gm7
C9sus
still in the cold. Still, I know De-cem - ber al - ways leads me
Slower
Dm7
Gm11
F/A
Bbsus2
C
Dm7
Gm11
F/A
home. I still be-lieve in mag - ic, al - ways leads me home. Still be-lieve in
Bbsus2
C
Dm7
Gm11
F/A
Bbsus2
C
mir - a - cles. I still be-lieve in Christ - mas.
Dm7
Gm11
F/A
Bb(9)
I still be-lieve in love.

# Deck the Halls

Traditional Welsh Carol

**Brightly**

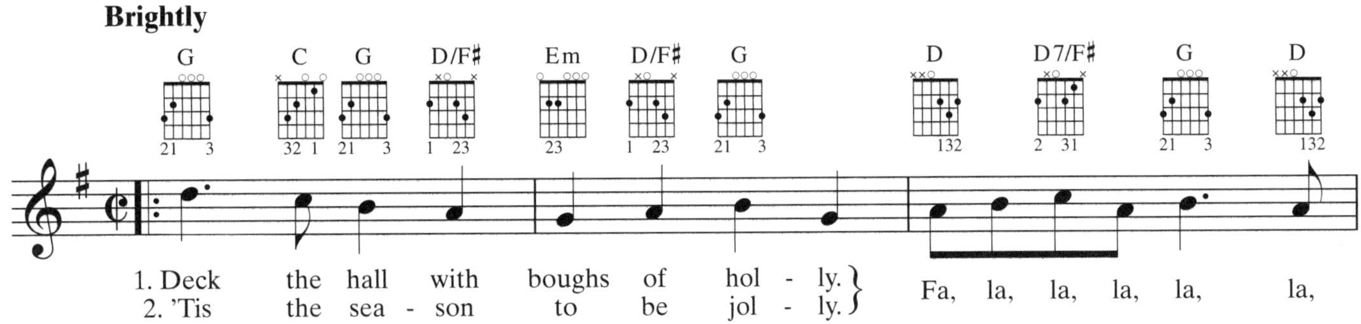


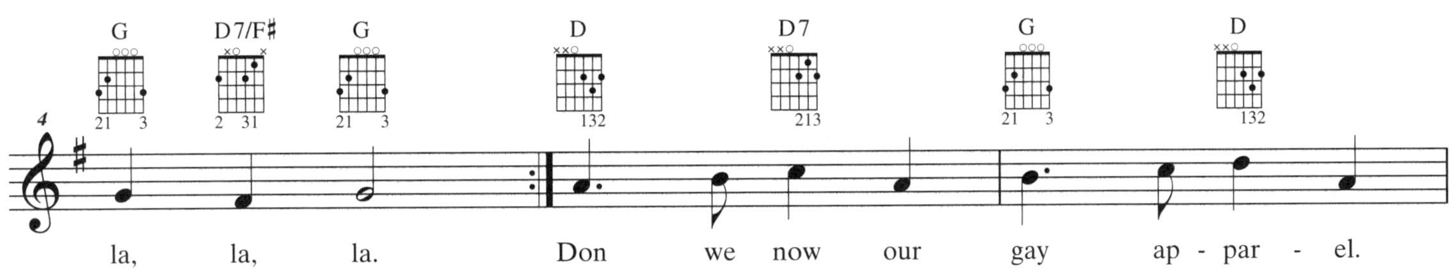


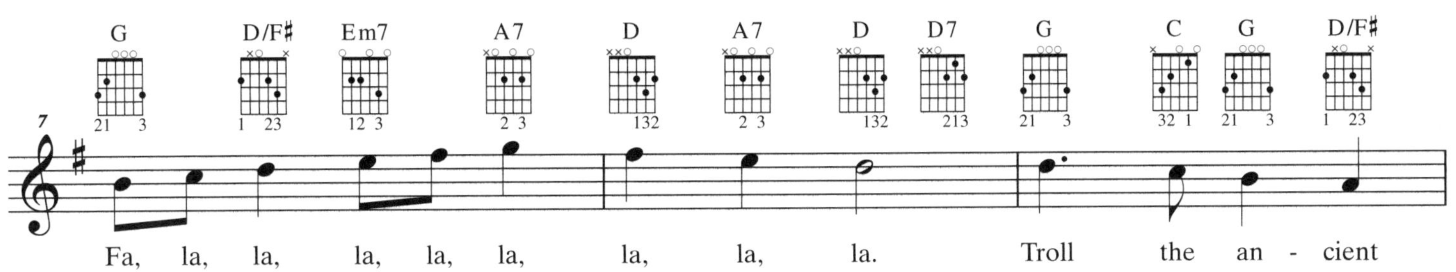


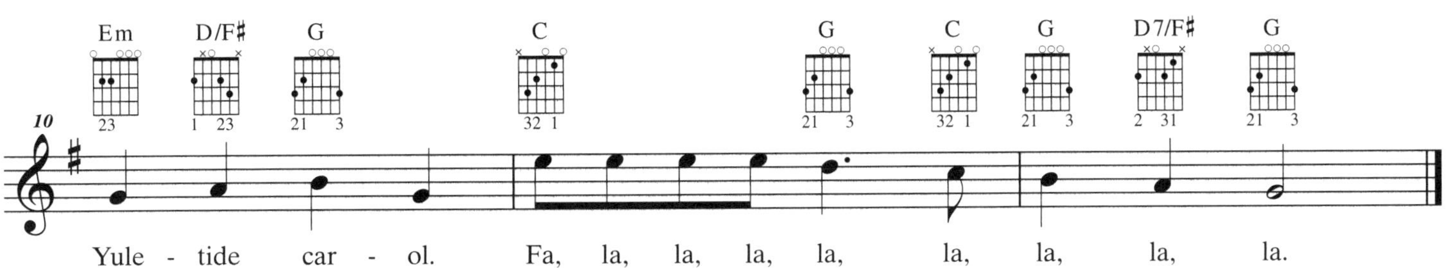

# Don't Save It All for Christmas Day

Words and Music by
PETER ZIZZO, RIC WAKE
and CELINE DION

Chorus:
E♭ G7sus/D G7(♭9) Cm9
all for Christ - mas Day. Find a way to
E♭ A♭(9) Fm7/B♭ E♭
give a lit - tle love ev - 'ry day. Don't save it all for Christ - mas
G7sus/D G7(♭9) Cm9 E♭ A♭(9)
Day, find your way. 'Cause hol - i - days have come and gone.
E♭ F7 Fm7/B♭ B♭7(♭9)
But love lives on if you give on love.
1. E♭ 2. E♭
2. How could you Let all the
Bridge:
E♭ Fm G7 G7/B Cm7 3fr. E♭
chil - dren know ev - er - y - where that they
A♭(9) E♭ Fm Cm/E♭ B♭/D
go, their whole life long,

*Verse 2:*
How could you wait another minute,
A hug is warmer when you're in it.
And, baby, that's a fact.
And sayin' I love you's always better,
Seasons, reasons, they don't matter.
So don't hold back.
How many people in this world
So needful in this world?
How many people are praying for love?
*(To Chorus:)*

# The First Noel

Traditional Carol

# Emmanuel

Words and Music by
JANIS IAN and KYE FLEMING

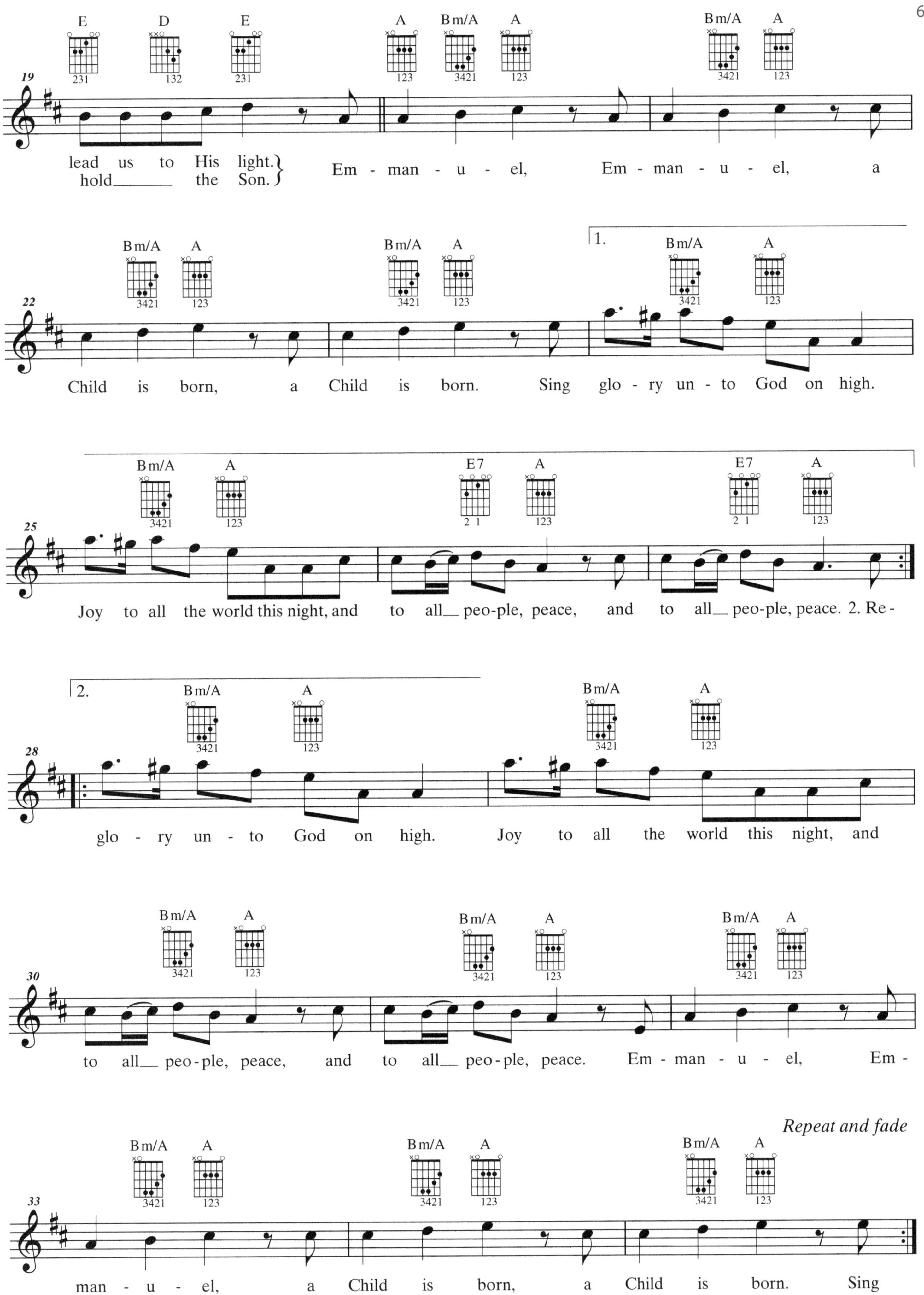
E D E A Bm/A A Bm/A A
lead us to His light. Em - man - u - el, Em - man - u - el, a
hold the Son.
Bm/A A Bm/A A 1. Bm/A A
Child is born, a Child is born. Sing glo - ry un - to God on high.
Bm/A A E7 A E7 A
Joy to all the world this night, and to all peo-ple, peace, and to all peo-ple, peace. 2. Re -
2. Bm/A A Bm/A A
glo - ry un - to God on high. Joy to all the world this night, and
Bm/A A Bm/A A Bm/A A
to all peo-ple, peace, and to all peo-ple, peace. Em - man - u - el, Em -
Repeat and fade
Bm/A A Bm/A A Bm/A A
man - u - el, a Child is born, a Child is born. Sing

# Feliz Navidad

Words and Music by
JOSÉ FELICIANO

Bm7
G
A7
I want to wish you a Mer - ry Christ - mas from the bot - tom of my heart.
D
N.C.
G
I want to wish you a Mer - ry Christ - mas.
A7
D
Bm7
I want to wish you a Mer - ry Christ - mas. I want to wish you a
G
A7
D
Mer - ry Christ - mas from the bot - tom of my heart.
1.2.
N.C.
3.
N.C.
G
Fe - liz Na - vi - Fe - liz Na - vi - dad.
A7
D
Fe - liz Na - vi - dad. Fe - liz Na - vi -
G
A7
D
dad. Pros - pe - ro a - ño y fe - li - ci - dad.

# The Friendly Beasts

Traditional Carol

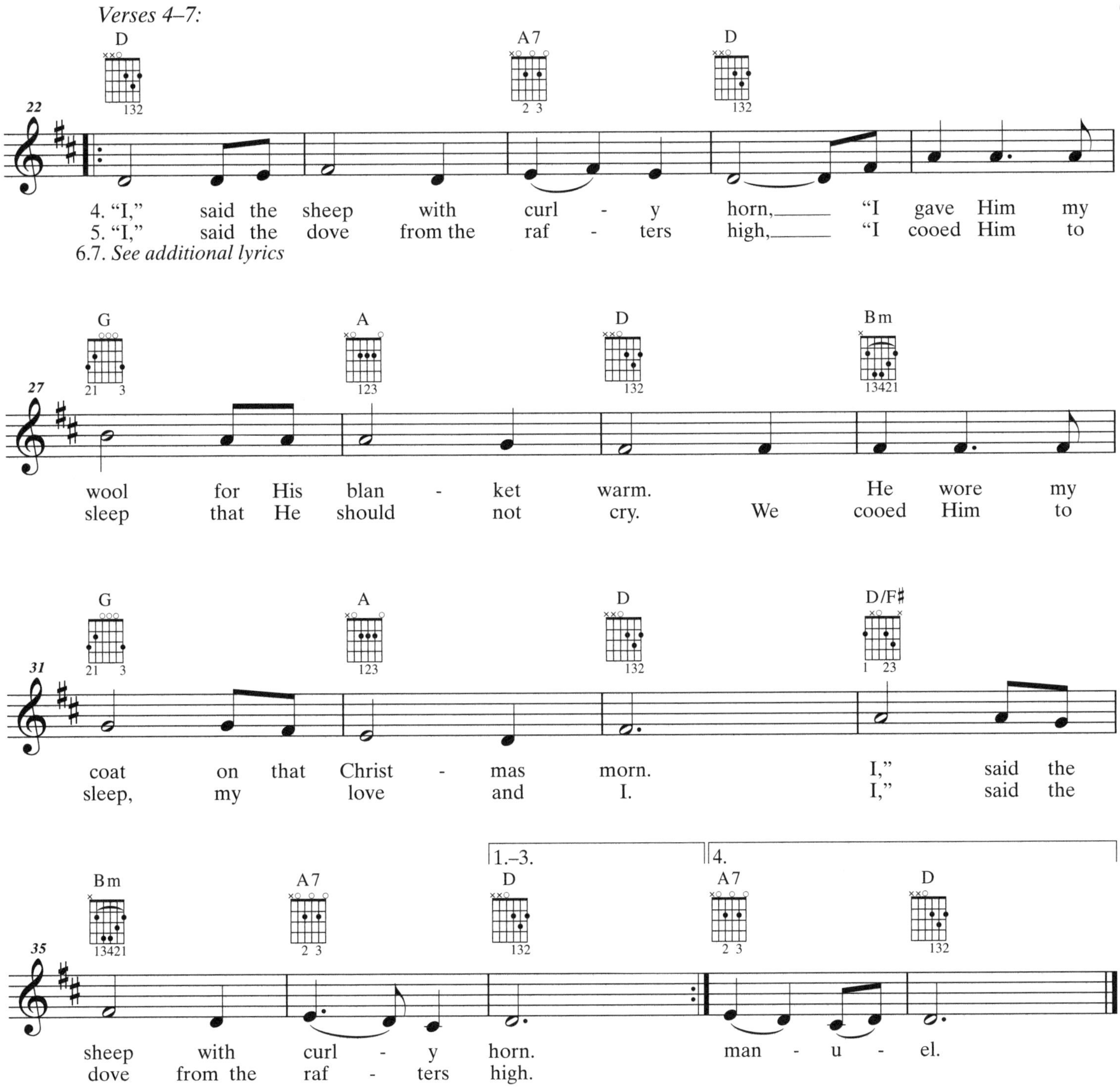
Verses 4–7:
D A7 D
4. "I," said the sheep with curl - y horn, "I gave Him my
5. "I," said the dove from the raf - ters high, "I cooed Him to
6.7. See additional lyrics
G A D Bm
wool for His blan - ket warm. He wore my
sleep that He should not cry. We cooed Him to
G A D D/F♯
coat on that Christ - mas morn. I," said the
sleep, my love and I. I," said the
1.–3. 4.
Bm A7 D A7 D
sheep with curl - y horn. man - u - el.
dove from the raf - ters high.

*Verse 3:*
"I," said the cow, all white and red,
"I gave Him my manger for a bed.
I gave Him my hay to pillow His head.
I," said the cow, all white and red.
*(To Verse 4:)*

*Verse 6:*
"I," said the camel, yellow and black,
"Over the desert upon my back,
I brought Him a gift in the wise man's pack.
I," said the camel, yellow and black.

*Verse 7:*
And thus, every beast, remembering it well,
In the stable dark was so proud to tell,
Of the gifts that they gave Emmanuel.
The gifts that they gave Emmanuel.

Gesu Bambino
(The Infant Jesus)
English Lyrics by
FREDERICK H. MARTENS
Music and Italian Lyrics by
PIETRO A. YON
Moderately
F/C C F/C C7
1. When blos - soms flow - ered 'mid___ the snows, up -
gain___ the heart___ with rap - ture glows to
F/C C F/C C7 F/C C F/C C7
on a win - ter night___ was born__ the Child,_ the Christ - mas Rose, the
greet the ho - ly night___ that gave__ the world_ it's Christ - mas Rose, it's
F/C C F/C Gm7 F
King__ of Love__ and Light.___ The an - gels sang,__ the shep - herds sang, the
King__ of Love__ and Light.___ Let ev - 'ry voice__ ac - claim His name, the
Gm7 B♭ F/C C7 Gm7(♭5) Fm7
grate - ful earth__ re - joiced.___ And at___ His bless - ed
grate - ful cho - rus swell.___ From par - a - dise___ to
C7 D♭ C7 Fm7 E♭
birth, the stars their ex - ul - ta - tion voiced.___
earth He came that we___ with Him might dwell.___
Oh,
A♭ E♭7 A♭ E♭7 A♭ E♭ A♭ E♭7 A♭ D♭
come let us a - dore Him,___ oh, come let us a -

Ab Eb Db Ab Bbm Eb7 Ab Db Ab Eb
13
dore Him, oh, come let us a - dore Him, Christ the
Ab C7 C7
17
1. 2.
Lord. 2. A - Ah!
F/C C F/C C7 F/C C F/C C7
20
Oh, come let us a - dore Him,
F/C C F/C C7 F/C C F/C F7
22
a - dore Him, Christ the Lord. Oh,
Bb F/A Bb F/A Ab7 Db Ab
24
come, oh, come, oh, come let us a -
C7 Db Bbm7 C7 Db Bbm7 C7(b9)
27
dore Him. Let us a - dore Him,
F C7 F
30
Christ the Lord.

# The Gift

Words and Music by
JIM BRICKMAN and TOM DOUGLAS

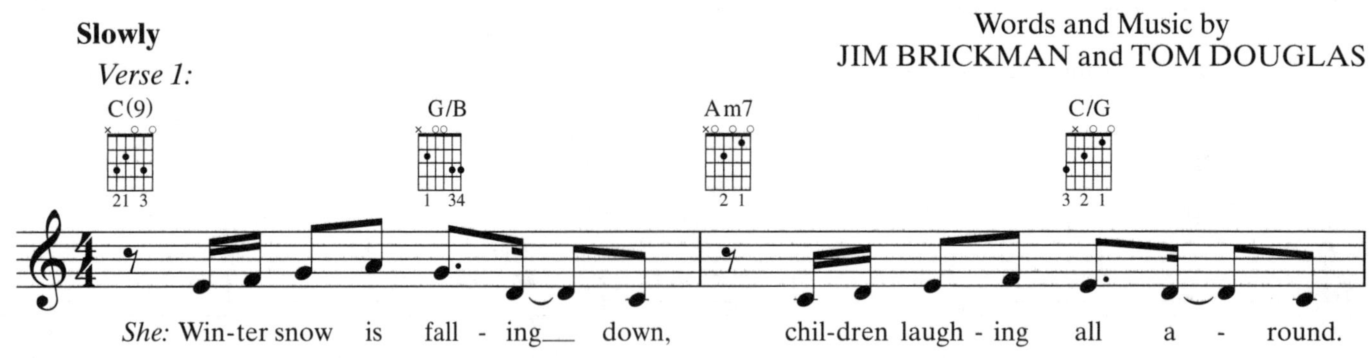


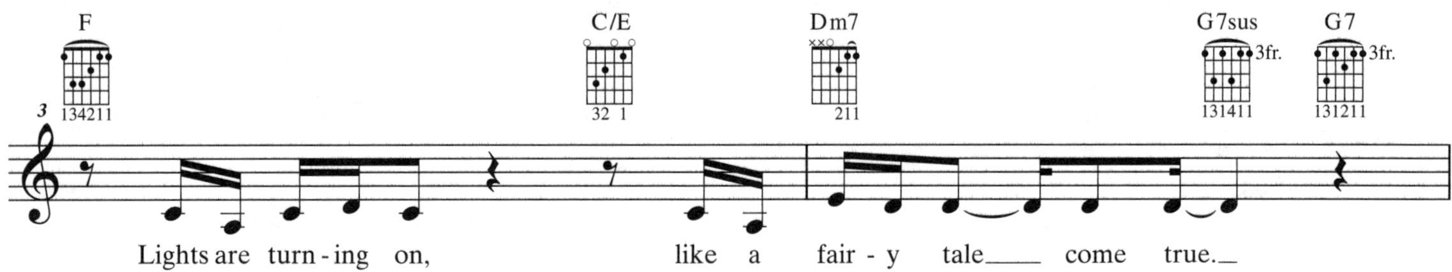


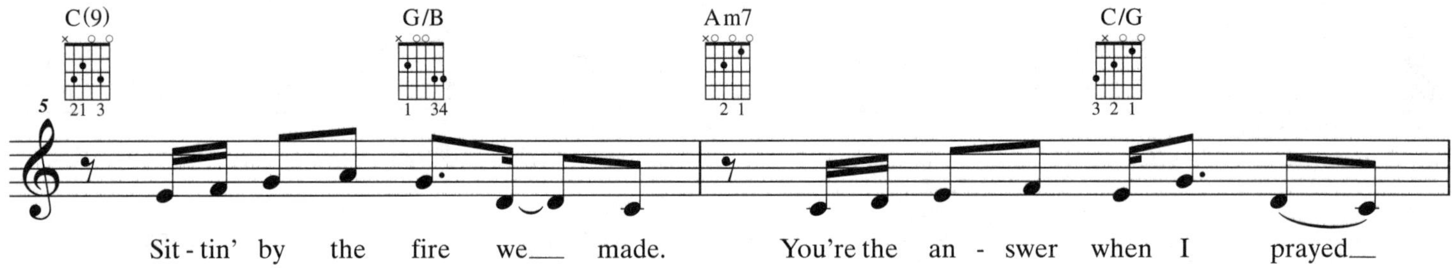


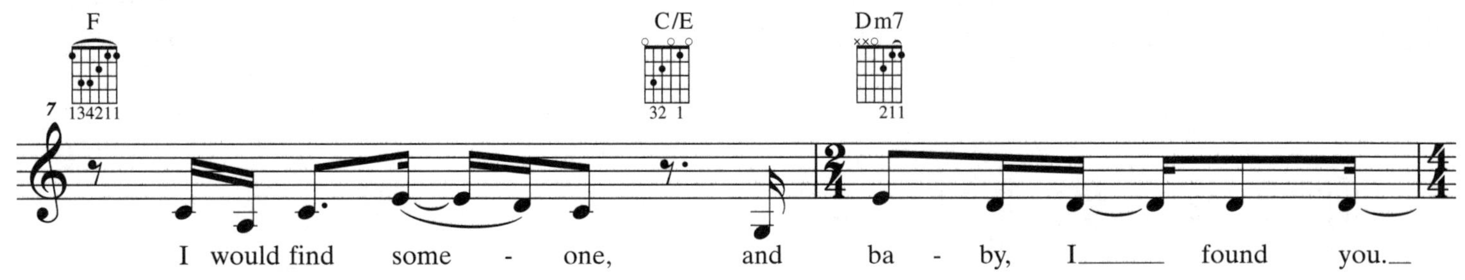

G7sus
G7
C/E
F
G7sus
G7
11
ev - er.
And all I need is you more ev - 'ry day.
C/E
E7
Am
C/G
F♯m7(♭5)
14
You saved my heart from be - ing bro - ken a - part. You gave your
Dm7
C/E
G7sus
16
love a - way, and I'm thank - ful ev - 'ry day for the
C(9)
G/B
Dm7
C/E
F
18
gift.
Verse 2:
G(9)
D/F♯
Em7
G/D
21
He: Watch-ing as you soft - ly sleep. What I'd give if I could keep
C(9)
G/B
Am7
D7
23
just this mo-ment. If on - ly time stood still.

G(9)
D/F♯
Em7
G/D
But the col-ors fade a-way and the years will make us gray.
C(9)
G/B
Am7
But, ba-by, in my eyes, you'll still be beau-ti-ful.
Chorus:
D7sus
D7
G/B
C(9)
Both: And all I want is to hold you for-ev-er.
All I need is you more ev-'ry day.
B7
To Coda
He: You saved my heart from be-ing bro-ken a-part.
Em
C♯m7(♭5)
She: You gave your love a-way,
He: and I'm thank-ful

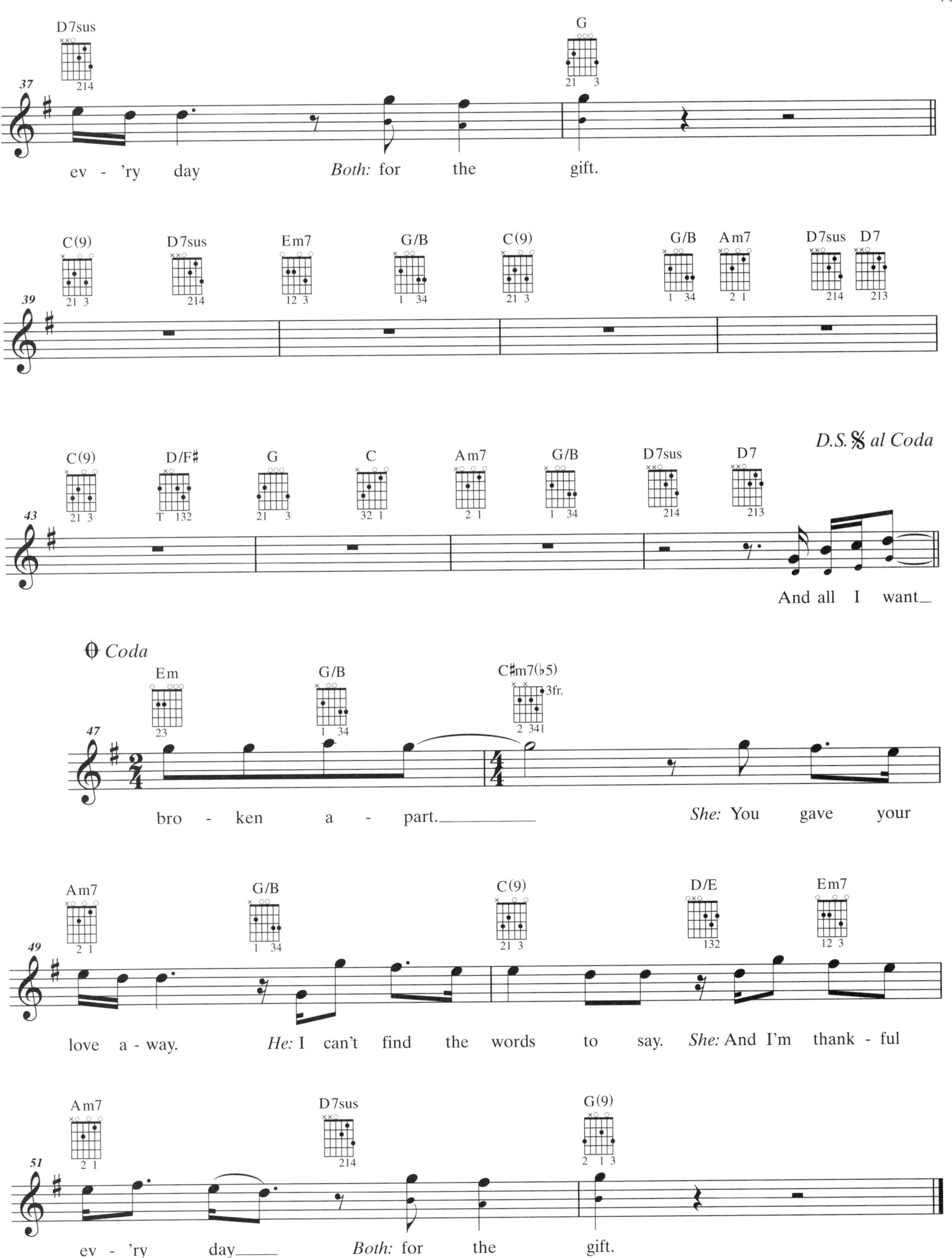
D7sus
G
ev - 'ry day Both: for the gift.
C(9) D7sus Em7 G/B C(9) G/B Am7 D7sus D7
C(9) D/F♯ G C Am7 G/B D7sus D7
D.S. 𝄋 al Coda
And all I want
𝄌 Coda
Em G/B C♯m7(♭5)
broken a - part.
She: You gave your
Am7 G/B C(9) D/E Em7
love a - way. He: I can't find the words to say. She: And I'm thank - ful
Am7 D7sus G(9)
ev - 'ry day Both: for the gift.

# Go Tell It on the Mountain

Traditional Spiritual

*Verse 3:*
While shepherds kept their watching
O'er wand'ring flock by night,
Behold, from out the Heavens
There shown a holy light.
(*To Chorus:*)

*Verse 4:*
And lo, when they had seen it,
They all bowed down and prayed.
Then they travelled on together,
To where the Babe was laid.
(*To Chorus:*)

# *God Rest Ye Merry, Gentlemen*

*Verse 3:*
In Bethlehem, in Jewry,
This Blessed Babe was born.
And laid within a manger
Upon this holy morn,
The which his Mother Mary
Did nothing take in scorn.
Oh, tidings…

*Verse 4:*
"Fear not then," said the angel,
"Let nothing you affright.
This day is born a Savior,
Of a pure Virgin bright,
To free all those who trust in Him
From Satan's power and might."
Oh, tidings…

*Verse 5:*
The shepherds at those tidings
Rejoiced much in mind,
And left their flocks a-feeding
In tempest, storm, and wind,
And went to Bethlehem straightway,
The Son of God to find.
Oh, tidings…

*Verse 6:*
And when they came to Bethlehem
Where our dear Savior lay,
They found Him in a manger
Where oxen feed on hay.
His Mother Mary kneeling down,
Unto the Lord did pray.
Oh, tidings…

*Verse 7:*
Now to the Lord sing praises,
All you within this place.
And with true love and brotherhood
Each other now embrace.
This holy tide of Christmas
All other doth deface.
Oh, tidings…

# Good Christian Men, Rejoice

Words by
HEINRICH SUSO

Traditional Melody

# Good King Wenceslas

Words by
JOHN M. NEALE

Traditional Carol

*Verse 3:*
"Bring me flesh and bring me wine, bring me pine logs hither.
Thou and I will see him dine, when we bear him thither."
Page and monarch forth they went, forth they went together,
Through the rude wind's wild lament and the bitter weather.

*Verse 4:*
"Sire, the night is darker now, and the wind blows stronger.
Fails my heart, I know not how, I can go no longer."
"Mark my footsteps, my good page, tread thou in them boldly.
Thou shalt find the winter's rage freeze thy blood less coldly."

*Verse 5:*
In his master's steps he trod, where the snow lay dinted.
Heat was in the very sod which the Saint had printed.
Therefore, Christian men, be sure, wealth or rank possessing;
Ye who will now bless the poor shall yourselves find blessing.

# A Great and Mighty Wonder

*Verse 2:*
The Word becomes incarnate
And yet remains on high!
And cherubim sing anthems
To shepherds from the sky.
*(To Chorus:)*

*Verse 3:*
While thus they sing your Monarch,
Those bright angelic bands,
Rejoice, ye vales and mountains;
Ye oceans, clap your hands.
*(To Chorus:)*

*Verse 4:*
Since all He comes to ransom,
By all be He adorned,
The infant born in Bethl'em,
The Savior and the Lord.
*(To Chorus:)*

*Verse 5:*
And idol forms shall perish,
And error shall decay,
And Christ shall wield His scepter,
Our Lord and God for aye.
*(To Chorus:)*

# Hallelujah Chorus

Composed by
G.F. HANDEL

D
G
Em
D
For the Lord God om - ni - po - tent reign - eth. Hal - le -
G D
lu - jah! Hal - le - lu - jah! Hal - le - lu - jah! Hal - le - lu - jah!
D A G A7 D A D
For the Lord God om - ni - po - tent reign - eth.
A Bm A D A E7 A
For the Lord God om - ni - po - tent reign - eth. Hal - le - lu - jah!
D A D A/C♯ G/B A
Hal - le - lu - jah! Hal - le - lu - jah! For the Lord God om - ni - po - tent
Asus D/F♯ G D
reign - eth. Hal - le - lu - jah! The

A/C♯
G/B
D/A
A/G
D/F♯
king - dom of this world is be -
D
A
Bm
Ddim
come the king - dom of our Lord, and of His
A
G
A7
N.C.
2fr.
Christ, and of His Christ. And He shall reign for - ev - er and
G♯dim7
E
ev - er. And He shall reign for - ev - er and ev -
Em
Asus
er. And He shall reign for - ev - er and ev - er. And
A/E
He shall reign for - ev - er and ev - er. King of

D A D A D A D A
49
Kings, for - ev - er and ev - er. Hal-le - lu - jah! Hal-le - lu - jah! and Lord of
D A D A D A D A D
52
Lords. For - ev - er and ev - er. Hal-le - lu - jah! Hal-le - lu - jah! King of
G D G D G D G D E
55
Kings. For - ev - er and ev - er. Hal-le - lu - jah! Hal-le - lu - jah! And Lord of
A E A E A E A E F♯
58
Lords. For - ev - er and ev - er. Hal-le - lu - jah! Hal-le - lu - jah! King of
Bm F♯ Bm F♯ Bm F♯ Bm G
61
Kings. For - ev - er and ev - er. Hal-le - lu - jah! Hal-le - lu - jah! And Lord of
A/C♯ D A
64
Lords. King of Kings and Lord of Lords. And He shall
D A D A/C♯ Bm A D G
67
reign, and He shall reign. And He shall reign for -

Em D/F♯ D/A A D/F♯ D G D
ev - er and ev - er. King of Kings, for - ev - er and
G D G D G D
ev - er, and Lord of Lords. Hal-le - lu - jah! Hal-le - lu - jah! And He shall
Bm D G D/F♯ A7 D Asus A D
reign for - ev - er, for - ev - er and ev - er. King of
Kings and Lord of Lords. King of Kings and Lord of Lords. And
D/F♯ Bm D G D/F♯ A7 D Asus A D
He shall reign for - ev - er and ev - er. King of
G D G D
Kings and Lord of Lords. Hal-le - lu - jah! Hal-le - lu - jah! Hal-le - lu - jah! Hal-le -
Largo
G D G D
lu - jah! Hal - le - lu - jah!

# Happy Xmas
(War Is Over)

Words and Music by
JOHN LENNON and YOKO ONO

Pre-chorus:
D
Dmaj9
Dsus2
D
Em
- mas,
I hope you have fun,
the near and the dear
Asus
A
A7sus2
A
D
Dmaj9
Dsus2
D
one,
the old and the young.
A ver-y Mer-ry
Chorus:
G
A
Christ-mas
and a hap-py New Year.
Let's hope it's a

Em
G
D
E
good one without an - y fear. 2. And so this is Christ-
Verses 2 & 3:
A
Asus2
Asus
A
Bm
Bsus2
Bm
Cont. rhy. simile
- mas for weak and for strong, for rich and the poor
(3.) Christ-mas and what have we done? An - oth - er year
War is o - ver if you want it!
Esus
E
A
Asus2
Asus
A
ones, the road is so long. And so hap - py
o - ver, and a new one just be - gun. And so hap - py
War is o - ver now!
Pre-chorus:
D
Dmaj9
Dsus2
D
Em
Christ-mas for black and for white, for yel - low and
Christ-mas, we hope you have fun, the near and the
War is o - ver if you want it!

Asus
A
A7sus2
A
D
Dmaj9
Dsus2
D
red ones, let's stop all the fight.
dear one, the old and the young.
A ver - y Mer-ry
War is o - ver now!
Chorus:
G
A
Resume chorus rhy. simile
Christ - mas and a hap - py New Year. Let's hope it's a
1.
D.S.
2.
Em
G
D
E
D
E
good one with-out an - y fear. 3. And so this is fear.
Outro:
Begin fade
A
Asus2
Asus
A
Bm
Bsus2
Bm
Esus
E
War is o - ver if you want it! War is o - ver
A
Asus2
Asus
A
Fade out
*D Dsus2 Dsus D Em Em(maj7) Em(9) Em
Gtrs. tacet
now!
*Chords implied by strings.

# Hark! The Herald Angels Sing

Traditional Carol

# Here Comes Santa Claus

Words and Music by
GENE AUTRY and OAKLEY HALDEMAN

# Have Yourself a Merry Little Christmas

Words and Music by
HUGH MARTIN and RALPH BLANE

**Medium two-beat**

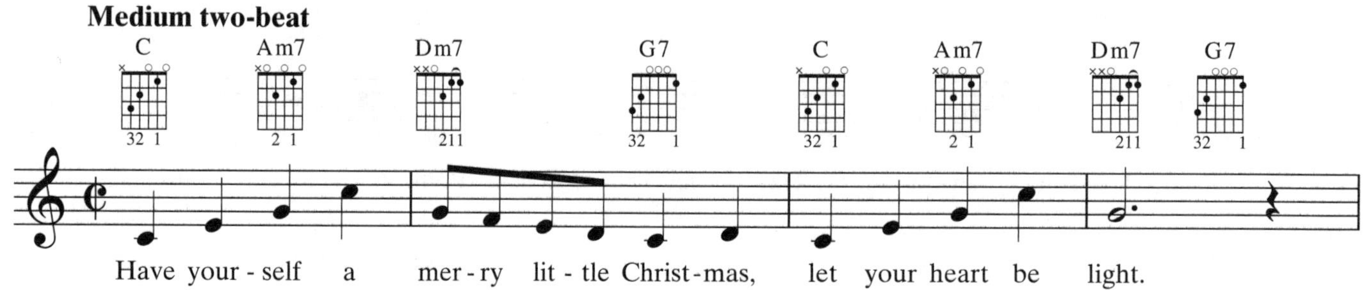


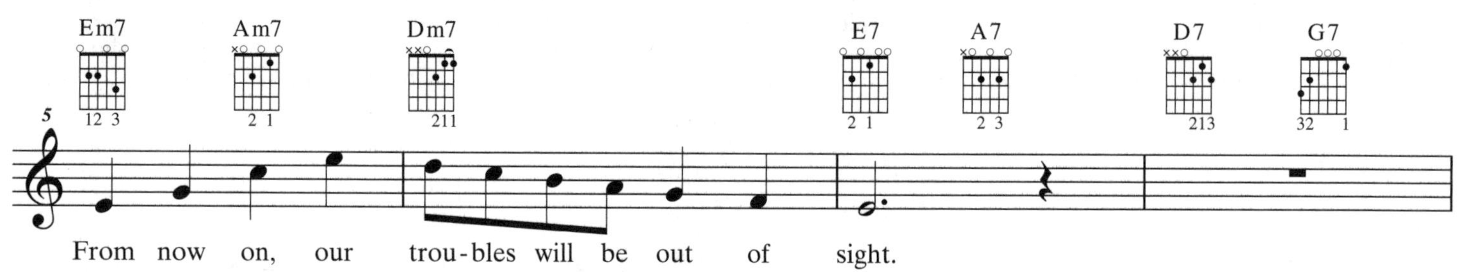


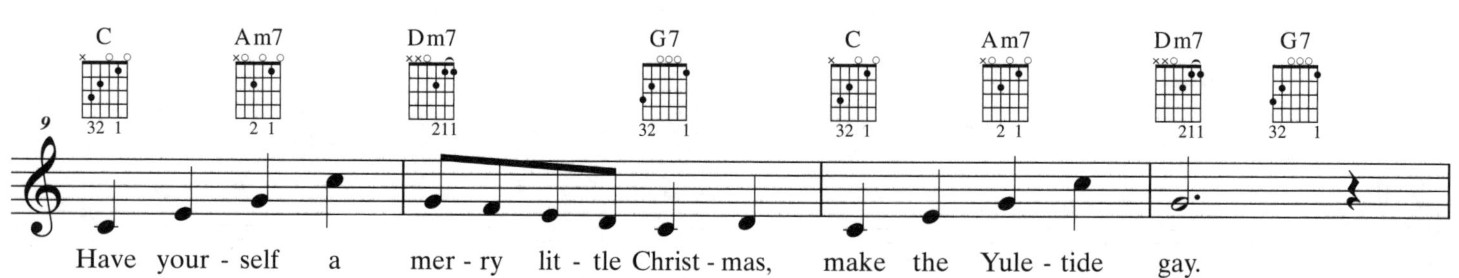


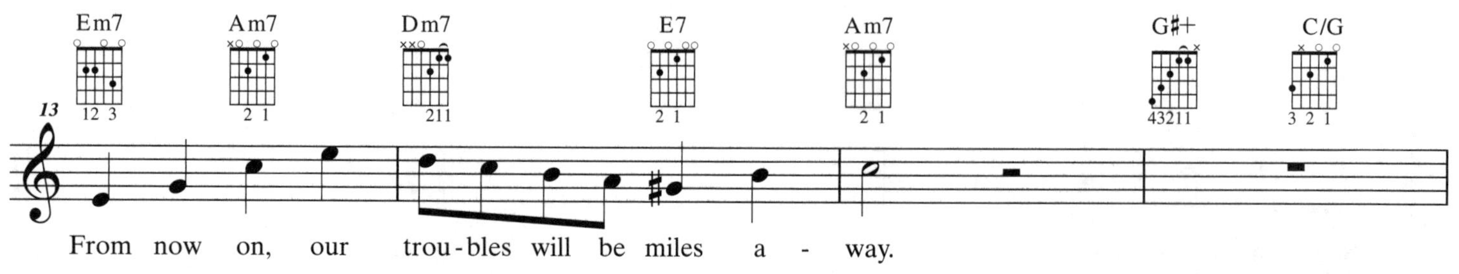

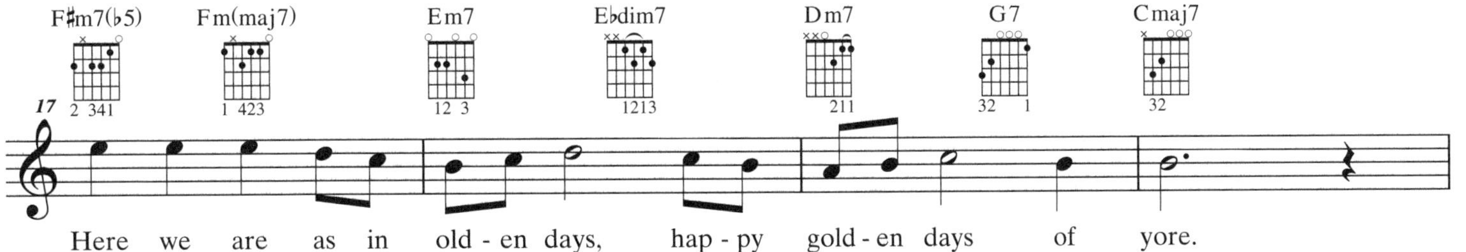
F♯m7(♭5)
Fm(maj7)
Em7
E♭dim7
Dm7
G7
Cmaj7
17
Here we are as in old - en days, hap - py gold - en days of yore.

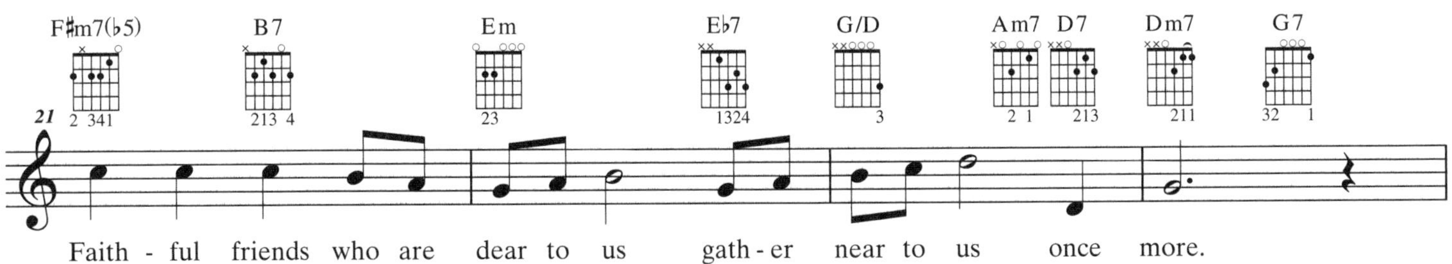
F♯m7(♭5)
B7
Em
E♭7
G/D
Am7
D7
Dm7
G7
21
Faith - ful friends who are dear to us gath - er near to us once more.

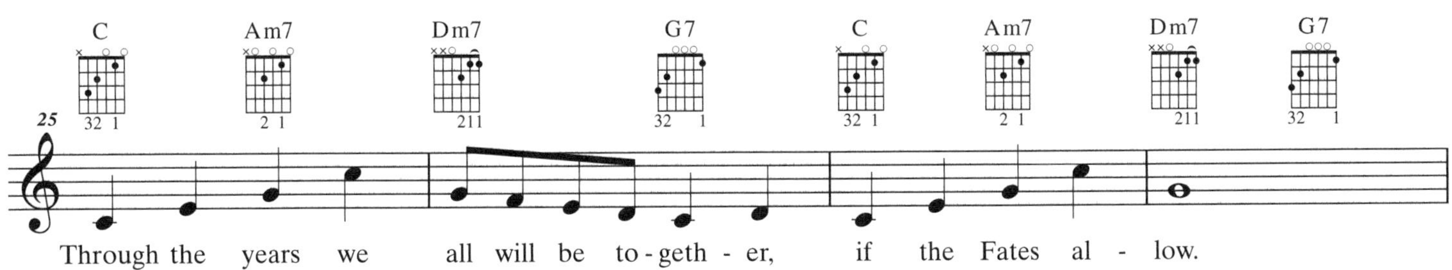
C
Am7
Dm7
G7
C
Am7
Dm7
G7
25
Through the years we all will be to - geth - er, if the Fates al - low.

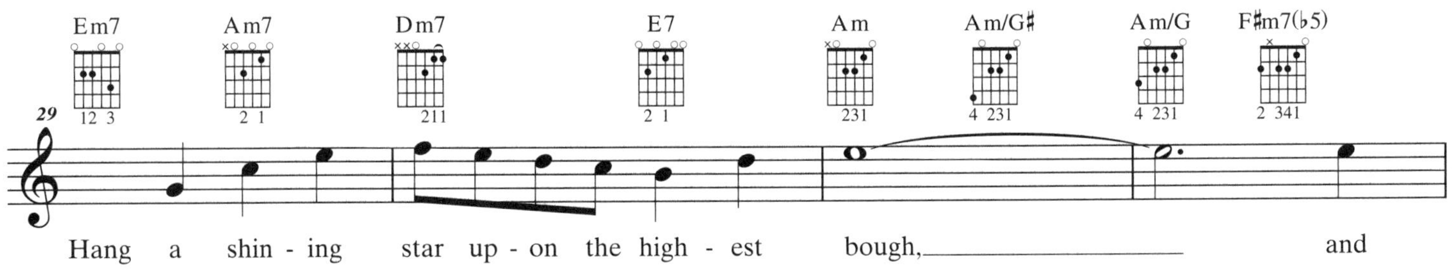
Em7
Am7
Dm7
E7
Am
Am/G♯
Am/G
F♯m7(♭5)
29
Hang a shin - ing star up - on the high - est bough, and

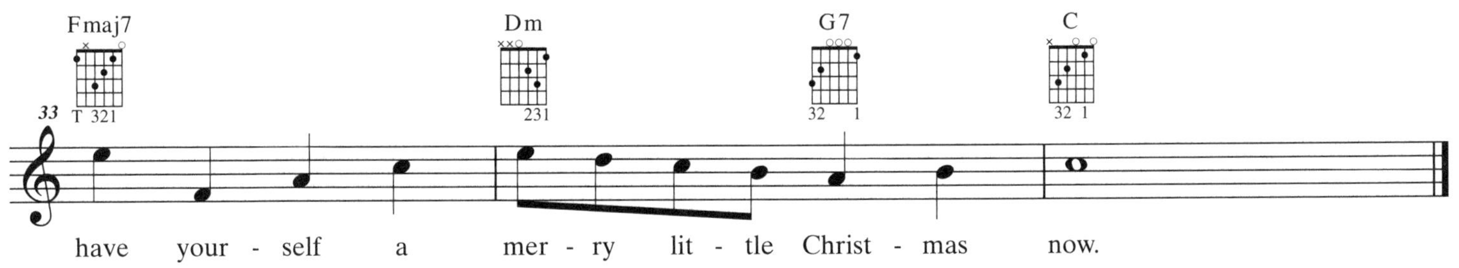
Fmaj7
Dm
G7
C
33
have your - self a mer - ry lit - tle Christ - mas now.

# Here We Come A-Wassailing

**Moderately**

Traditional Carol

*Verse 2:*
We are not daily beggars
That beg from door to door.
But we are neighbors' children
Whom you have seen before.
*(To Chorus:)*

*Verse 3:*
We have got a little purse
Of stretching leather skin,
We want a little of your money
To line it well within.
*(To Chorus:)*

*Verse 4:*
Bring us out a table,
And spread it with a cloth;
Bring us out a moldy cheese,
And some of your Christmas loaf.
*(To Chorus:)*

*Verse 5:*
God bless the master of this house,
Likewise the mistress too,
And all the little children
That 'round the table go.
*(To Chorus:)*

# The Holly and the Ivy

*Verse 2:*
The holly bears a blossom
As white as lily flow'r,
And Mary bore sweet Jesus Christ
To be our sweet Savior.
*(To Refrain:)*

*Verse 3:*
The holly bears a berry
As red as any blood,
And Mary bore sweet Jesus Christ
To do poor sinners good.
*(To Refrain:)*

# The Holiday Season

Words and Music by
KAY THOMPSON

The Holiday Season - 2 - 1

Em7 A7 Dm7 G7 C C/G
bun - dle of joy when he's com - ing down the chim - ney down. He'll have a
Dm7 G7 C Dm7 G7 C F Em
big fat pack up - on his back and lots of good - ies for you
Dm C Dm7 G7 C Dm7 G7 C
and for me. So leave a pep - per - mint stick for Old Saint Nick hang-
D7 G7 C C/G
- ing on the Christ - mas tree. It's the hol - i - day sea - son
C C♯dim7 3fr. Dm7 G7 Dm7 G7
so hoop de doo and dick - o - ry dock and
Dm7 G7 C Am Dm7 G7
don't for - get to hang up your sock. 'Cause just ex - act - ly at
Em7 A7 Dm7 G7 C
twelve o' clock, he'll be com - ing down the chim - ney down.

# A Holly Jolly Christmas

Words and Music by
JOHNNY MARKS

**Bright two-beat**

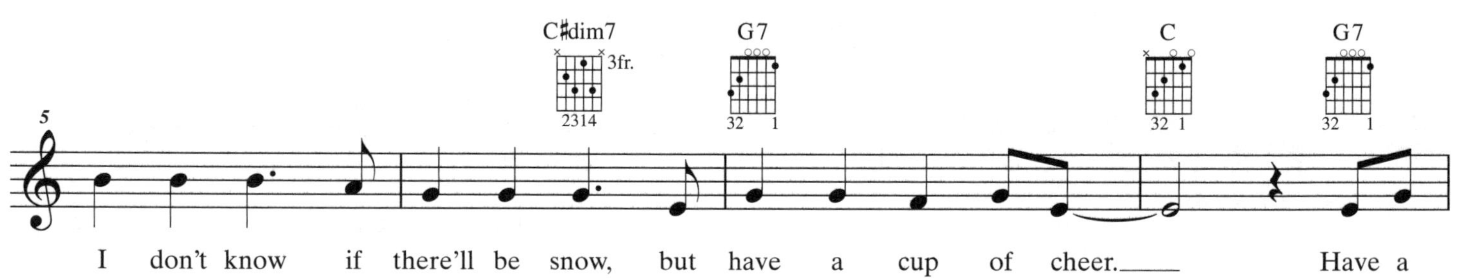

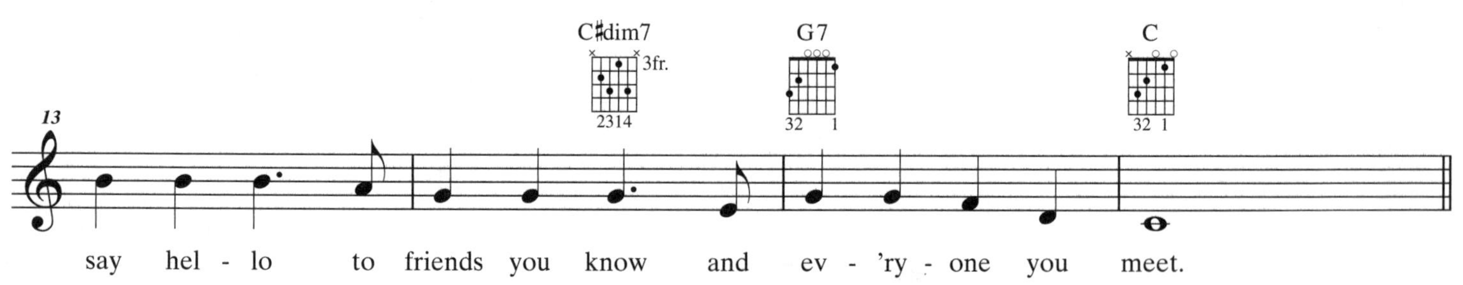


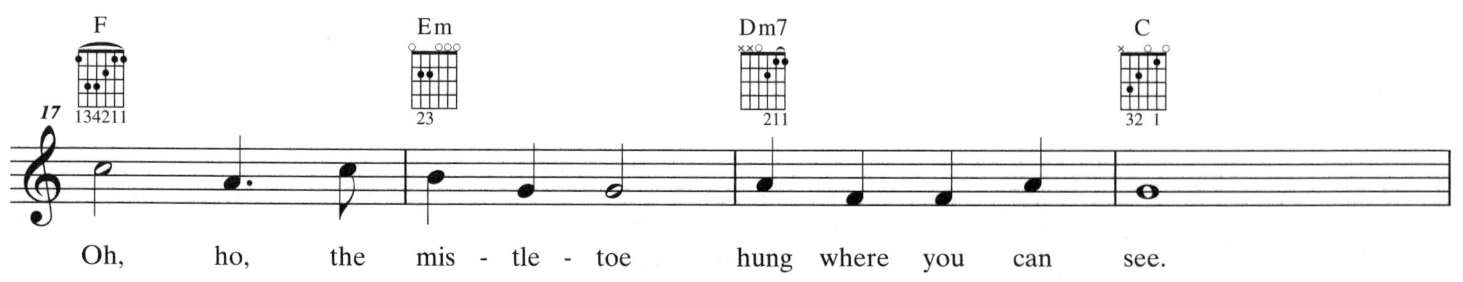

21
Dm Am D7 Am7 D7 G G7
Some - bod - y waits for you, kiss her once for me. Have a
25
C Cmaj7 C6 C♯dim7 G7
3fr.
hol - ly jol - ly Christ - mas, and in case you did - n't hear,
29
Em Am7
1.
D7 G7 C G7
oh, by gol - ly, have a hol - ly jol - ly Christ - mas this year. Have a
2.
33
D7 G7 C F C G7 C
Christ - mas this year.

# Holy Night, Peaceful Night

Words by
REV. JOSEPH MOHR
English Translation by
JANE MONTGOMERY CAMPBELL

Music by
ALONZO P. HOWARD

# Hush, My Babe, Lie Still and Slumber

Words by
ISAAC WATTS

Music by
JEAN-JACQUES ROUSSEAU

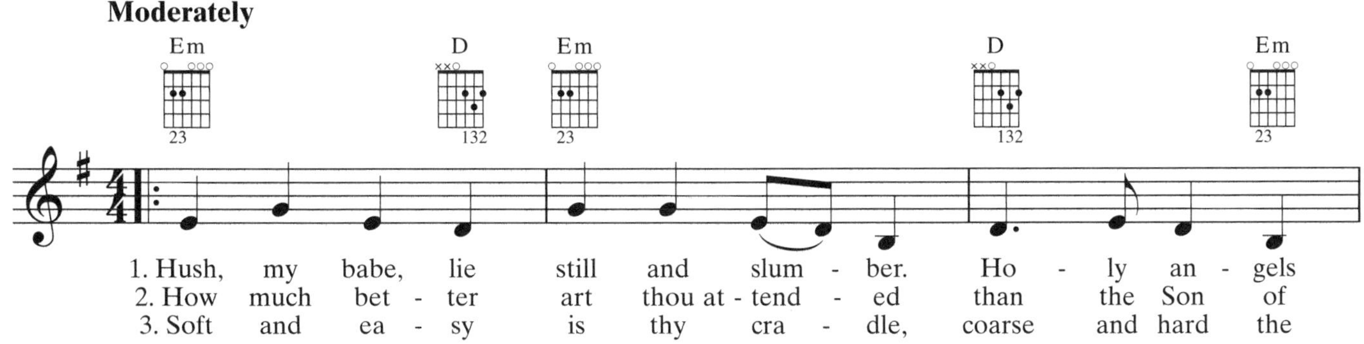

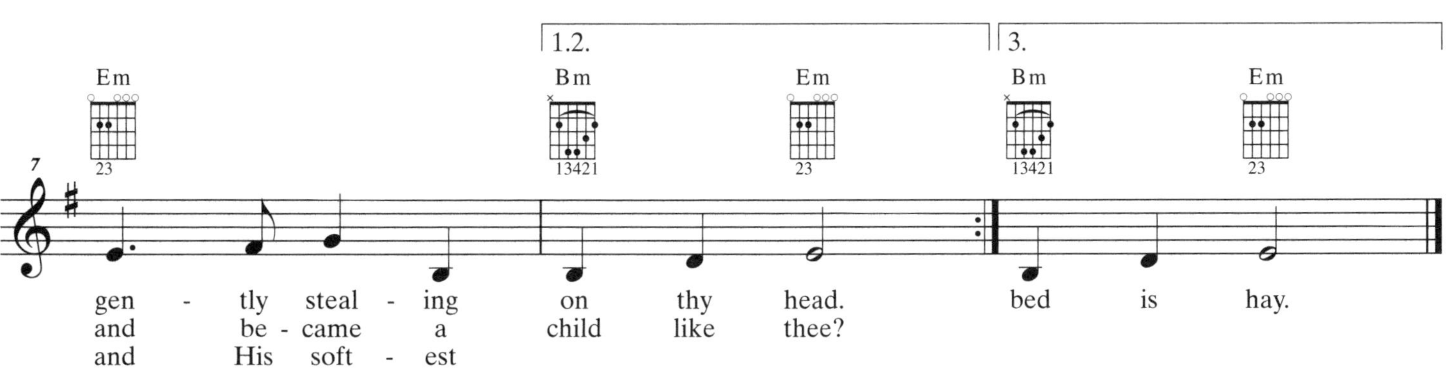

(There's No Place Like)

# Home for the Holidays

Words by
AL STILLMAN

Music by
ROBERT ALLEN

**Bright two-beat**

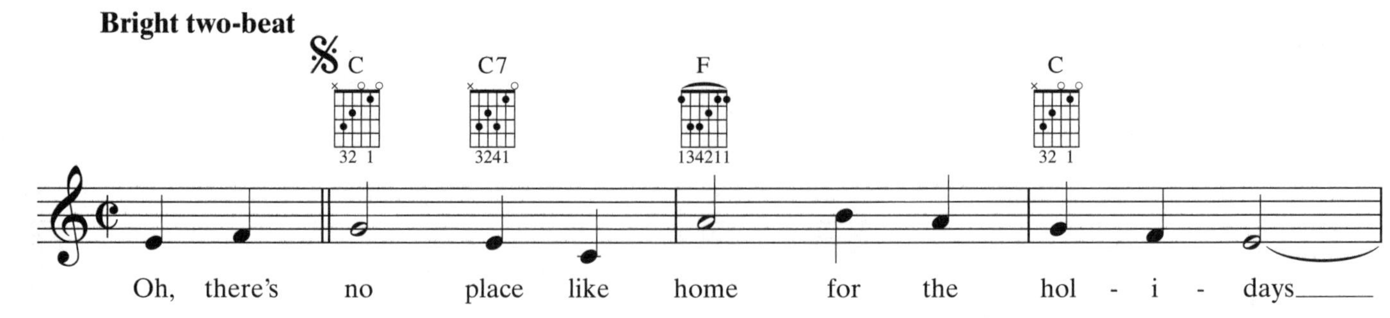


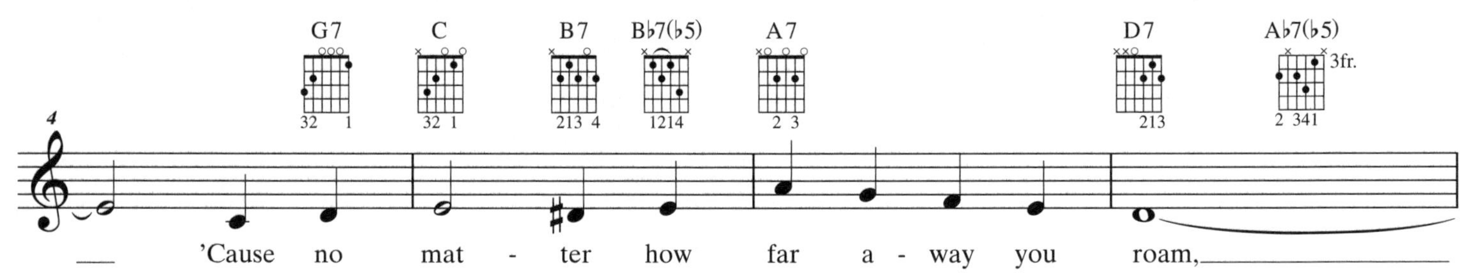


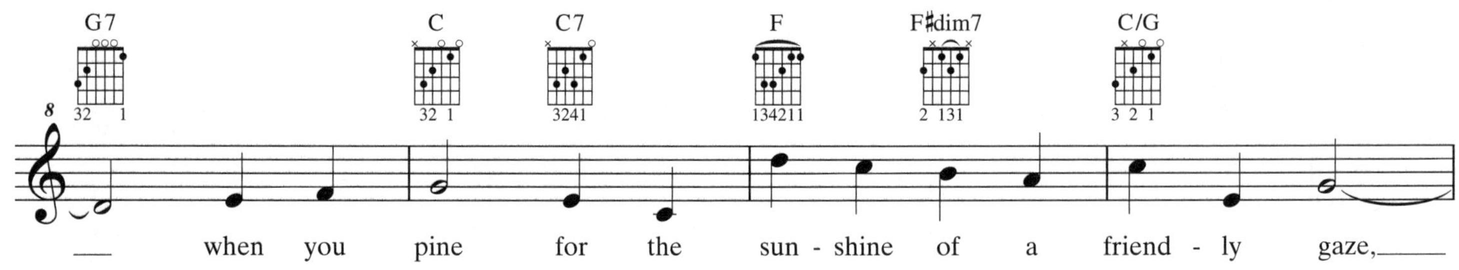


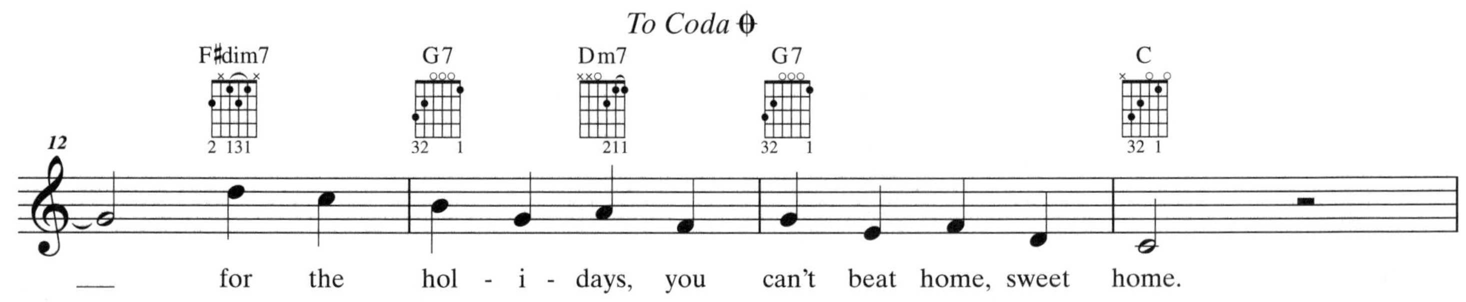


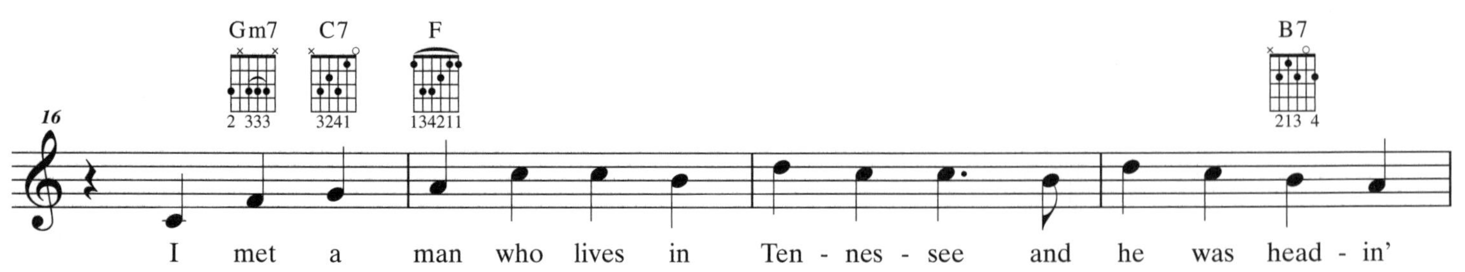


(There's No Place Like) Home for the Holidays - 2 - 1

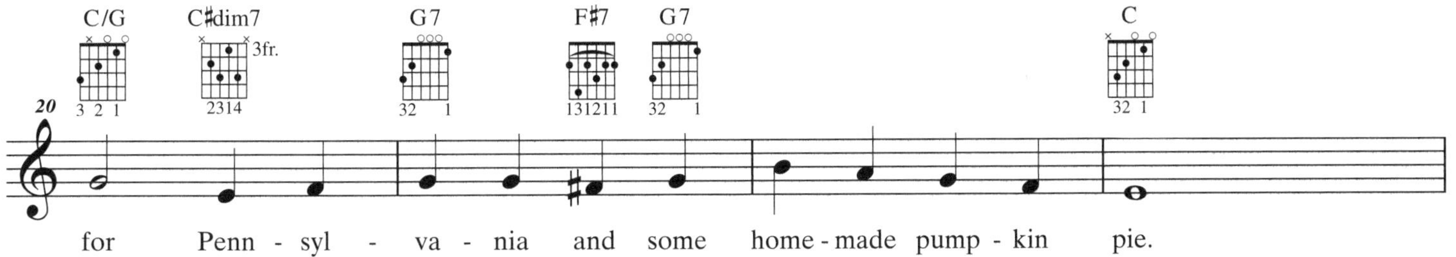
C/G
C♯dim7
G7
F♯7
G7
C
20
for Penn - syl - va - nia and some home - made pump - kin pie.

Gm7
C7
F
24
From Penn - syl - va - nia, folks are trav - 'lin' down to

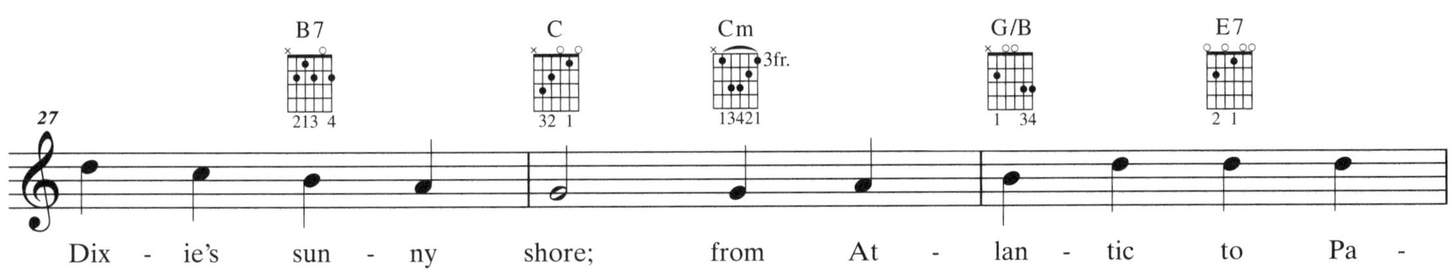
B7
C
Cm
G/B
E7
27
Dix - ie's sun - ny shore; from At - lan - tic to Pa -

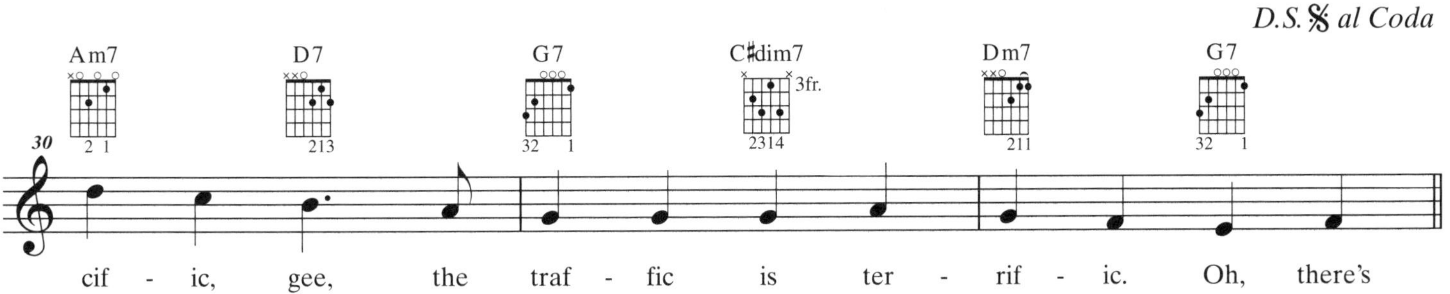
D.S. 𝄋 al Coda
Am7
D7
G7
C♯dim7
Dm7
G7
30
cif - ic, gee, the traf - fic is ter - rif - ic. Oh, there's

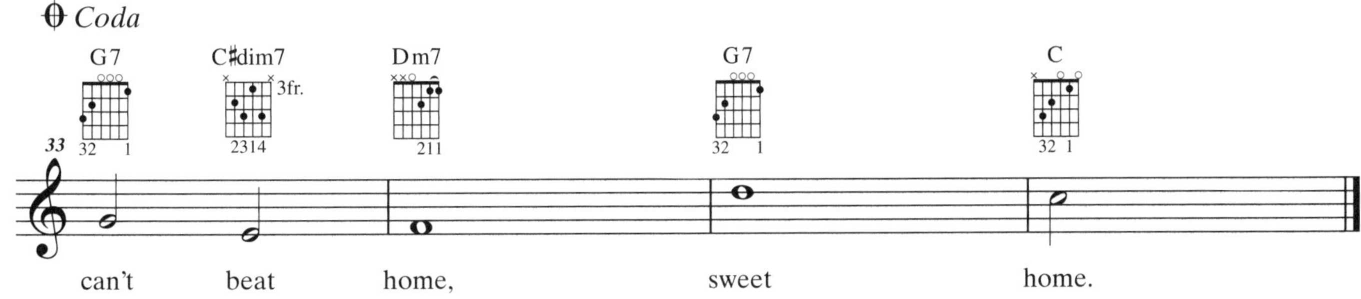
Coda
G7
C♯dim7
Dm7
G7
C
33
can't beat home, sweet home.

# *I Heard the Bells on Christmas Day*

Words by
HENRY WADSWORTH LONGFELLOW

Music by
JOHN BAPTISTE CALKIN

# I Saw Three Ships

Traditional Carol

**Moderately**

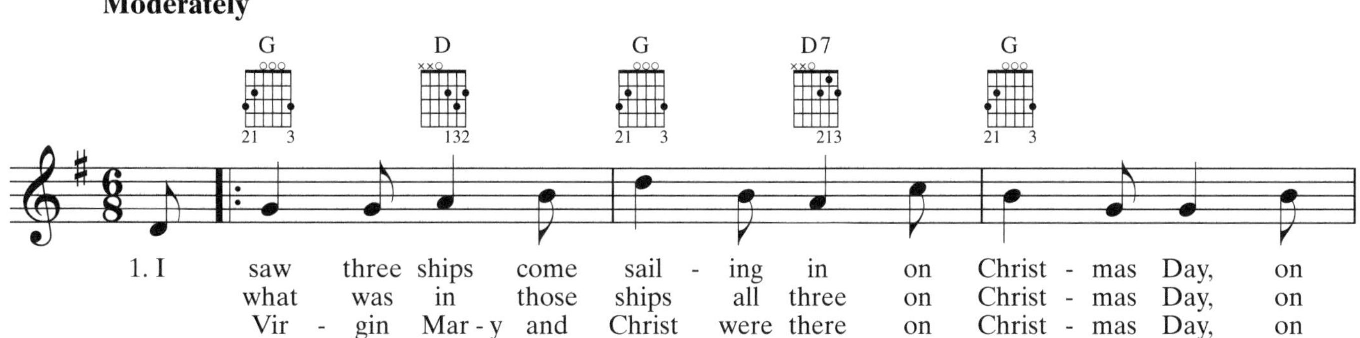


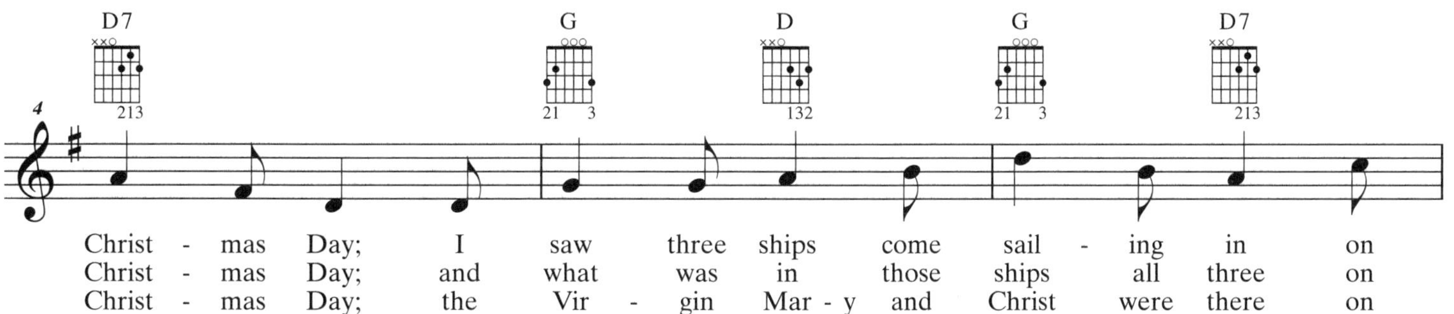


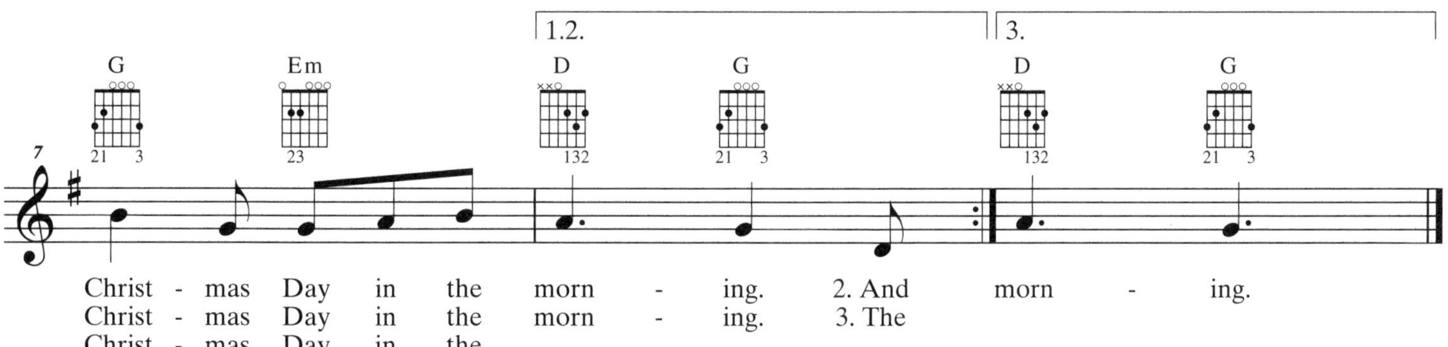

# I Wonder as I Wander

Traditional Appalachian Carol

**Medium waltz**

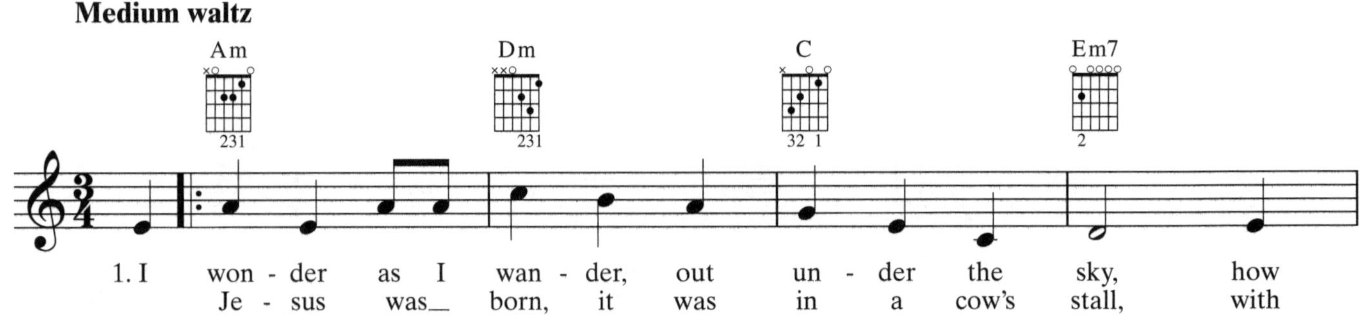


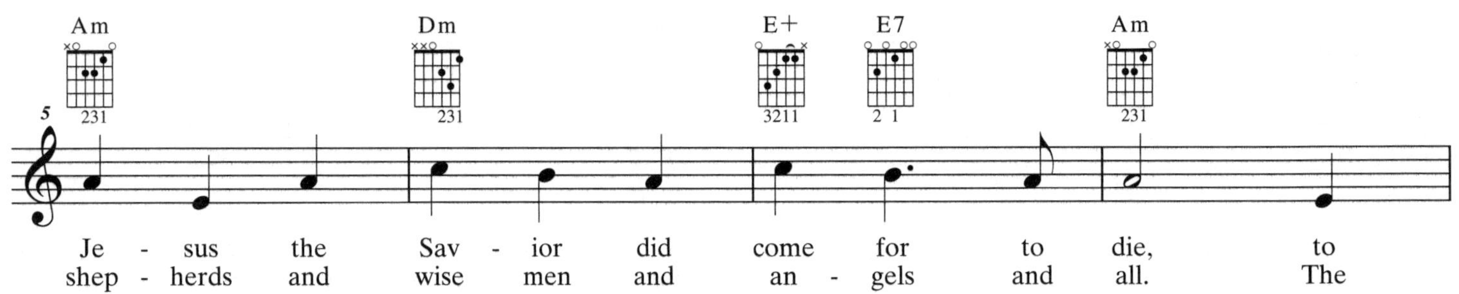


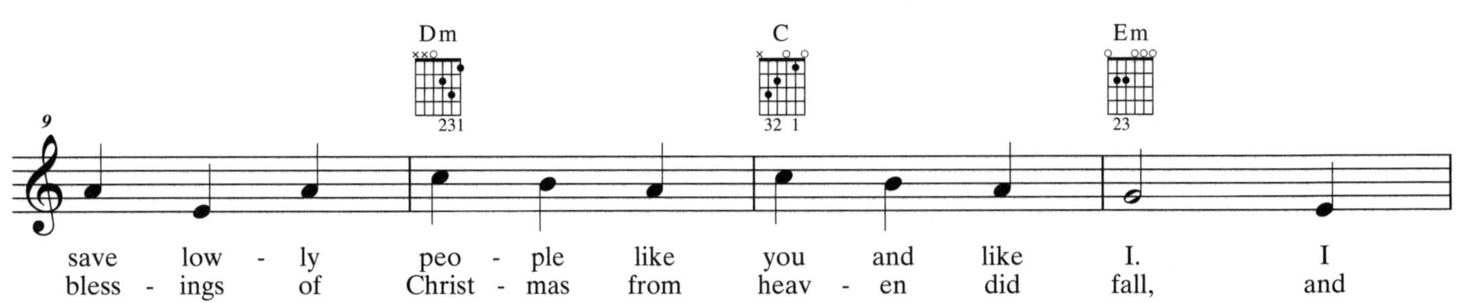


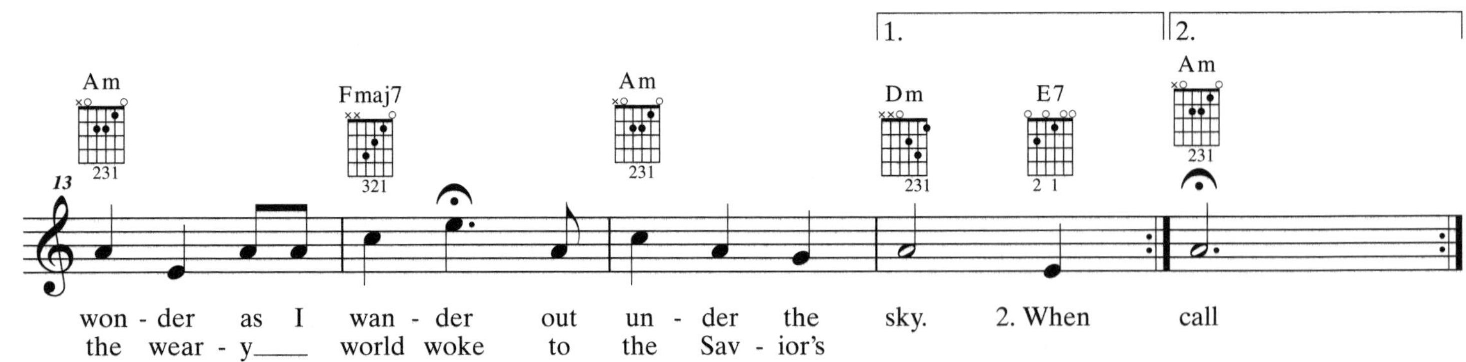

# I'll Be Home for Christmas

Words by
KIM GANNON

Music by
WALTER KENT

**Moderately**

C F6/G Dm7 G7 Dm7 G7 C6

I'll be home for Christ - mas, you can

Gm7 A7 Dm Gm6 Dm A7 Dm Fm(9) G7

plan on me. Please have snow and

C G Am Am7 D7 Am7 D7 G C♯dim7 3fr.

mis - tle - toe and pres - ents on the tree.

Dm7 G7 C F6/G Dm7 G7 Dm7 G7

Christ - mas Eve will find me

C6 Gm7 A7 Dm Gm6 Dm A7 Dm7

where the love - light gleams. I'll be

Fm C B♭7 A7 Dm C♯dim7 3fr. Fm G

home for Christ - mas, if on - ly in my

1. C G7 2. C

dreams. dreams.

# In a Christmas Mood

Words by
JUDY SPENCER

Music by
EARL ROSE

Bridge:
A13 D7sus G(9) C(9) D7
Christ - mas mood? With shop - pers fill - ing
G(9) Am7 D7 G(9)
down - town stores and toy shelves al - most cleared, with
C♯m7 F♯7 Bm7 E7 D7 A♯dim7
young - sters sit - ting on San - ta's lap, tell - ing him se - crets and
Refrain:
Am7 D7 G(9) Am7 Bm7 Am7
rum - pling his beard. The light - ed trees and fall - ing snow,
Gmaj7 G♯dim7 Am7 D7 Gmaj7 E13
cards from ev - 'ry - one I know, a kitch - en full of
Am7 D7 Bm7 E9
friends and par - ty food. No
Am7 D7sus D7 G(9)
won - der that I'm in a Christ - mas mood!

# It Came Upon the Midnight Clear

Traditional Carol

**Medium waltz**

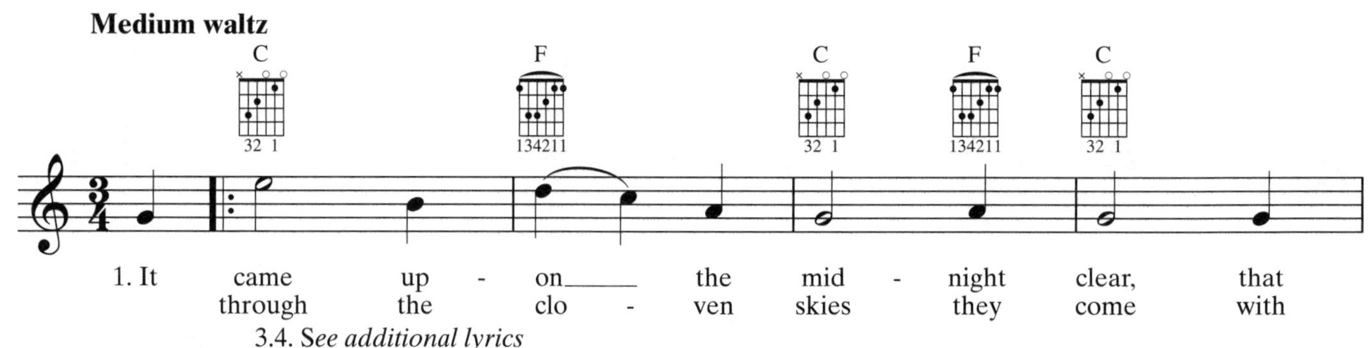


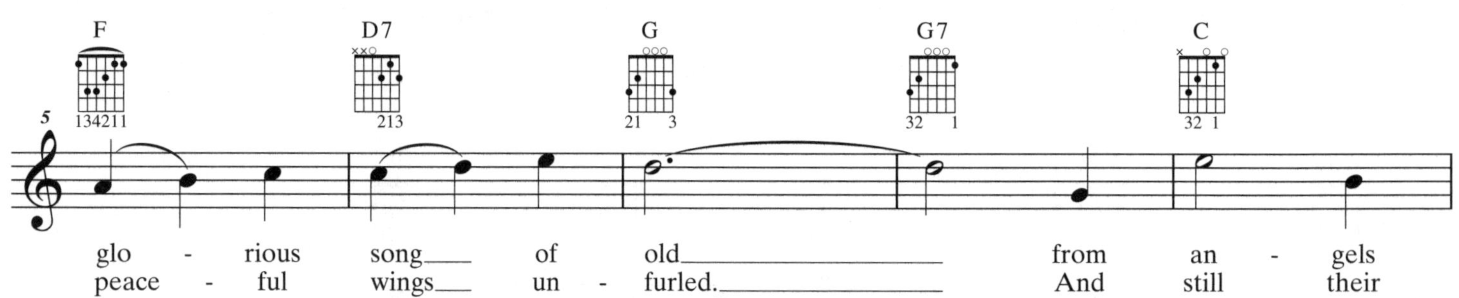


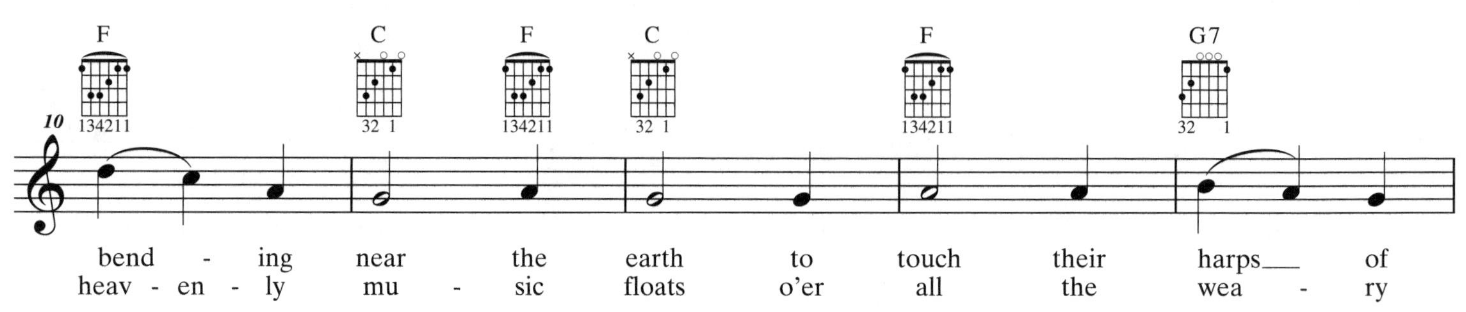


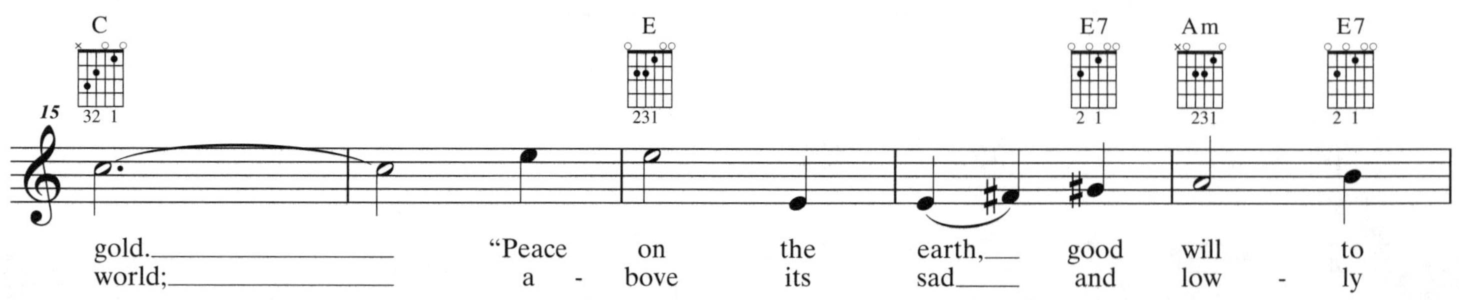

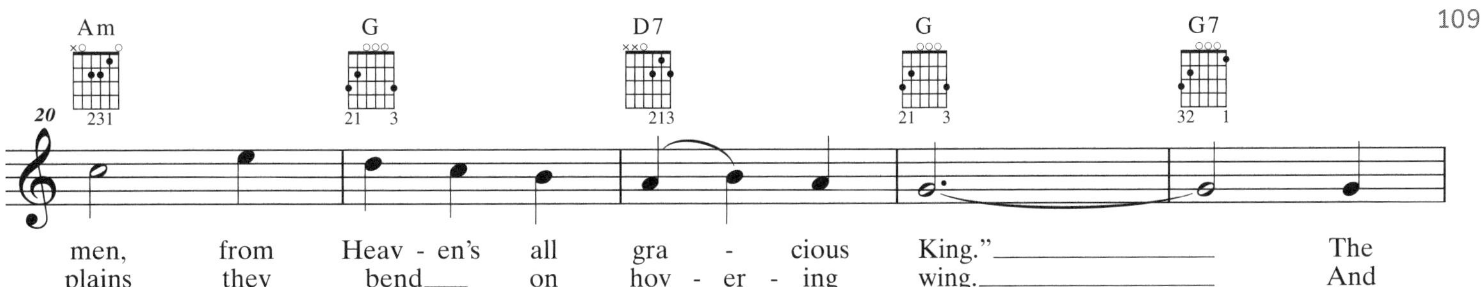


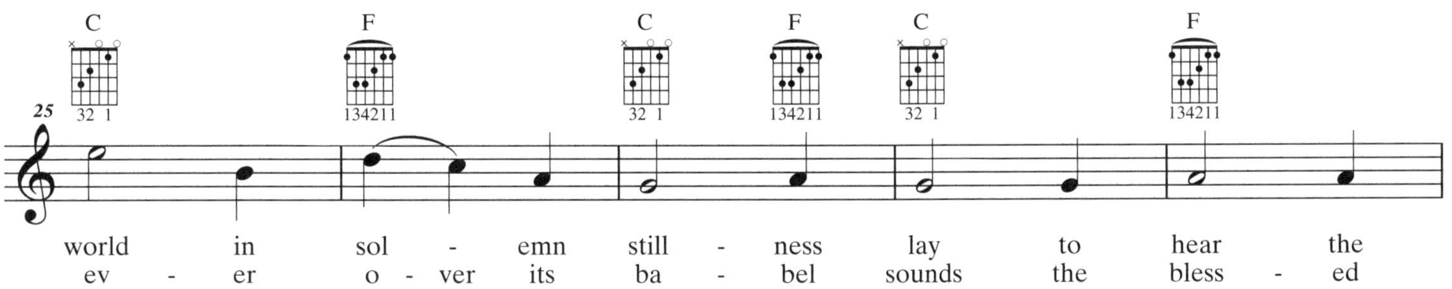


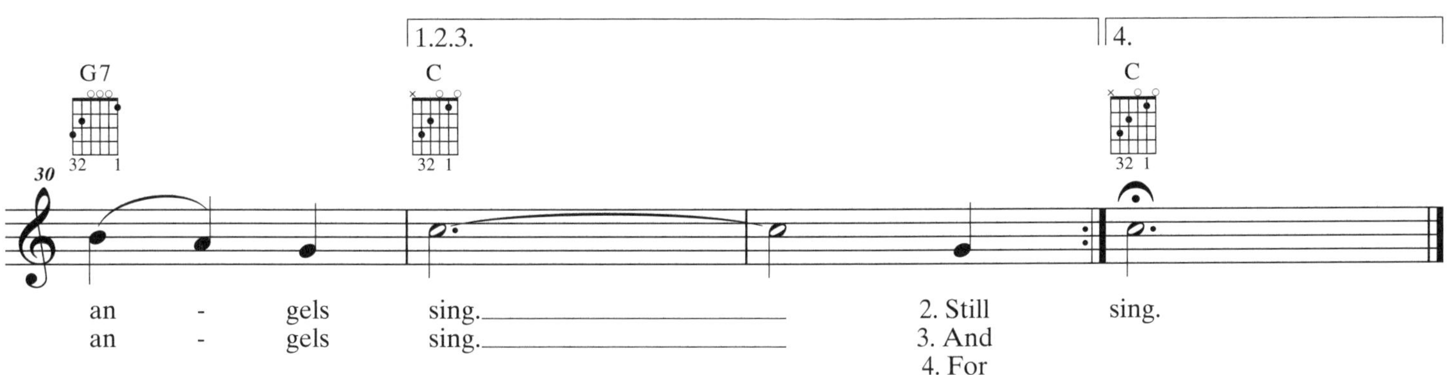


*Verse 3:*
And ye beneath life's crushing load,
Whose forms are bending low,
Who toil along the climbing way,
With painful steps and slow,
Look now! For glad and golden hours
Come swiftly on the wing.
O rest beside the weary road
And hear the angels sing.

*Verse 4:*
For lo, the days are hast'ning on,
By prophet bards foretold.
When, with the evercircling years,
Comes 'round the age of gold,
When peace shall over all the earth
Its ancient splendor fling,
And the whole world give back the song
Which now the angels sing.

# It's Christmas in New York

*Verse 3:*
Stockings are filling, champagne is chilling.
It's all so thrilling, it's Christmas in New York.
Log fires are burning,
Santa's returning, filling each yearning,
It's Christmas in New York.
*(To Verse 4:)*

# It's the Most Wonderful Time of the Year

Words and Music by
EDDIE POLA and GEORGE WYLE

G♯dim7
D/A
Bm7
Em7
A7
30
host - ing, marsh - mal - lows for toast - ing, and car - ol - ing out in the
D
D7
Gm7
C7
Fmaj7
35
snow. There'll be scar - y ghost sto - ries and tales of the
Dm7
Em7(♭5)
B♭7
Em7
A7
40
glo - ries of Christ-mas - es long, long a - go.
D
Bm
Em7
A7
46
It's the most won - der - ful time of the
D
Bm
Em7
A7
Em7
51
year. There'll be much mis - tle -
A7
D
D7
G
56
toe - ing, and hearts will be glow - ing when loved ones are near.
G♯dim7
D
Bm
Em7
61
It's the most won - der - ful time
A7
D
B♭
Gm
3fr.
D
66
of the year.

# Jingle Bells

Words and Music by
JAMES PIERPONT

Jingle Bells - 2 - 1

*Chorus:*

G
17
Jin - gle bells, jin - gle bells, jin - gle all the way.

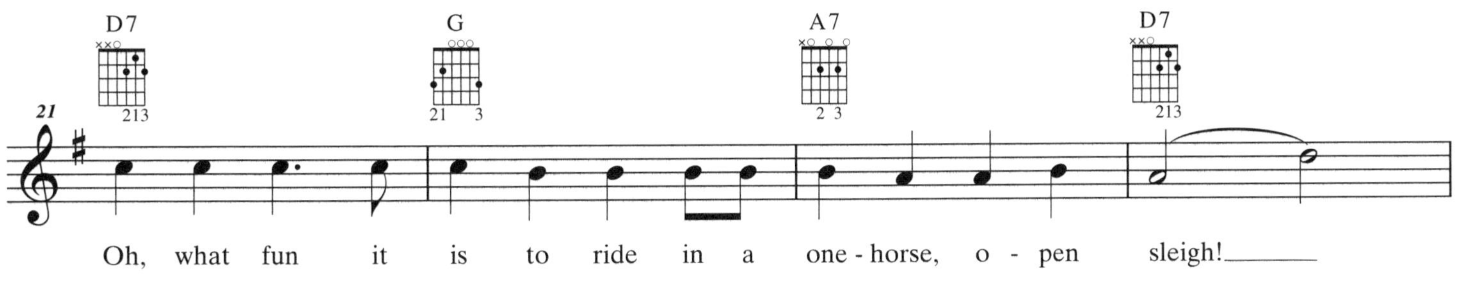
D7
G
A7
D7
21
Oh, what fun it is to ride in a one - horse, o - pen sleigh!

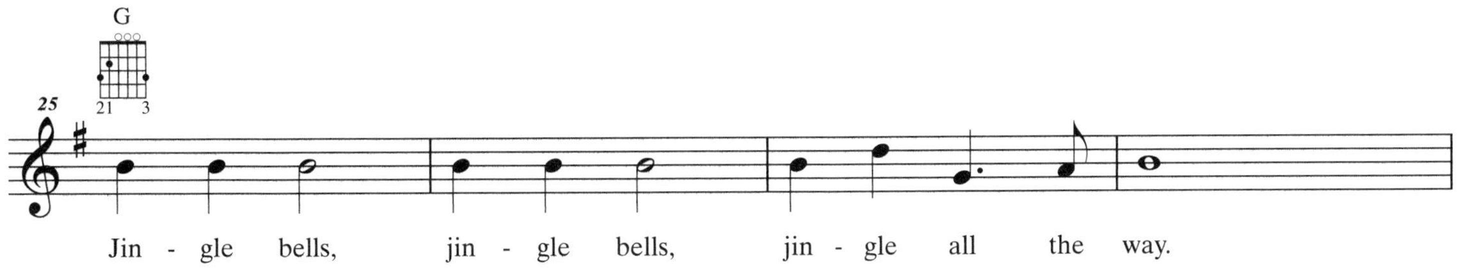
G
25
Jin - gle bells, jin - gle bells, jin - gle all the way.

1.2.
3.
D7
G
D7
G
G
29
Oh, what fun it is to ride in a one-horse, o - pen sleigh! 2. A sleigh!

# Jolly Old Saint Nicholas

Traditional American Carol

**Moderately fast**

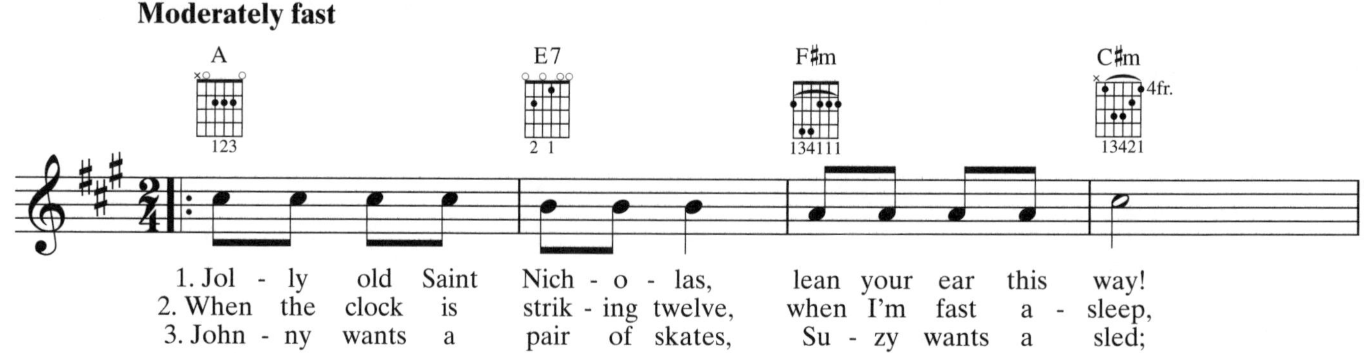


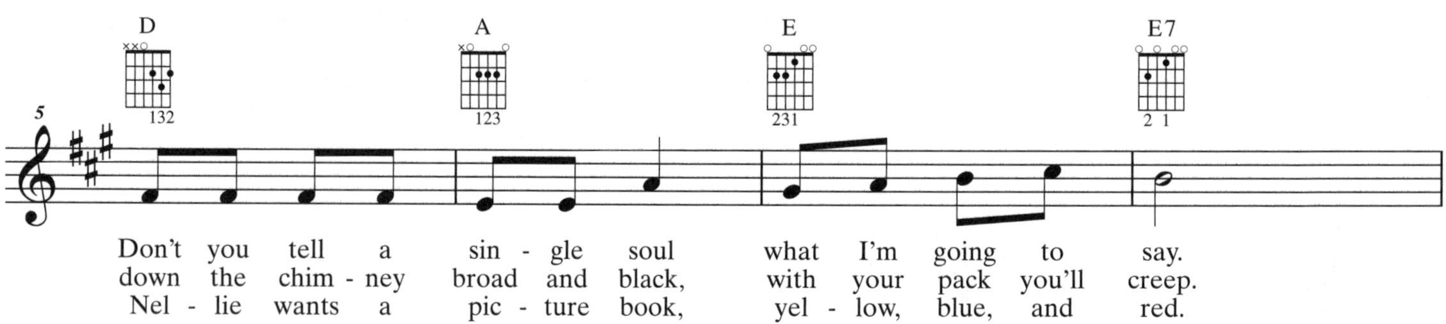

# Joy to the World

Words by
ISAAC WATTS

Music by
G. F. HANDEL

# Let There Be Peace on Earth

## (Let It Begin with Me)

Word and Music by
SY MILLER and JILL JACKSON

**Slowly, in one ♩. = 48**

C Am Dm7 G7 C F C

32 1 / 231 / 211 / 32 1 / 32 1 / 134211 / 32 1

Let there be peace on earth, and let it be - gin with

7

Dm7 G C B B7 Em

211 / 21 3 / 32 1 / 1333 / 213 4 / 23

me.______ Let there be peace on earth, the peace that was

14

B G(9) G Am Em C7

1333 / 2 1 3 / 21 3 / 231 / 23 / 3241

meant to be.______ With God as our Fa - ther,______

21

F G G7 C Am D

134211 / 21 3 / 32 1 / 32 1 / 231 / 132

{broth - ers / fam - 'ly} all are we.______ Let {me / us} walk with {my / each

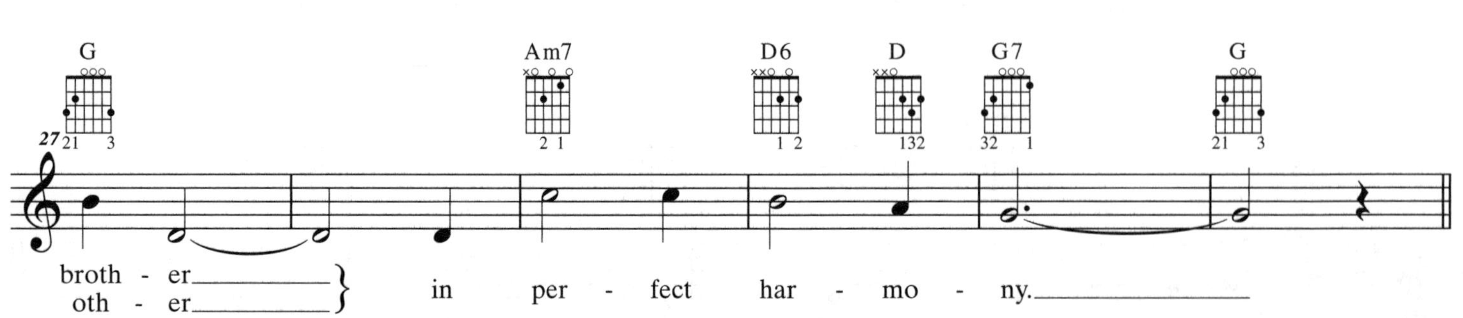

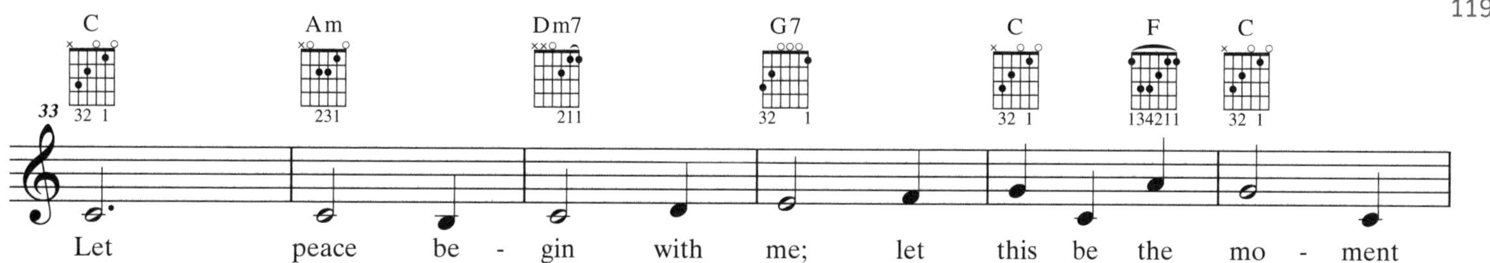
C Am Dm7 G7 C F C
33
Let peace be - gin with me; let this be the mo - ment

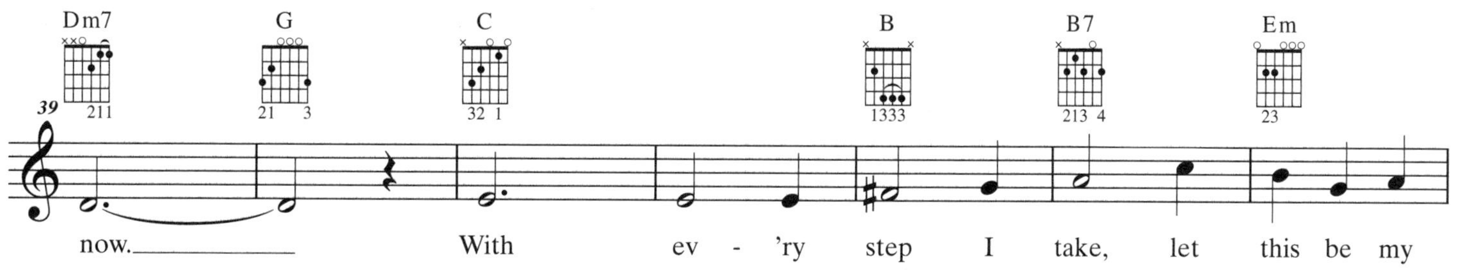
Dm7 G C B B7 Em
39
now. With ev - 'ry step I take, let this be my

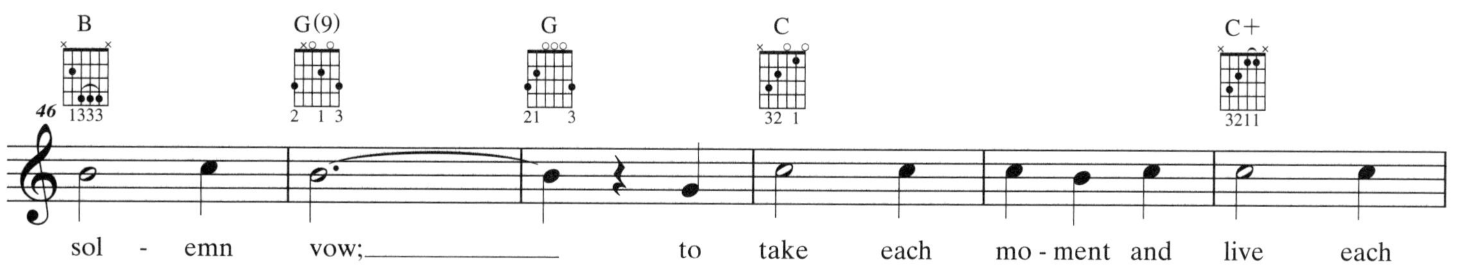
B G(9) G C C+
46
sol - emn vow; to take each mo - ment and live each

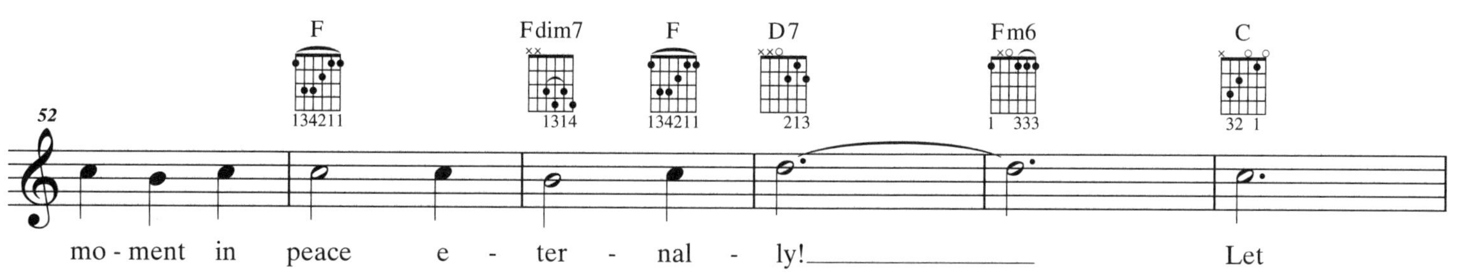
F Fdim7 F D7 Fm6 C
52
mo - ment in peace e - ter - nal - ly! Let

E7 F C F G(9) G7sus C
58
there be peace on earth, and let it be - gin with me.

# Let's Have an Old-Fashioned Christmas

Words by
HAROLD ADAMSON

Music by
JIMMY McHUGH

G7 Dm7 G7 C Cdim7
things we know and love while each
Dm7 G7 G+ C Am7(♭5)
car - ol rings and the King of Kings sends his
G/D D7 G7
bless - ing from a - bove.
Chorus:
C Cdim7 G7 Gdim7
Let's stay at home by the fi - re with the
Dm7 C♯dim7 Dm7 G7 C
ones that we hold so dear. Let's have an
Cdim7 G7 Gdim7 Dm7 G7
old - fash - ioned Christ - mas and let's pray for
1. C 2. C
a hap - py new year.

# The Little Drummer Boy

Words and Music by
HARRY SIMEONE, HENRY ONORATI
and KATHERINE DAVIS

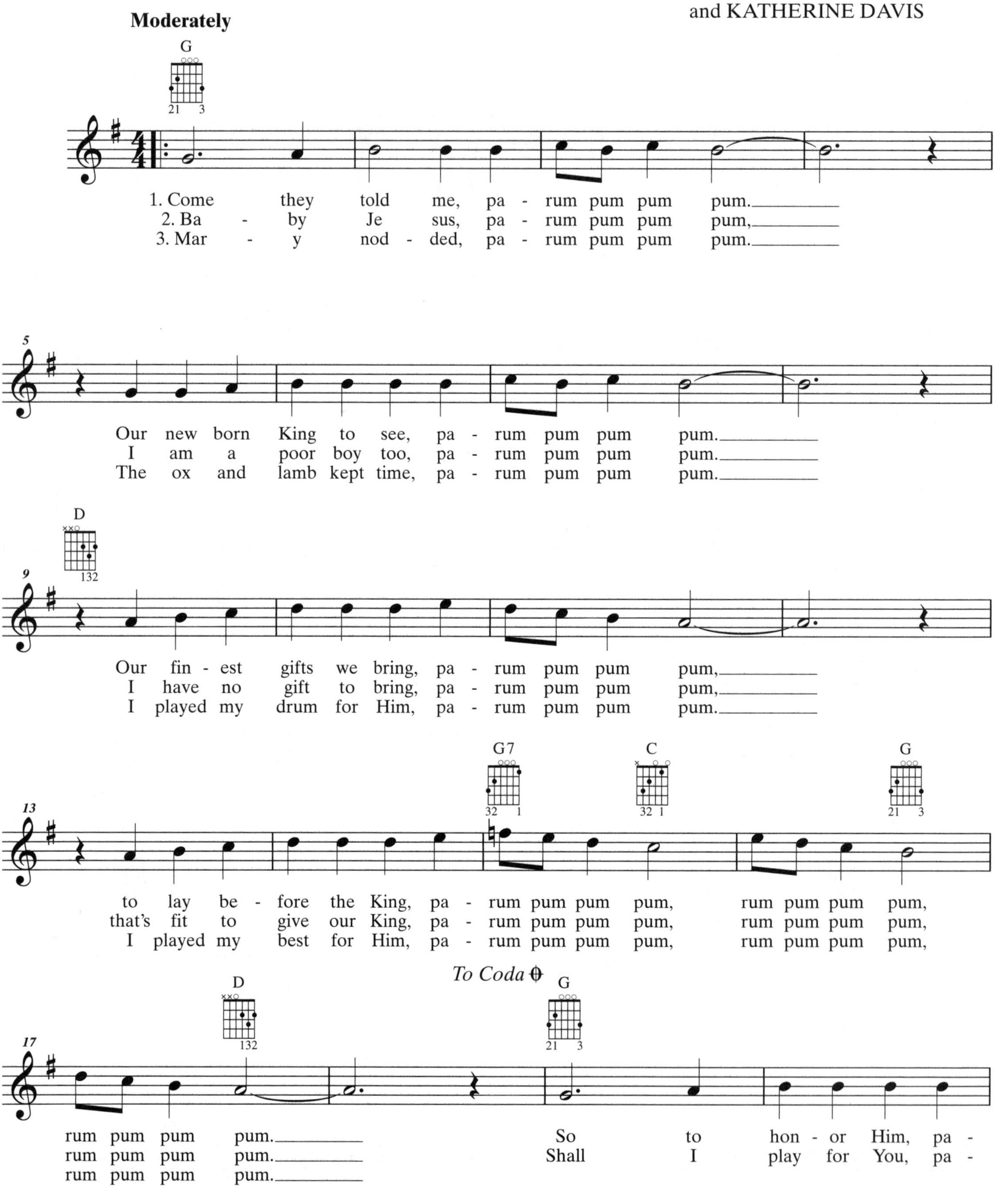

**Moderately**

G

1. Come they told me, pa - rum pum pum pum.
2. Ba - by Je sus, pa - rum pum pum pum,
3. Mar - y nod - ded, pa - rum pum pum pum.

5

Our new born King to see, pa - rum pum pum pum.
I am a poor boy too, pa - rum pum pum pum.
The ox and lamb kept time, pa - rum pum pum pum.

D

9

Our fin - est gifts we bring, pa - rum pum pum pum,
I have no gift to bring, pa - rum pum pum pum,
I played my drum for Him, pa - rum pum pum pum.

G7 C G

13

to lay be - fore the King, pa - rum pum pum pum, rum pum pum pum,
that's fit to give our King, pa - rum pum pum pum, rum pum pum pum,
I played my best for Him, pa - rum pum pum pum, rum pum pum pum,

D7
G
21
rum pum pum pum,
rum pum pum pum,
when we come.
on my drum?

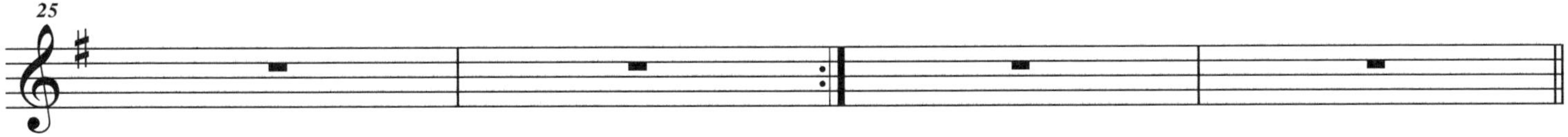
1.
2.
D.S. al Coda
25

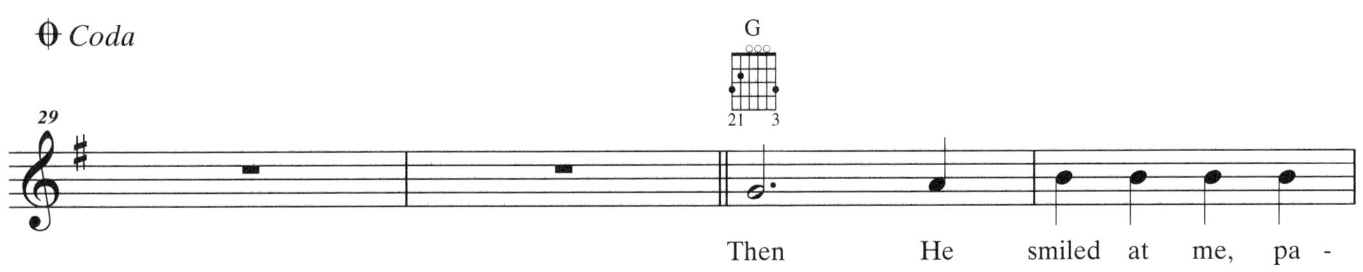
Coda
G
29
Then He smiled at me, pa -

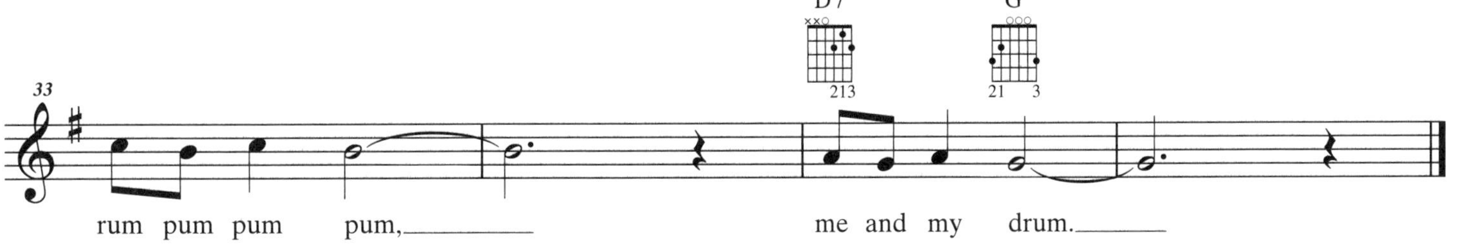
D7
G
33
rum pum pum pum,
me and my drum.

# Mary Had a Baby

Traditional Carol

**Moderately**

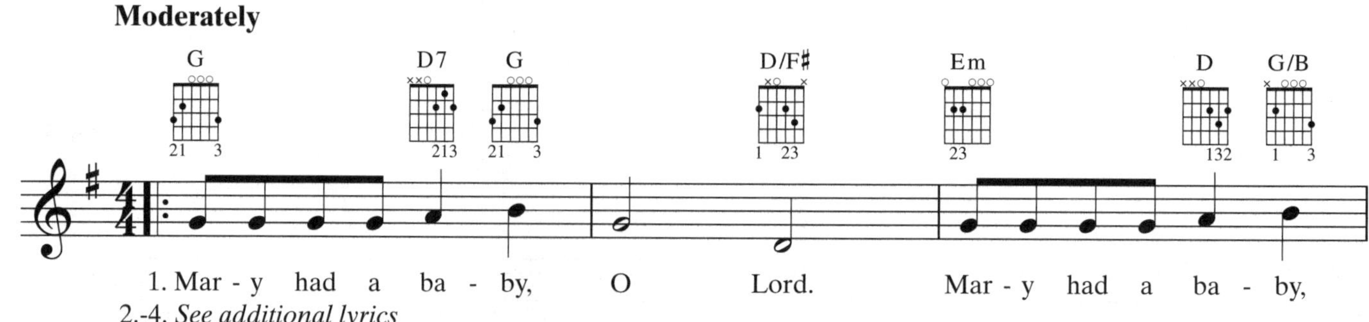

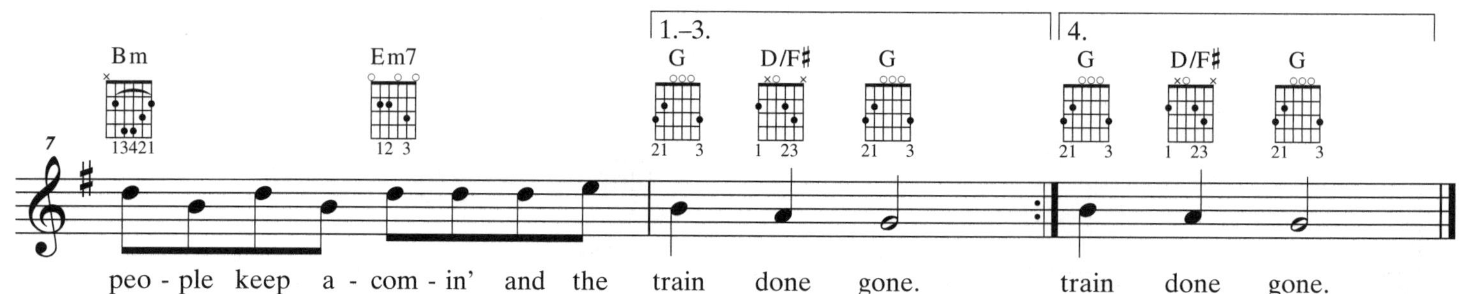


*Verse 2:*
Laid Him in a manger, O Lord.
Laid Him in a manger, O my Lord.
Laid Him in a manger, O Lord.
The people keep a-comin' and the train done gone.

*Verse 3:*
Shepherd came to see Him, O Lord.
Shepherd came to see Him, O my Lord.
Shepherd came to see Him, O Lord.
The people keep a-comin' and the train done gone.

*Verse 4:*
Named Him King Jesus, O Lord.
Named Him King Jesus, O my Lord.
Named Him King Jesus, O Lord.
The people keep a-comin' and the train done gone.

# Noel! Noel!

Traditional Carol

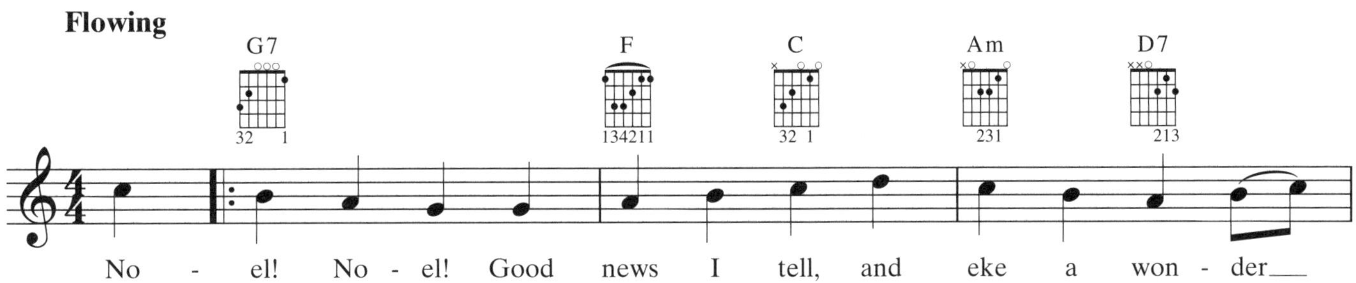

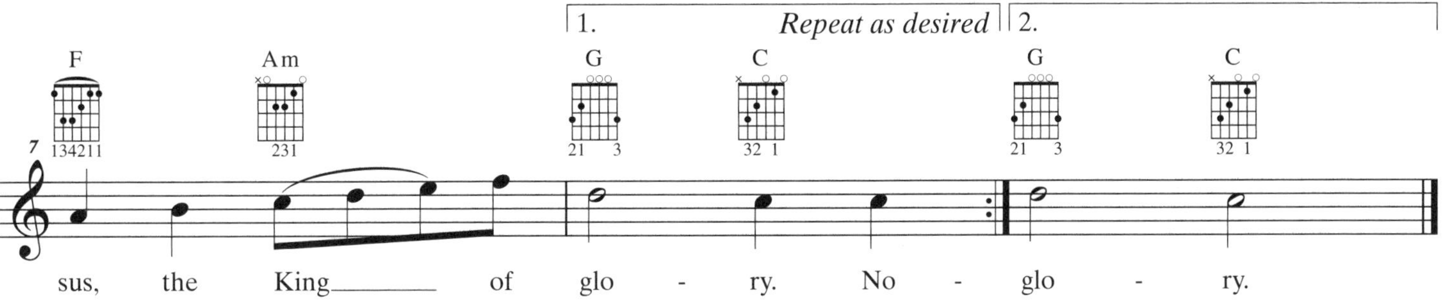

# Mary, Did You Know?

1.
2.
E7sus
E7
soon de - liv - er you? 2. Ma - ry, did you
kissed the face of God?
Am
G6
3fr.
Fmaj7
The
Bridge:
F
G
blind will see, the deaf will hear, the dead will live a - gain.
Dm7
The lame will leap, the dumb will speak the prais - es of the lamb.
D.S. al Coda
Coda
3. Ma - ry, did you
great I
Am?
know?
Repeat ad lib. and fade
Ma - ry, did you

# Mele Kalikimaka

Word and Music by
R. ALEX ANDERSON

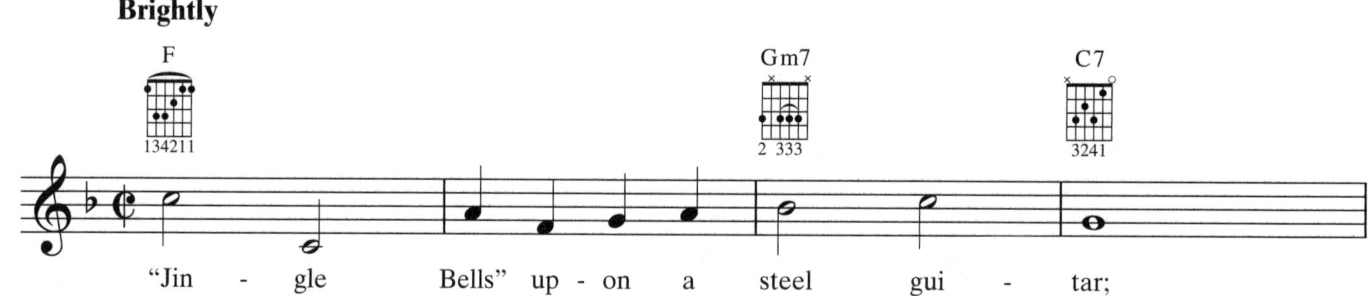


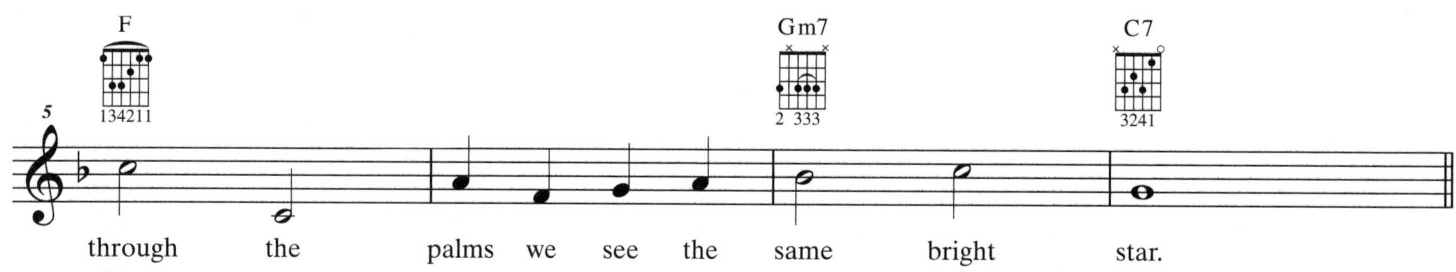

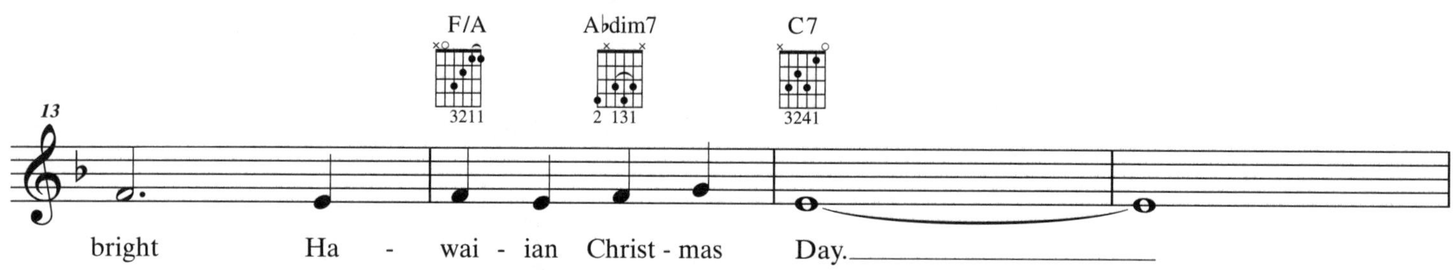

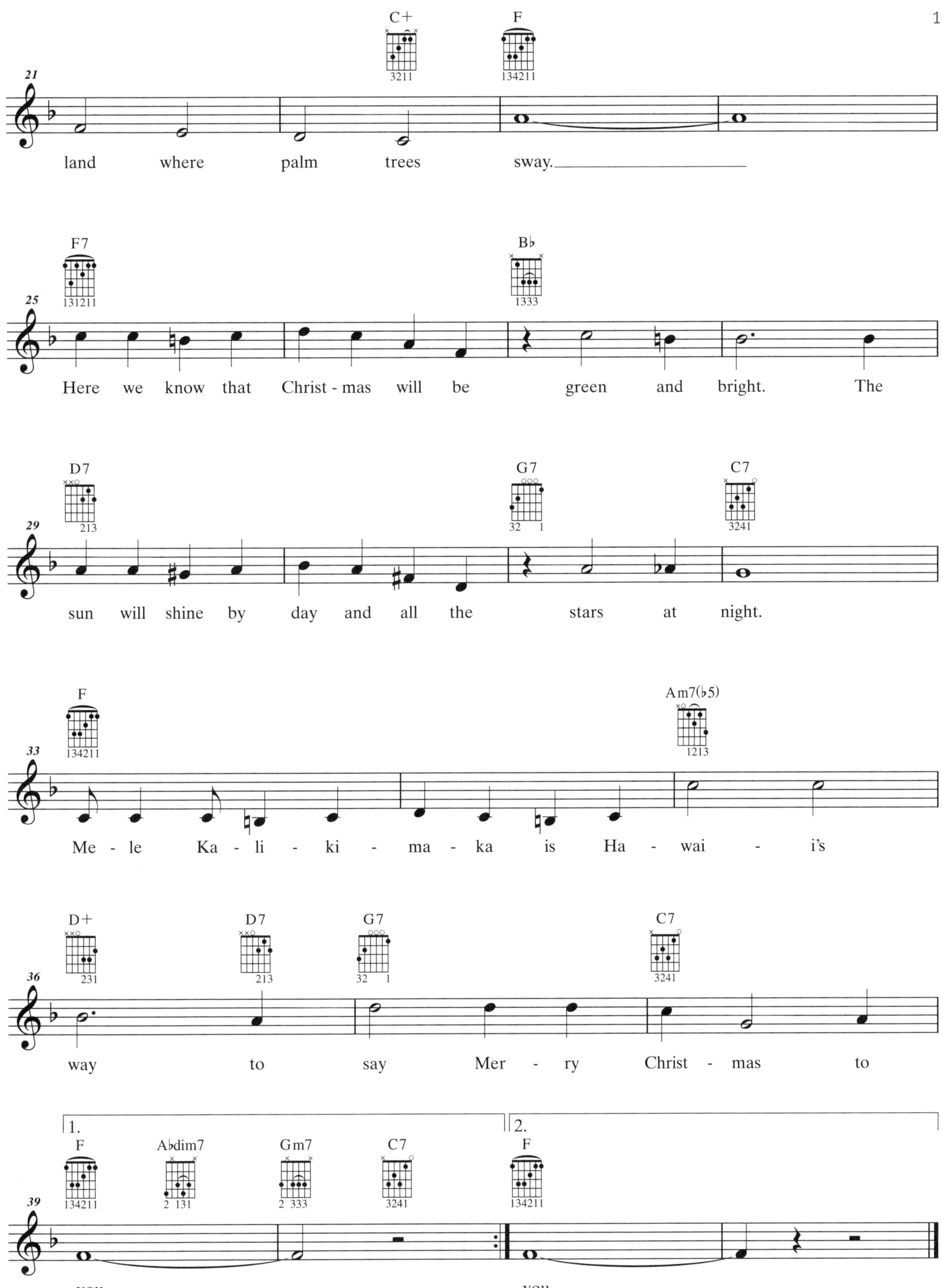
21
C+
F
land where palm trees sway.
F7
B♭
25
Here we know that Christ - mas will be green and bright. The
D7
G7
C7
29
sun will shine by day and all the stars at night.
F
Am7(♭5)
33
Me - le Ka - li - ki - ma - ka is Ha - wai - i's
D+
D7
G7
C7
36
way to say Mer - ry Christ - mas to
1.
2.
F
A♭dim7
Gm7
C7
F
39
you.
you.

# O Christmas Tree

(O Tannenbaum)

Traditional Carol

# O Come, All Ye Faithful

(Adeste Fideles)

English Words by
FREDERICK OAKELEY
Latin Words Attributed to
JOHN FRANCIS WADE

Music by
JOHN READING

# O Come, Little Children

Words by CHRISTOPH von SCHMID
English Words by MELANIE SCHULTE

Music by
JOHANN A.P. SCHULZ

# O Come, O Come Emmanuel

*Verse 3:*
O come, Thou Day-Spring, come and cheer
Our spirits by Thine advent here;
Disperse the gloomy clouds of night,
And death's dark shadows put to fight.
*(To Chorus:)*

*Verse 4:*
O come, Thou Key of David, come,
And open wide our heav'nly home;
Make safe the way that leads on high,
And close the path to misery.
*(To Chorus:)*

*Verse 5:*
O come, O come, Thou Lord of might,
Who to Thy tribes, on Sinai's height,
In ancient times did'st give the law,
In cloud and majesty and awe.
*(To Chorus:)*

# O Holy Night

Words and Music by
J.S. DWIGHT and ADOLPHE ADAM

# O Little Town of Bethlehem

Music by
LEWIS H. REDNER

**Moderately**

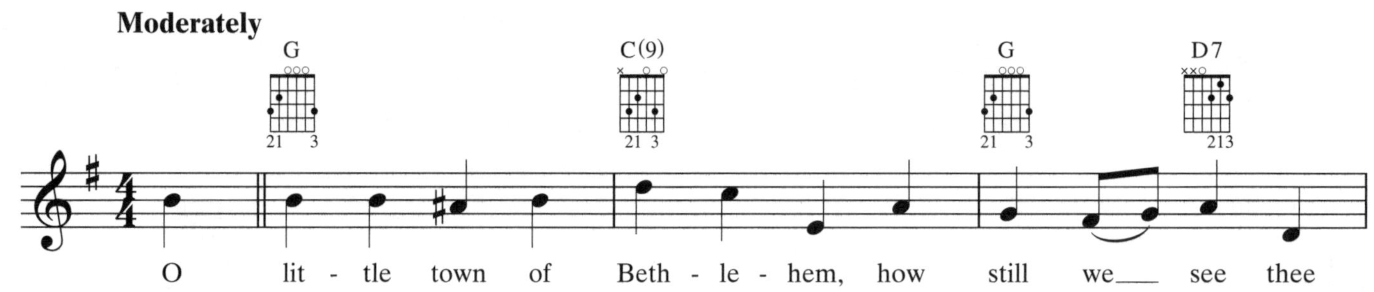


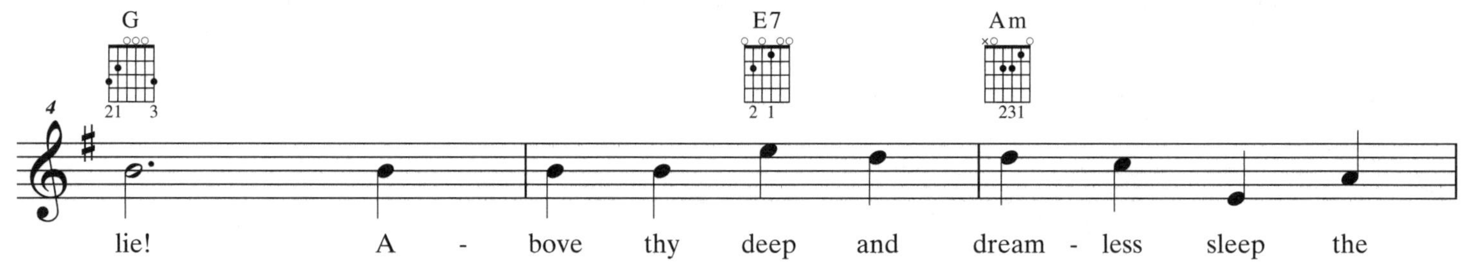


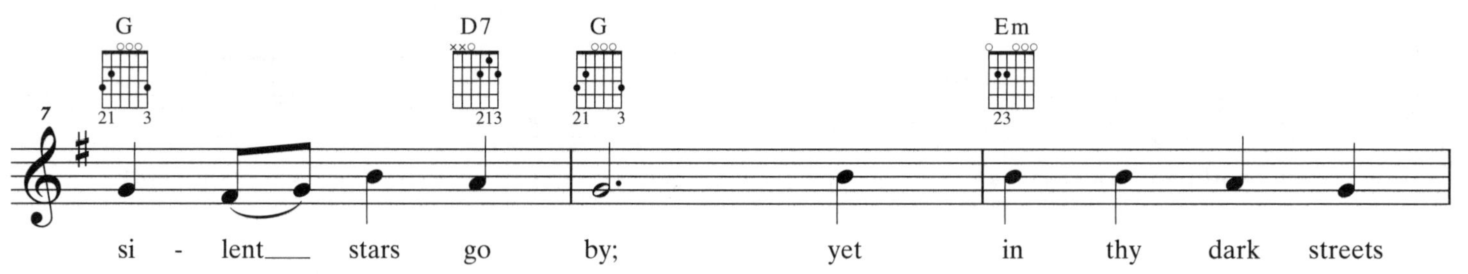


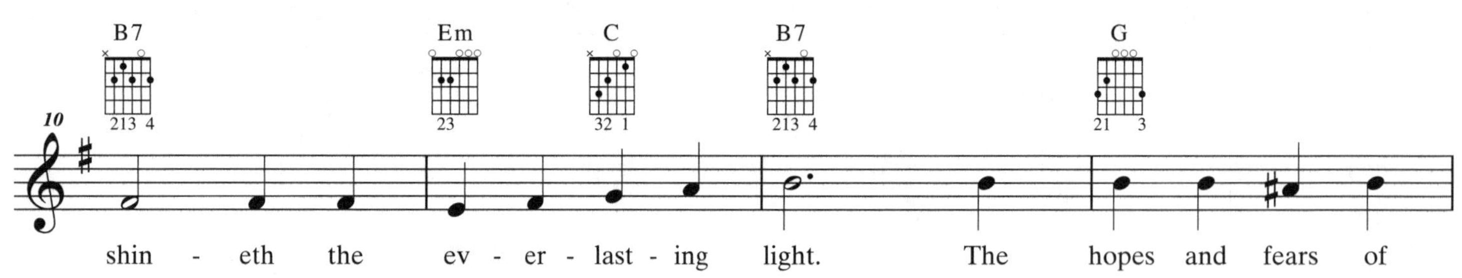


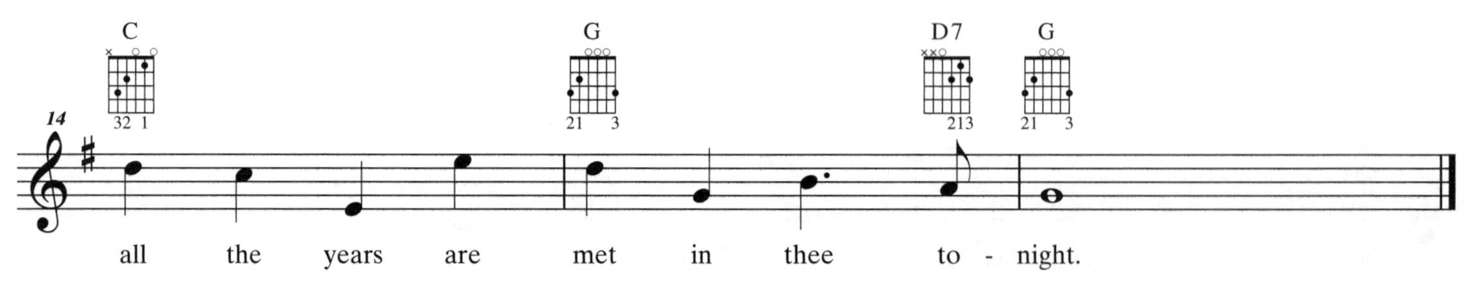

# On Christmas Night All Christians Sing

Traditional Carol

# Once in Royal David's City

Words by
Mrs. C. F. ALEXANDER

Music by
H. J. GAUNTLETT

*Verse 2:*
He came down to Earth from Heaven,
Who is God and Lord of all.
And His shelter was a stable,
And His cradle was a stall.
With the poor and mean and lowly,
Lived on earth our Savior holy.

*Verse 3:*
And our eyes at last shall see Him,
Through His own redeeming love.
For that Child so dear and gentle
Is our Lord in Heaven above.
And He leads His children on
To the place where He is gone.

# Patapan

Composed by
BERNARD DE LA MONNOYE

**Bright two-beat**

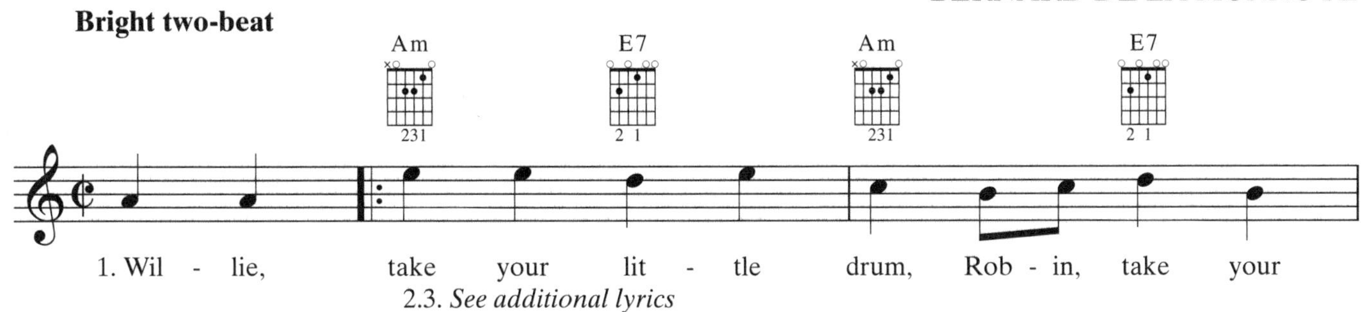

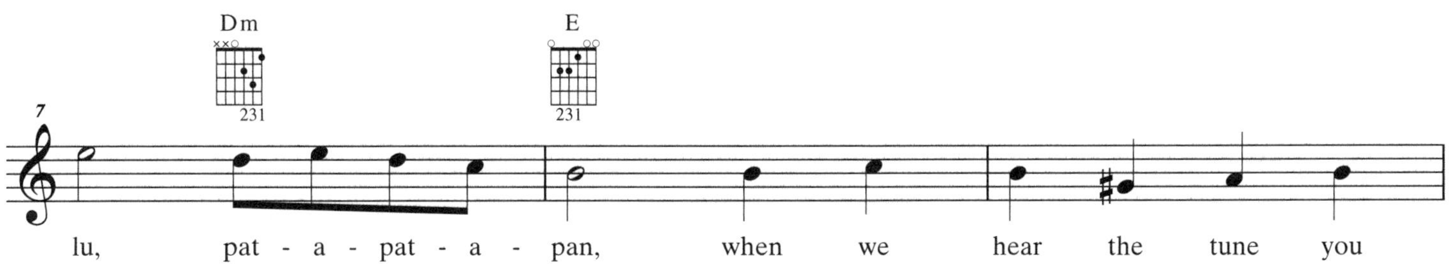


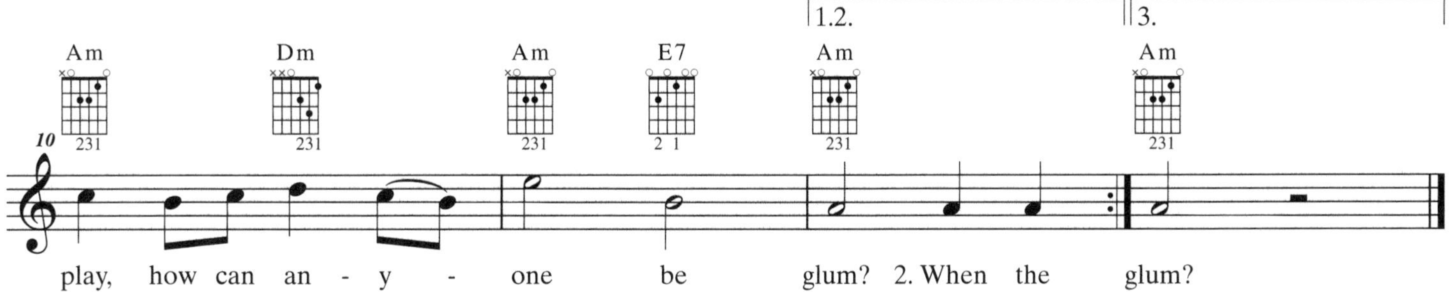


*Verse 2:*
When the men of olden days
Gave the King of Kings their praise,
They had pipes on which to play,
Turelurelu, patapatapan.
They had drums on which to play,
Full of joy, on Christmas Day.

*Verse 3:*
God and man this day become
Joined as one with flute and drum.
Let the happy time play on,
Turelurelu, patapatapan.
Flute and drum together play,
As we sing on Christmas Day.

# *Put a Little Love in Your Heart*

Words and Music by
JIMMY HOLIDAY, RANDY MYERS
and JACKIE DE SHANNON

**Moderately**

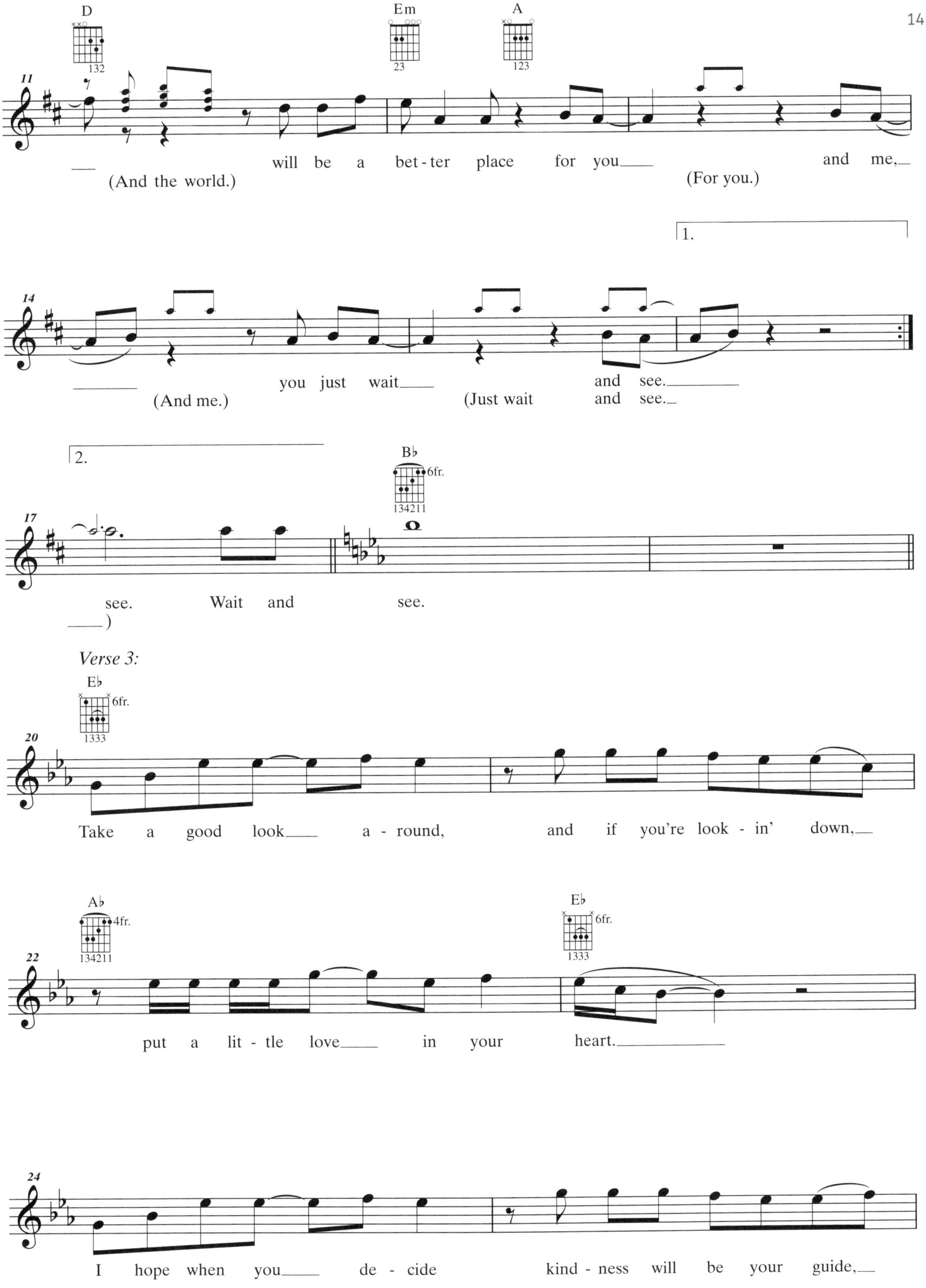

D Em A

11

will be a bet - ter place for you___ and me,_
(And the world.) (For you.)

1.

14

you just wait___ and see.____
(And me.) (Just wait and see._

2.

B♭

17

see. Wait and see.
____)

*Verse 3:*

E♭

20

Take a good look___ a - round, and if you're look - in' down,_

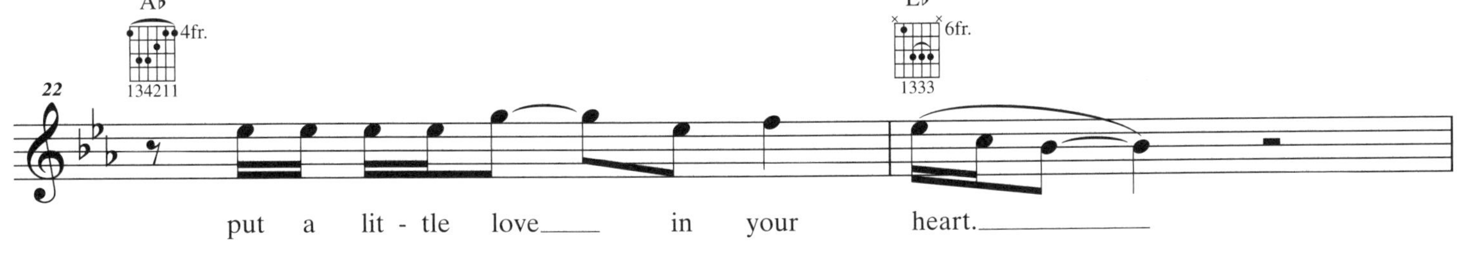

A♭
4fr.
134211
E♭
6fr.
1333
26
put a lit - tle love in your heart. And the world

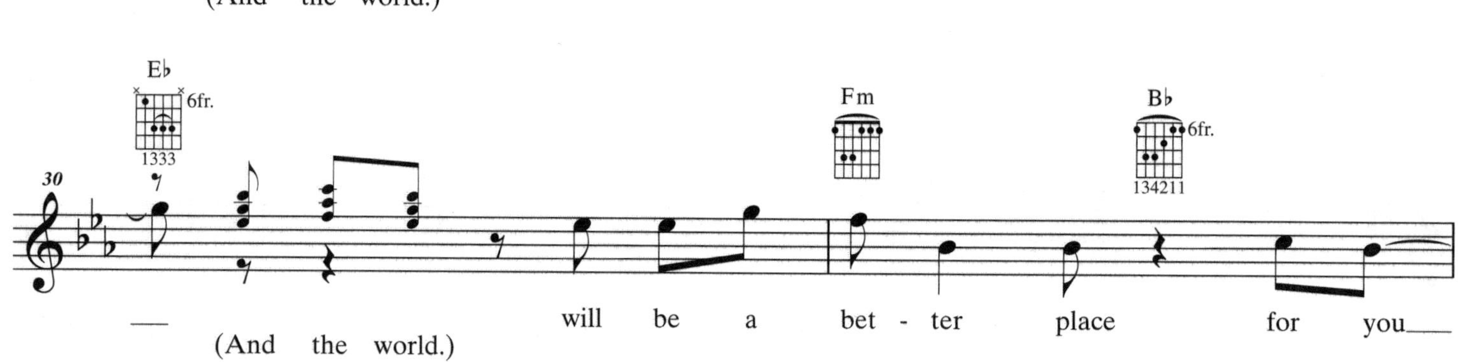
Fm
B♭
6fr.
134211
28
will be a bet - ter place and the world
(And the world.)

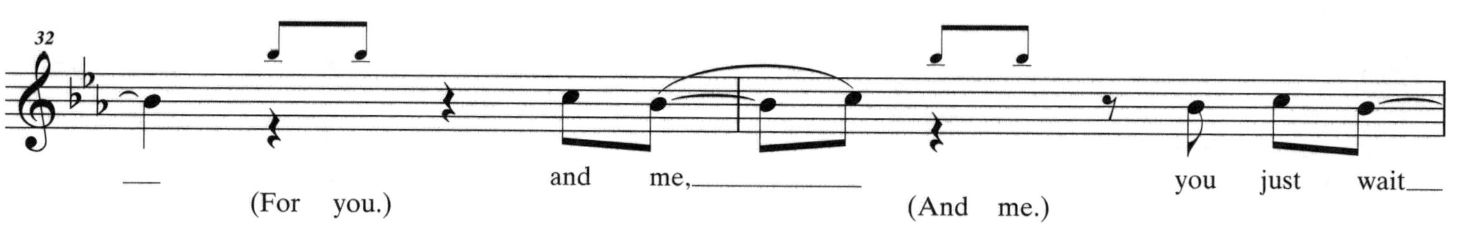
E♭
6fr.
1333
Fm
B♭
6fr.
134211
30
will be a bet - ter place for you
(And the world.)
32
and me, you just wait
(For you.) (And me.)

34
and see.
(Just wait and see.)
Peo - ple, now.
Outro:
Repeat ad lib. & fade
A♭
4fr.
134211
E♭
6fr.
1333
36
Put a lit - tle love in your heart.

# Rúu, Rúu, Chúu

Traditional Spanish Carol

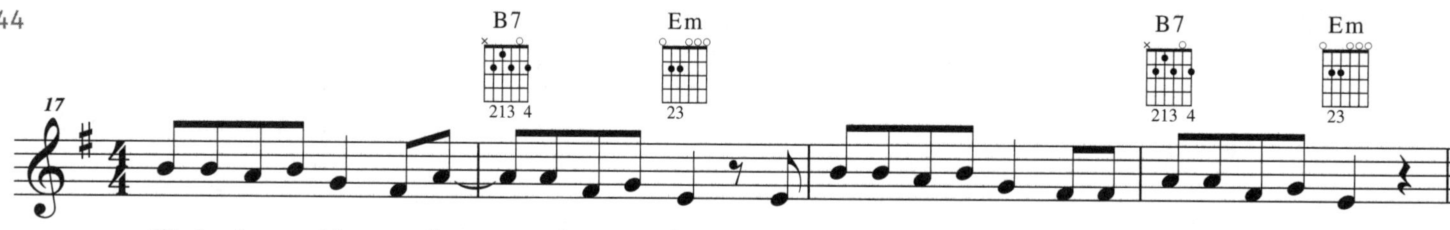
B7
213 4
Em
23
B7
213 4
Em
23
17
El lo-bo ra-bio so la___ qui-so mor-der. Mas Di-os po-de-ro-so la su-po de-fen-der.

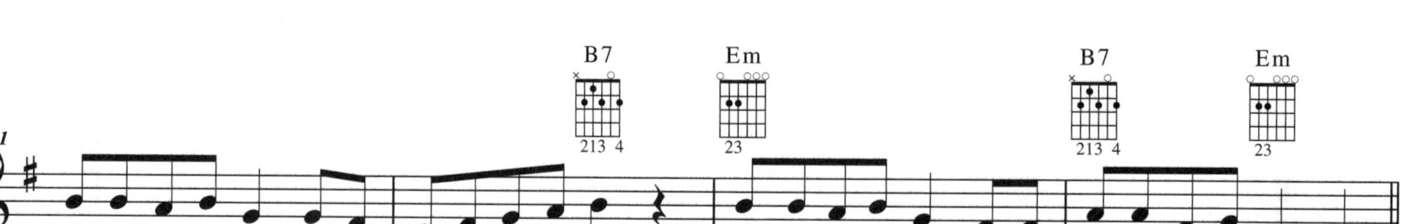
B7
213 4
Em
23
B7
213 4
Em
23
21
Quí-so le ha-cer que no pu-dies se pe-car. ni aun o-ri-gi-nal es-ta Vir-gen no tu-vie-ra.

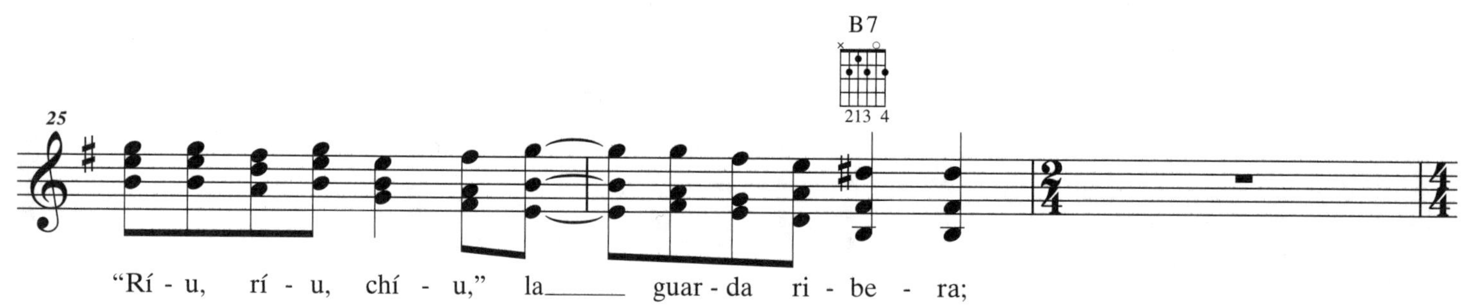
B7
213 4
25
"Rí-u, rí-u, chí-u," la___ guar-da ri-be-ra;

Em
23
28
Dios guar-dó el lo-bo, el lo-bo de___ nues-tra cor-de-ra.
Dios guar-dó el lo, el lo-bo de___ nues-tra cor-de-ra.
Dios guar-dó el lo-bo de___ nues-tra cor-de-ra.

B7
213 4
Em
23
31
Dios guar-dó el lo-bo, el lo-bo de___ nue-stra cor-de-ra.
Dios guar-dó el lo, el lo-bo de___ nues-tra cor-de-ra.
Dios guar-dó el lo-bo de___ nues-tra cor-de-ra.

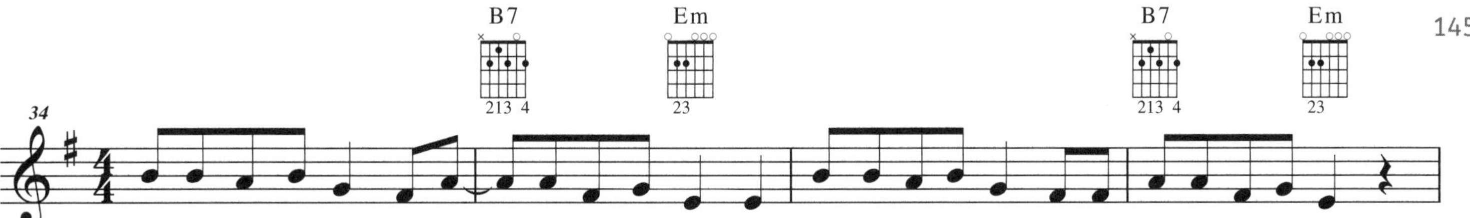
B7
Em
B7
Em
34
Es - te qu'es na - ci - do es___ el gran mo - nar - ca, Chris - to pa - tri - ar - ca de car - ne ves - ti - do.

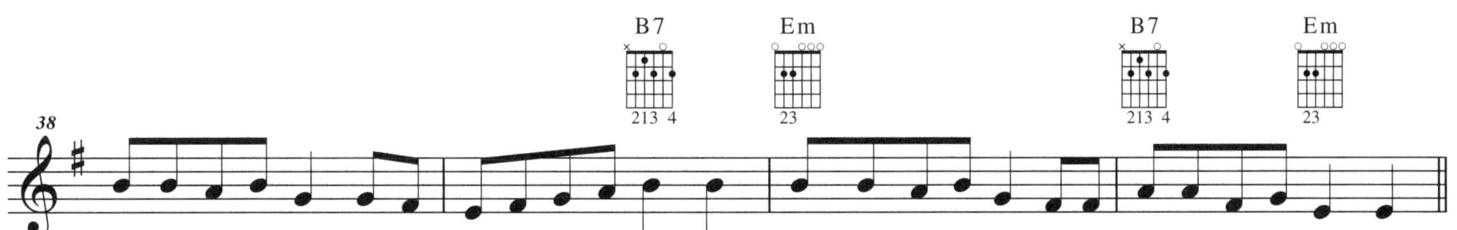
B7
Em
B7
Em
38
Ha nos re - di - mi - do con se ha - cer chi - qui - to. Aun - que in - fi - ni - to, fi - ni - to se hi - cie - ra.

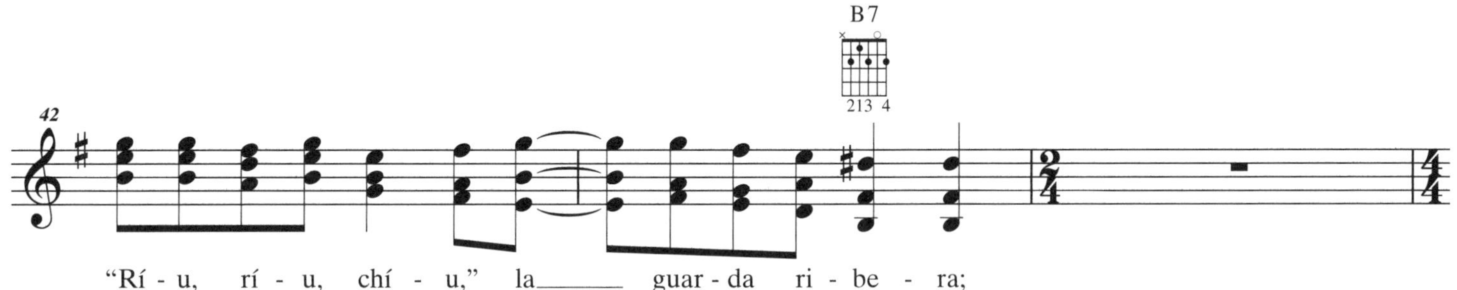
B7
42
"Rí - u, rí - u, chí - u," la___ guar - da ri - be - ra;

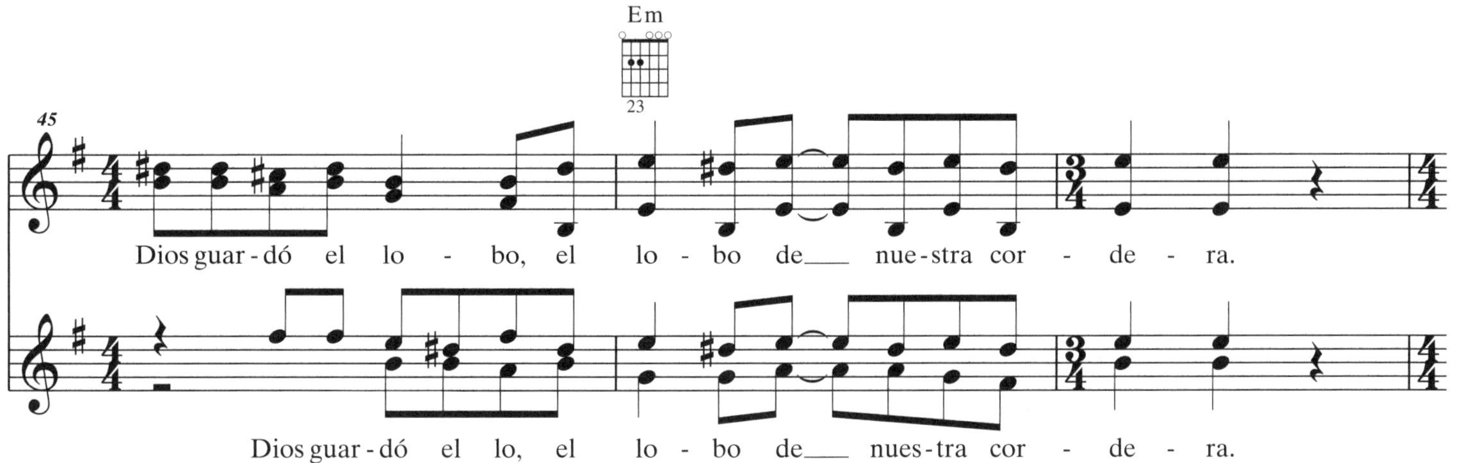
Em
45
Dios guar - dó el lo - bo, el lo - bo de___ nue - stra cor - de - ra.
Dios guar - dó el lo, el lo - bo de___ nues - tra cor - de - ra.
Dios guar - dó el lo - bo de___ nues - tra cor - de - ra.

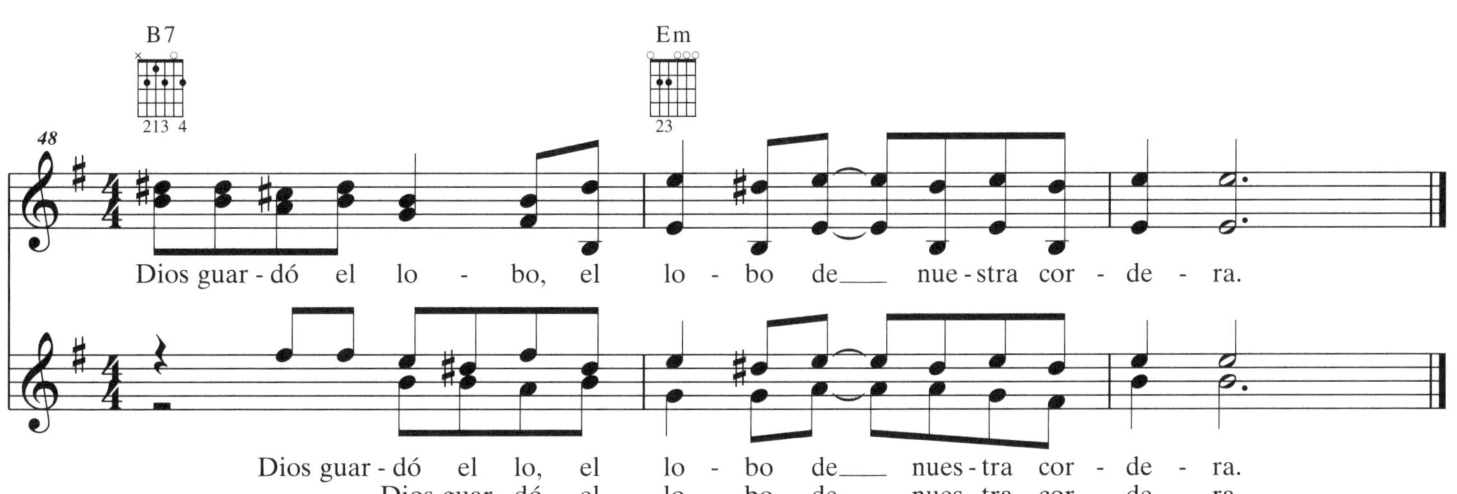
B7
Em
48
Dios guar - dó el lo - bo, el lo - bo de___ nue - stra cor - de - ra.
Dios guar - dó el lo, el lo - bo de___ nues - tra cor - de - ra.
Dios guar - dó el lo - bo de___ nues - tra cor - de - ra.

River
Words and Music by
JONI MITCHELL
Moderately
Intro:
C
Am
Piano
mf
F(9)
Fmaj7
G7
C/G
G7
C/G
1. It's
Verse:
Csus
C
Csus
C
Cont. rhy. simile
(1.3.) com-ing on Christ-mas, they're cut-ting down trees. They're
2. See additional lyrics
Csus
C
Csus
C
put-ting up rein-deer and sing-ing songs of joy and peace. Oh, I
Am
To Coda
G
wish I had a riv - er I could skate a - way on.

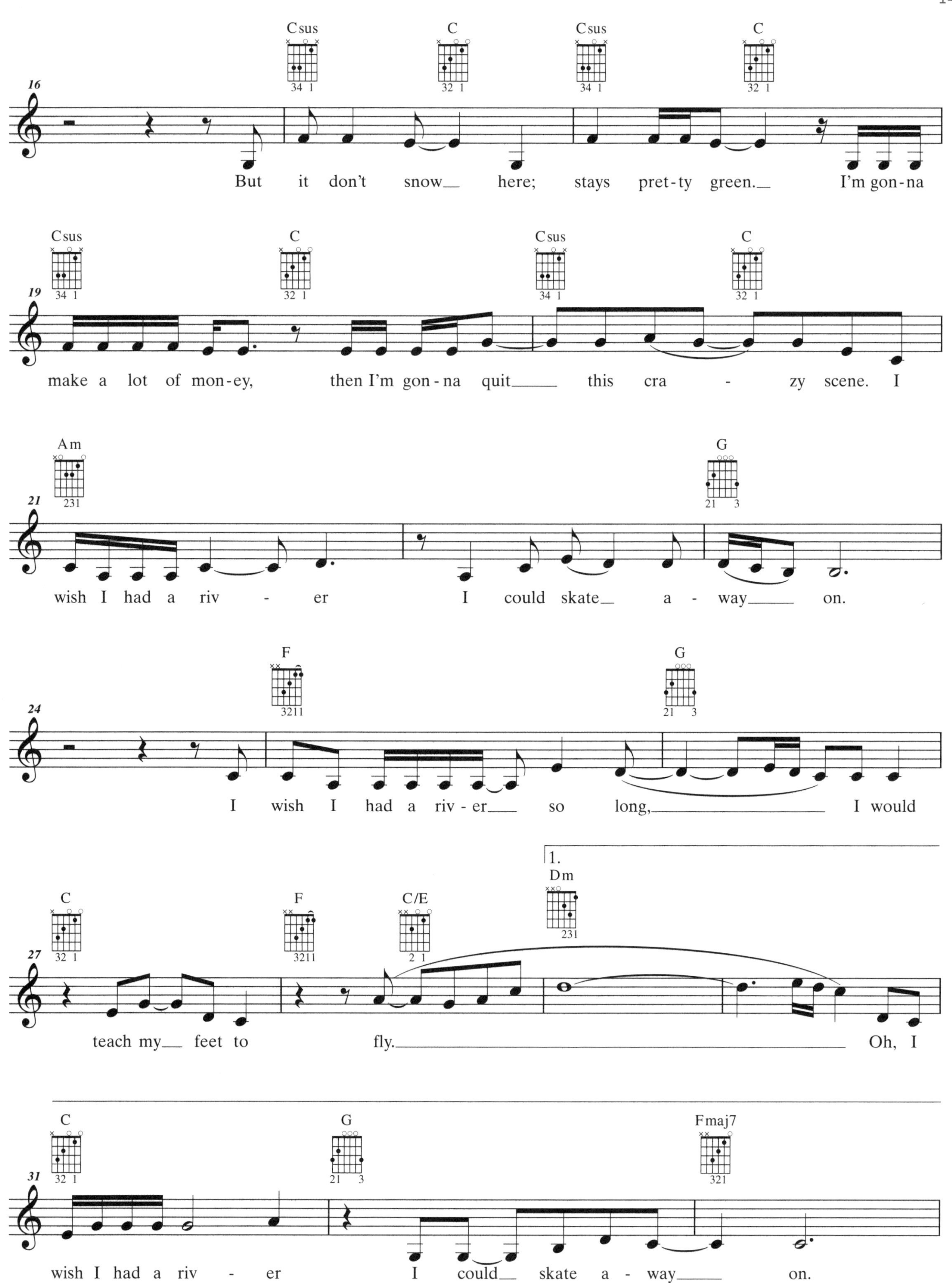
Csus
C
16
But it don't snow here; stays pret-ty green. I'm gon-na
19
make a lot of mon-ey, then I'm gon-na quit this cra - zy scene. I
Am
G
21
wish I had a riv - er I could skate a - way on.
F
24
I wish I had a riv-er so long, I would
F
C/E
1.
Dm
27
teach my feet to fly. Oh, I
Fmaj7
31
wish I had a riv - er I could skate a - way on.

F
C
34
I made my ba - by cry.
Am
Asus2
Am
Asus2
G
38
2. He
2.
Dm
42
Oh, I
C
G
Fmaj7
46
wish I had a riv - er I could skate a - way on.
F
C
49
I made my ba - by say good - bye.
Am
G
D.S. al Coda
53
3. It's

*Verse 2:*
He tried hard to help me
You know he put me at ease
And he loved me so naughty
Made me weak in the knees
Oh, I wish I had a river
I could skate away on
I'm so hard to handle
I'm selfish and I'm sad
Now I've gone and lost the best baby
That I ever had
Oh, I wish I had a river
I could skate away on
I wish I had a river so long
I would teach my feet to fly
*(To 2nd ending:)*

# Rockin' Around the Christmas Tree

Words and Music by
JOHNNY MARKS

**Lively rock and roll**

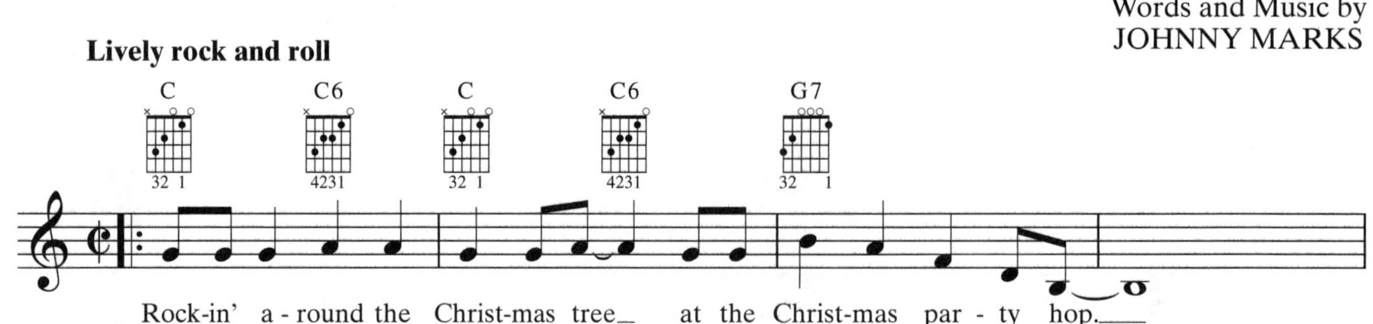


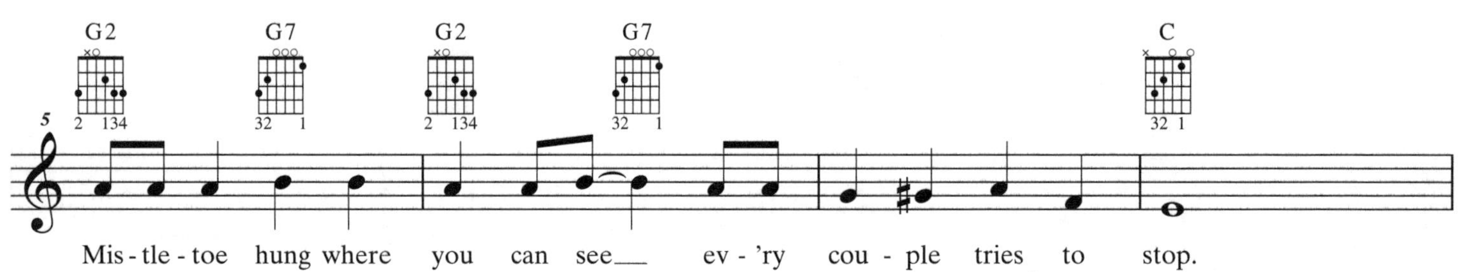


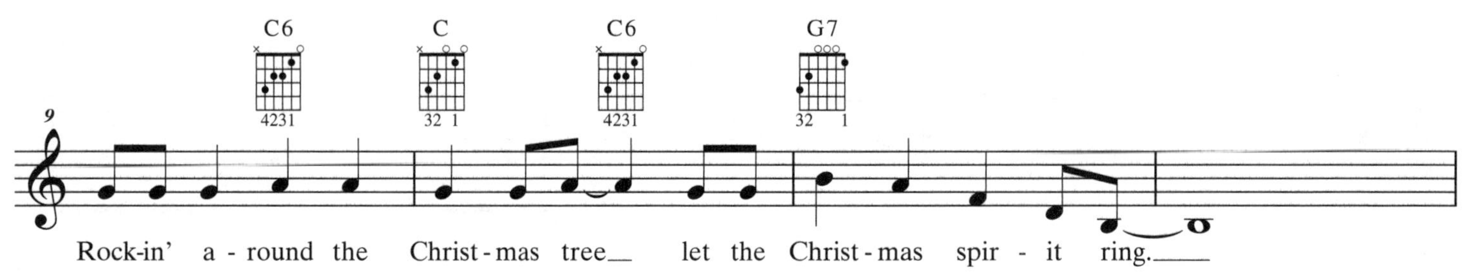


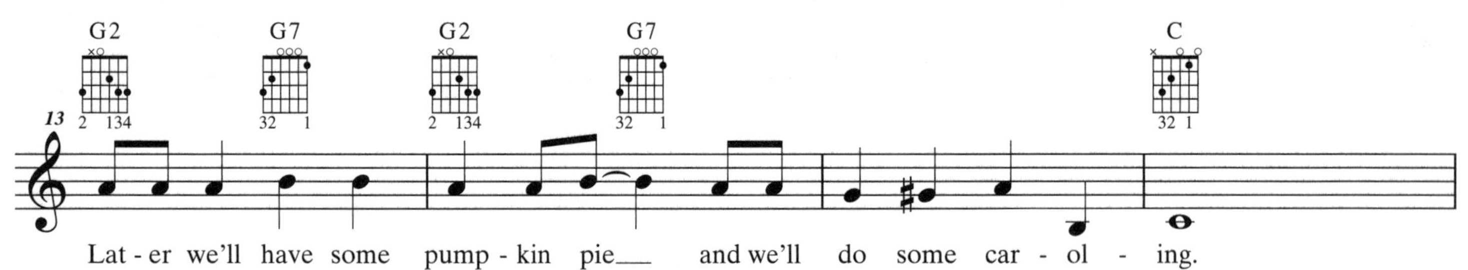


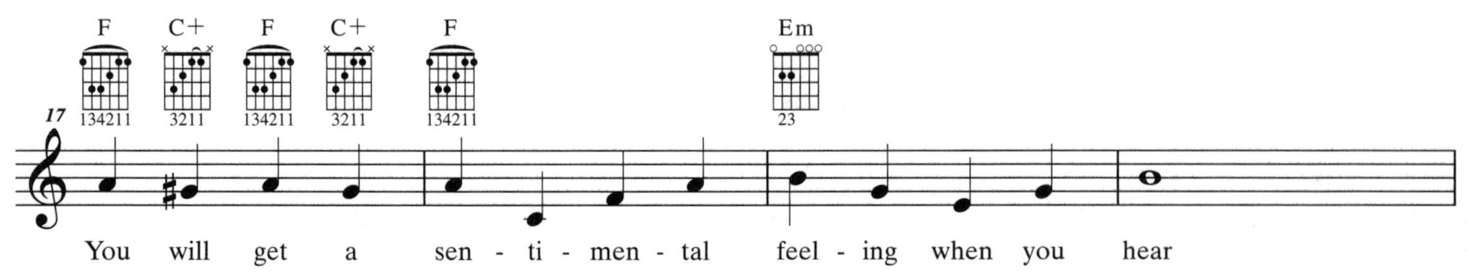

Am
Am(maj7)
Am7
D7
G7

21
voic - es sing - ing, "Let's be jol - ly, deck the halls with boughs of hol - ly."

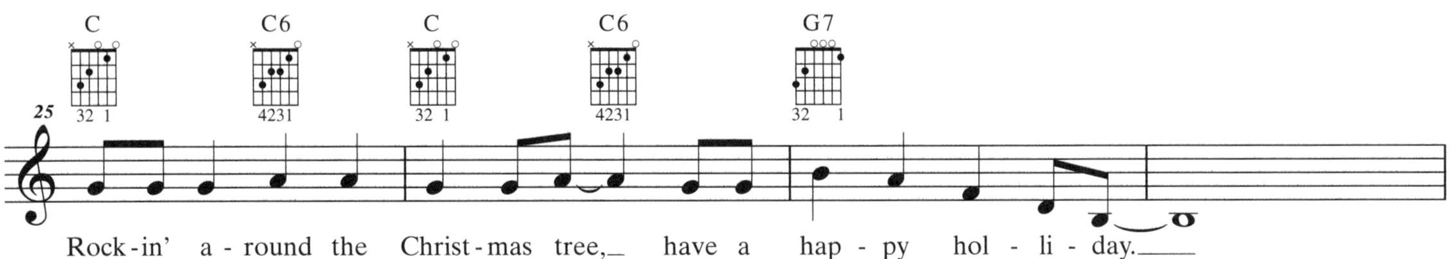
C
C6
C
C6
G7
25
Rock - in' a - round the Christ - mas tree, have a hap - py hol - li - day.

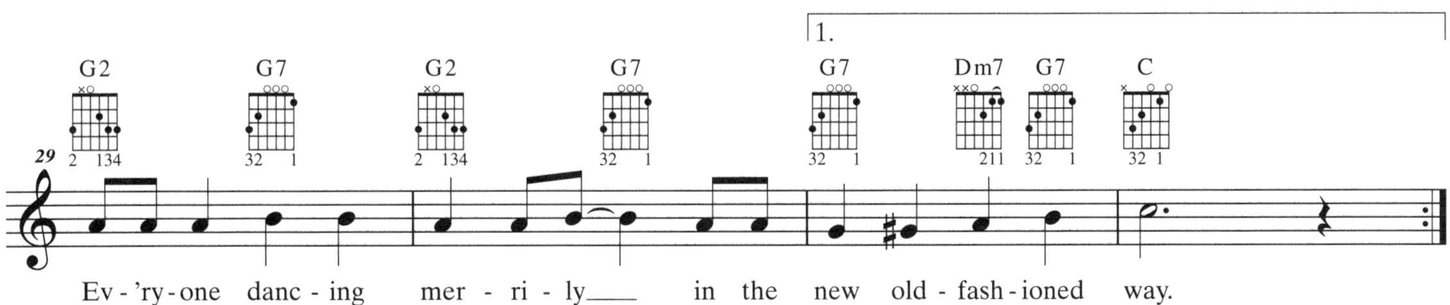
1.
G2
G7
G2
G7
G7
Dm7
G7
C
29
Ev - 'ry - one danc - ing mer - ri - ly in the new old - fash - ioned way.

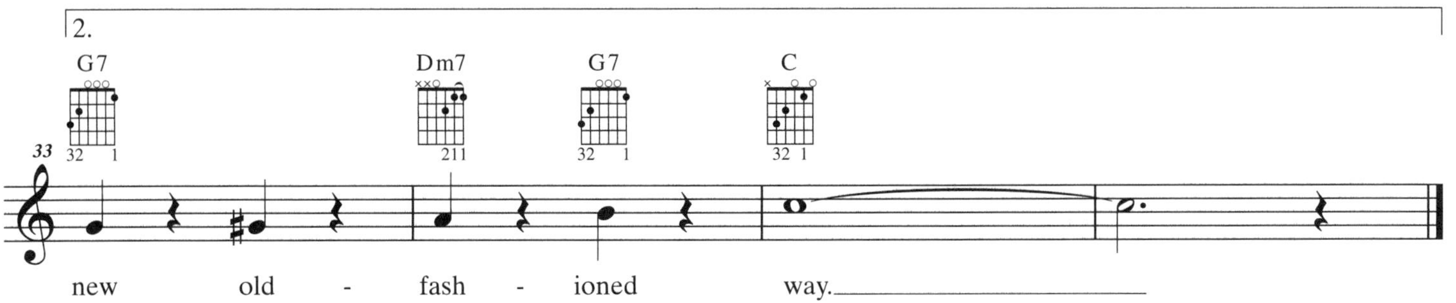
2.
G7
Dm7
G7
C
33
new old - fash - ioned way.

# Rudolph, the Red-Nosed Reindeer

Words and Music by
JOHNNY MARKS

**Freely**

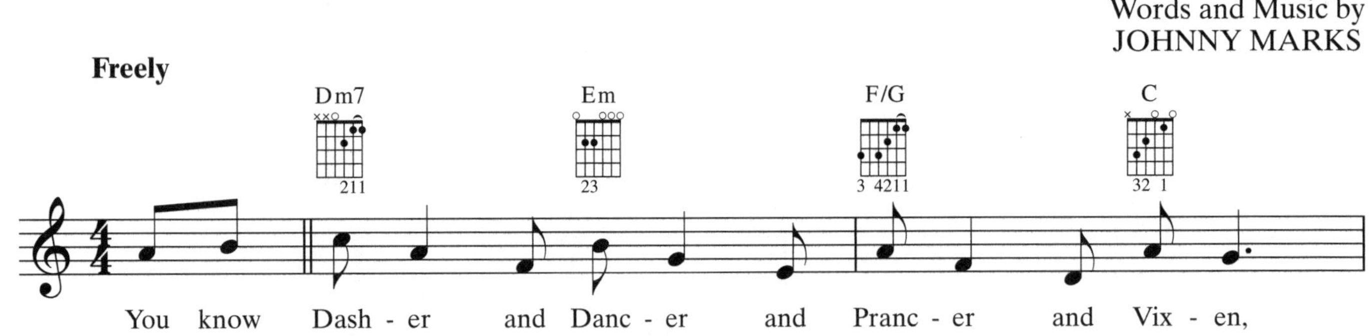


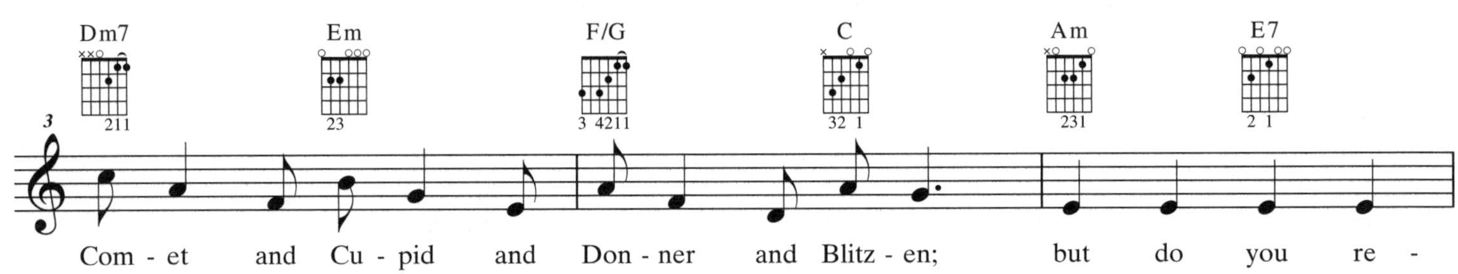

**Bright two-beat**

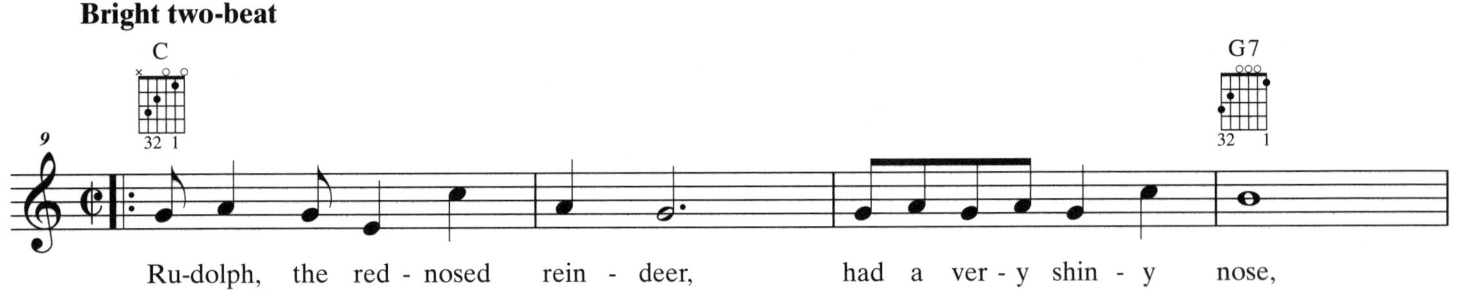

17
G7
All of the oth - er rein - deer used to laugh and call him names.
21
C
C7
They nev - er let poor Ru - dolph join in an - y rein - deer games.
F
C
Dm7
G7
C
C♯dim7
3fr.
25
Then one fog - gy Christ - mas Eve, San - ta came to say:
G/D
Ddim7
Am7
D7
G7
29
"Ru - dolph with your nose so bright, won't you guide my sleigh to - night?"
C
G7
33
Then how the rein - deer loved him as they shout - ed out with glee:
37
"Ru-dolph, the red - nosed rein - deer, you'll go down in his - to -
1.
2.
C
Dm7
G7
C
G7
C
40
ry."
ry."

# Santa Baby

Words and Music by
JOAN JAVITS, PHILIP SPRINGER
and TONY SPRINGER

Am7
D7
G
B7
Think of all the fun I've missed.
Come and trim my Christ - mas tree
E7
A7
Think of all the fel - las that I have - n't kissed.
with some dec - o - ra - tions bought at Tif - fa - ny.
Next year I could be
I real - ly do be -
D7
just as good if you check off my Christ - mas list.
lieve in you. Let's see if you be - lieve in me.
G
Em
A7
D7
San - ta Ba - by, I want a yacht and real - ly that's not a - lot.
San - ta Ba - by, for - got to men - tion one lit - tle thing, a ring!
Been an an - gel all year, San - ta Ba - by, so hur - ry down the chim - ney to - night.
I don't mean on the phone, San - ta Ba - by, so hur - ry down the chim - ney to - night.
1.
2.
G6/9

# Santa Claus Is Comin' to Town

Words by
HAVEN GILLESPIE

Music by
J. FRED COOTS

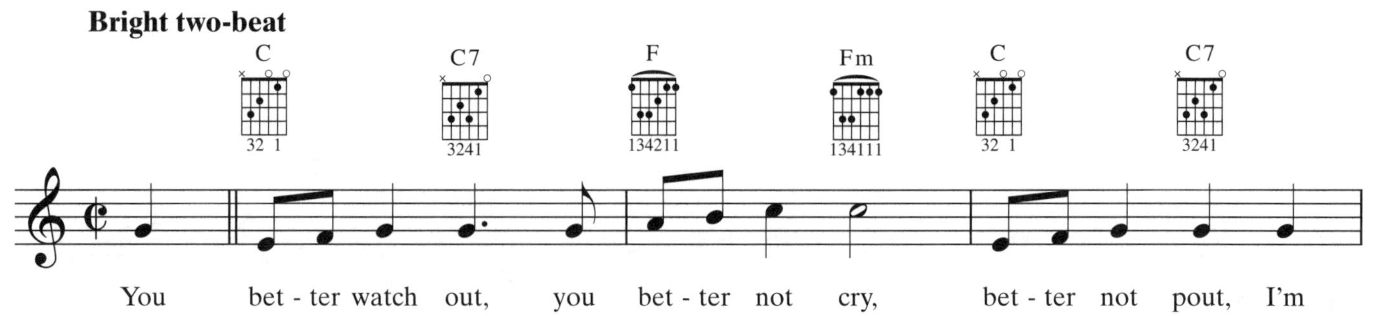


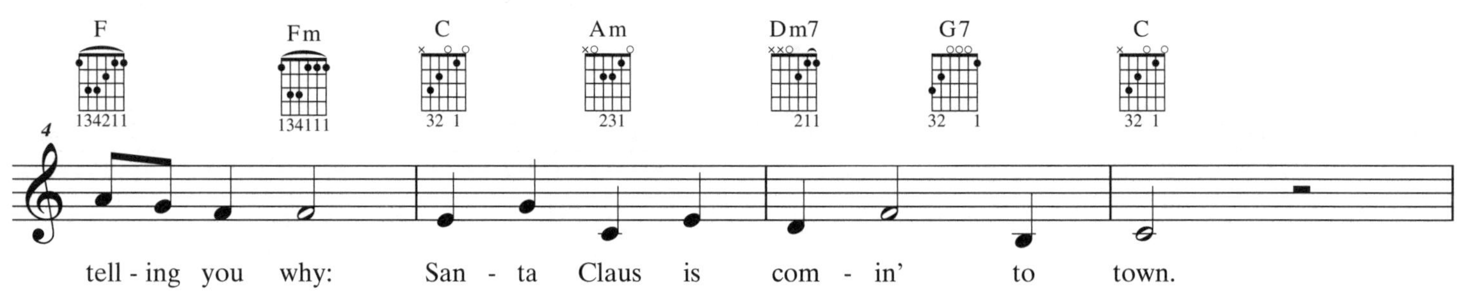


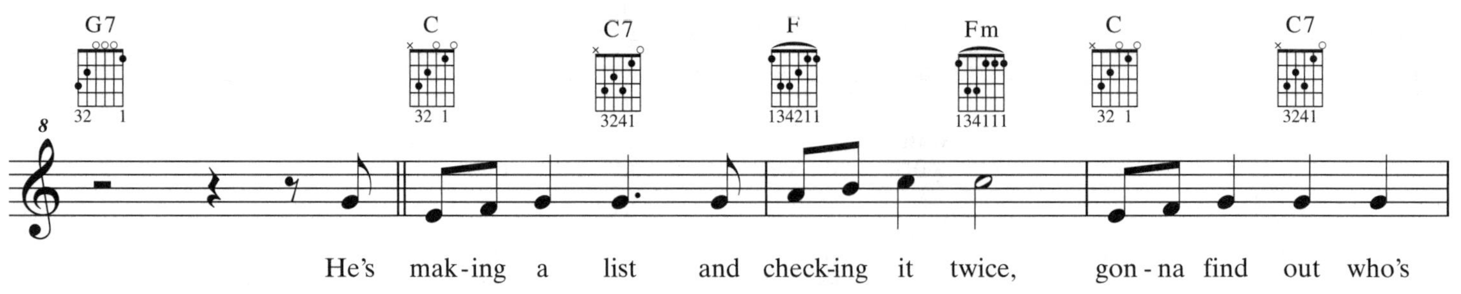


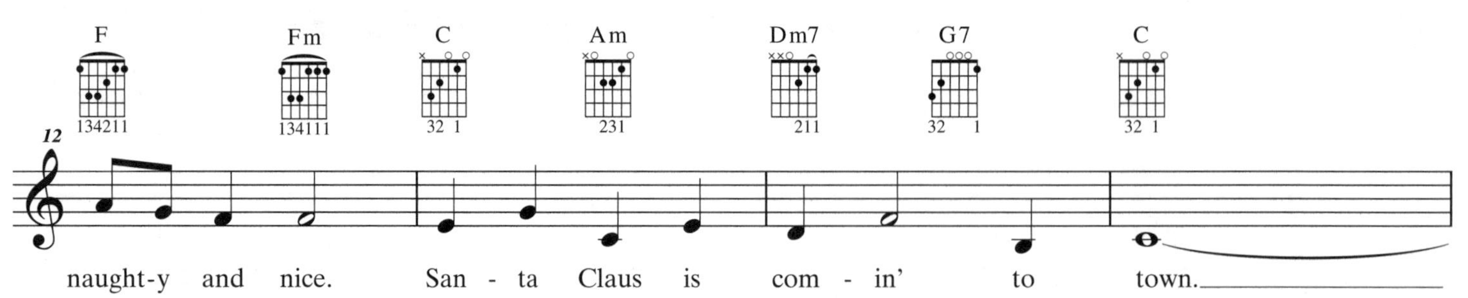


Santa Claus Is Comin' to Town - 2 - 1

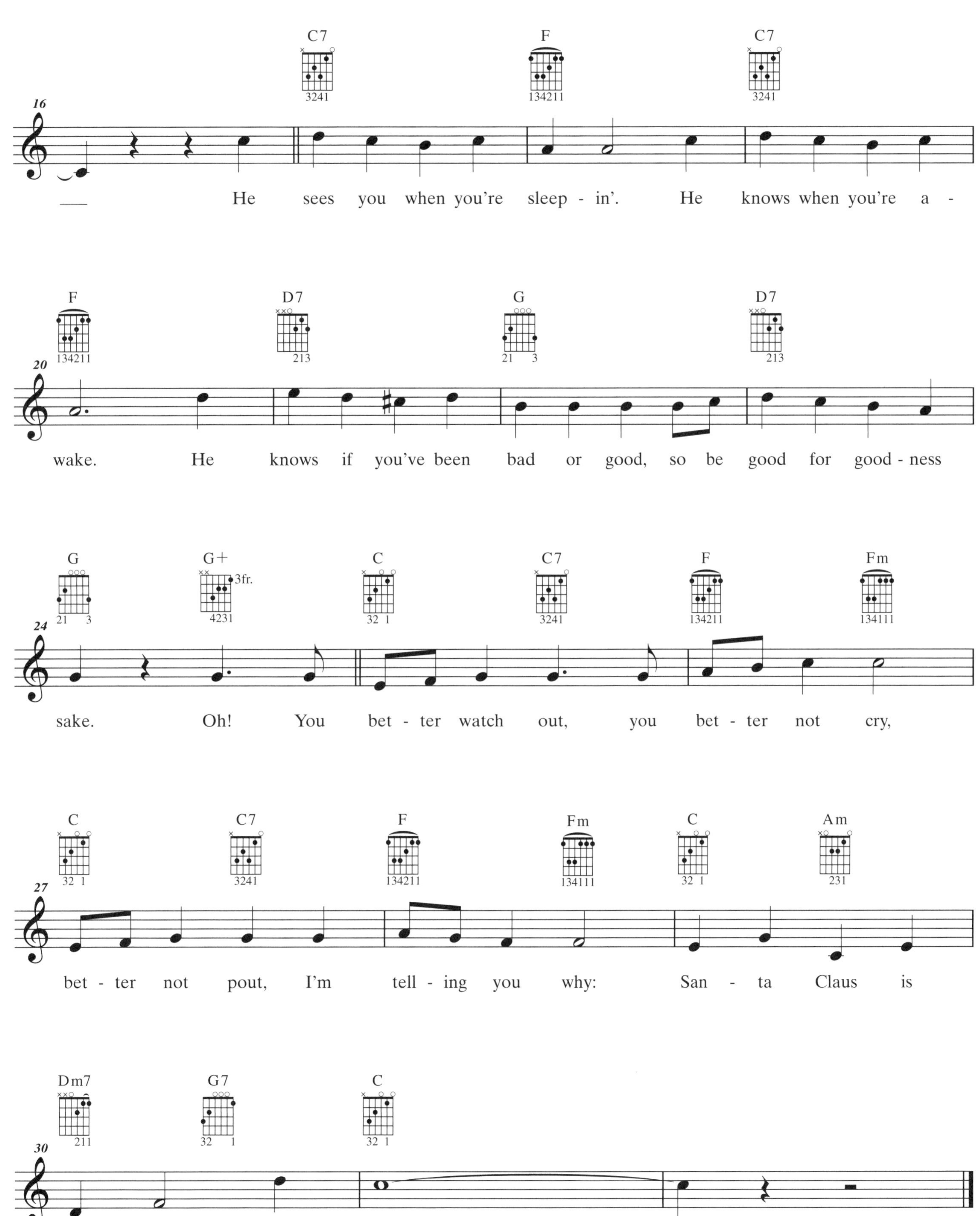
C7
3241
F
134211
C7
3241
16
He sees you when you're sleep - in'. He knows when you're a -
F
134211
D7
213
G
21 3
D7
213
20
wake. He knows if you've been bad or good, so be good for good - ness
G
21 3
G+
3fr.
4231
C
32 1
C7
3241
F
134211
Fm
134111
24
sake. Oh! You bet - ter watch out, you bet - ter not cry,
C
32 1
C7
3241
F
134211
Fm
134111
C
32 1
Am
231
27
bet - ter not pout, I'm tell - ing you why: San - ta Claus is
Dm7
211
G7
32 1
C
32 1
30
com - in' to town.

Words and Music by
JOSEPH MOHR and
FRANZ GRUBER

**Gentle waltz**

C

1. Si - lent night, ho - ly night,
2. Si - lent night, ho - ly night,
3. Si - lent night, ho - ly night,

5 G C

all is calm, all is bright.
shep - herds quake at the sight.
Son of God, love's pure light.

9 F C

'Round yon Vir - gin Moth - er and Child.
Glo - ries stream____ from heav - en a - far.
Ra - diant beams____ from Thy ho - ly face,

13 F C

Ho - ly In - fant so ten - der and mild.
Heav - en - ly hosts sing Al - le - lu - ia.
with the dawn of re - deem - ing grace.

17 G C

Sleep in heav - en - ly peace,____
Christ the Sav - ior is born!____
Je - sus Lord at Thy birth.____

21 G7 | 1.2. C | 3. C

sleep____ in heav - en - ly peace! | birth!
Christ____ the Sav - ior is born!
Je - sus Lord at Thy

# Silver and Gold

Words and Music by
JOHNNY MARKS

# Simple Gifts

Words and Music by
ELDER JOSEPH BRACKETT

Star of the East
Words by
GEORGE COOPER
Music by
AMANDA KENNEDY
Moderately
G C G
Star of the east, O Beth - le - hem's star,
C D7
guid - ing us on to heav - en a - far!
G C G
Sor - row and grief are lulled by thy light, thou
D G D7 G
hope of each mor - tal, in death's lone - ly night!
C G
1. Fear - less and tran - quil we look up to thee!
2. Help us to fol - low where thou still dost guide!
1.
D7 G
Know - ing thou beams thru e - ter - ni - ty!
2.
D7 G
Pil - grims of earth so wide.

Sleigh Ride
Words by
MITCHELL PARISH
Music by
LEROY ANDERSON
Bright two-beat
G Em7 Am7 D7
Just hear those sleigh bells jin - gle - ing, ring - ting - tin - gle - ing
too. Come on, it's love - ly weath-er for a sleigh ride to-geth-er with
you. Out - side the snow is fall - ing and friends are call - ing "Yoo -
hoo." Come on, it's love - ly weath-er for a sleigh ride to-geth-er with
C♯m7 F♯7
you. Gid - dy - yap, gid - dy - yap, gid - dy - yap, let's go,
Sleigh Ride - 4 - 1

B
G♯m
C♯m7
F♯7
let's look at the show. We're rid-ing in a won-der-land of
B
Bm
Bm7
E7
snow. Gid-dy-yap, gid-dy-yap, gid-dy-yap, it's grand
A
F♯m
Am7
just hold-ing your hand. We're glid-ing a-long with a song of a
D7
Am7
D7
G
Em7
Am7
D7
win-ter-y fair-y-land. Our cheeks are nice and ros-y, and com-fy co-zy are
G
Em7
Am7
D7
G
Em7
Am7
D7
we. We're snug-gled close to-geth-er like two birds of a feath-er would
G
D7
G
Em7
Am7
D7
be. Let's take that road be-fore us and sing a cho-rus or

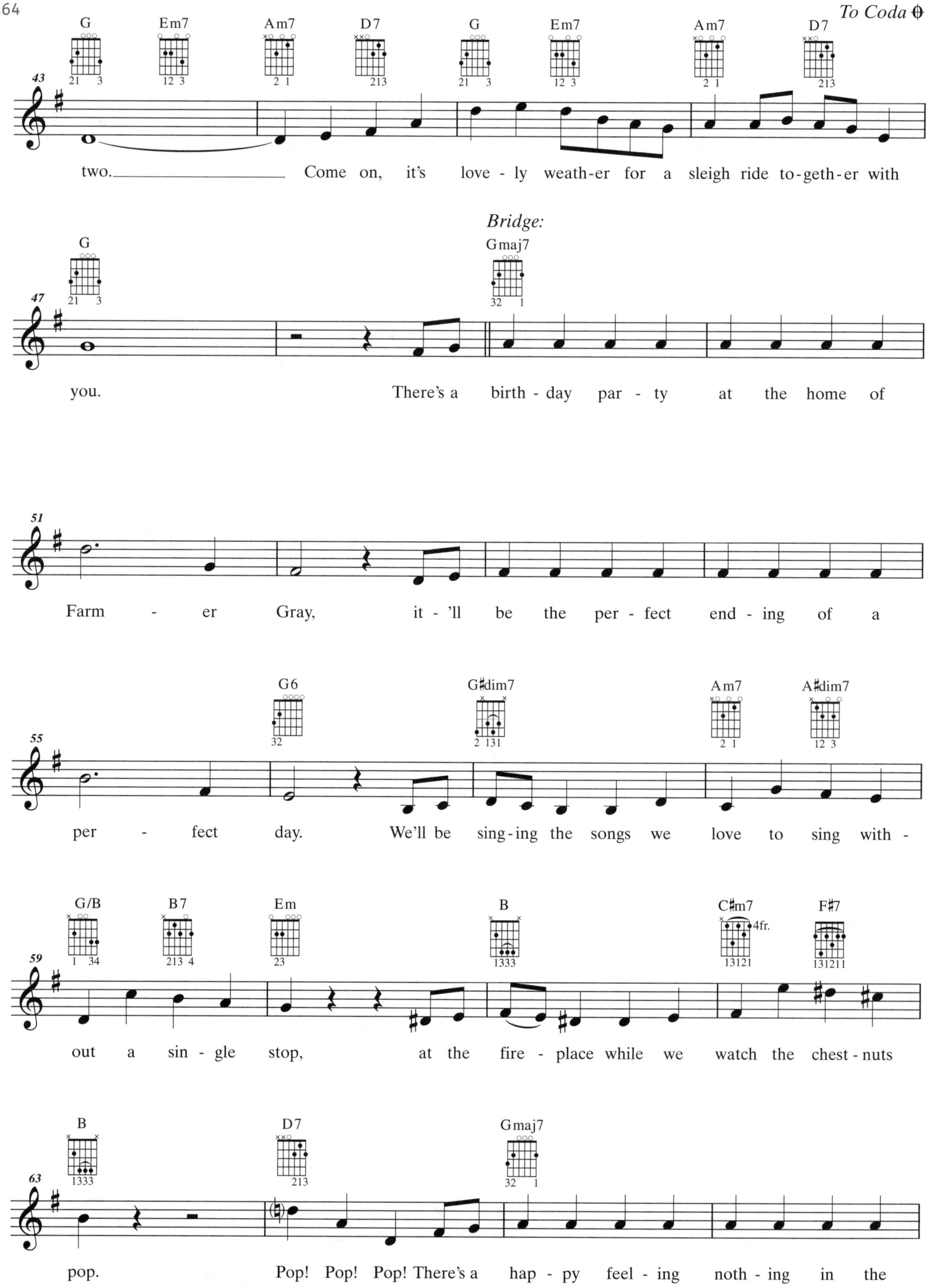

*To Coda* ⊕

43
G Em7 Am7 D7 G Em7 Am7 D7

two.______ Come on, it's love - ly weath-er for a sleigh ride to-geth-er with

*Bridge:*

47
G Gmaj7

you. There's a birth - day par - ty at the home of

51

Farm - er Gray, it - 'll be the per - fect end - ing of a

55
G6 G♯dim7 Am7 A♯dim7

per - fect day. We'll be sing-ing the songs we love to sing with -

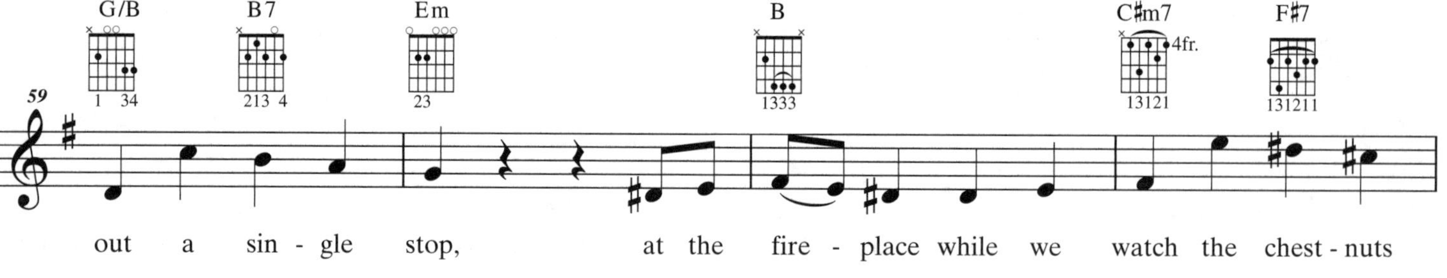


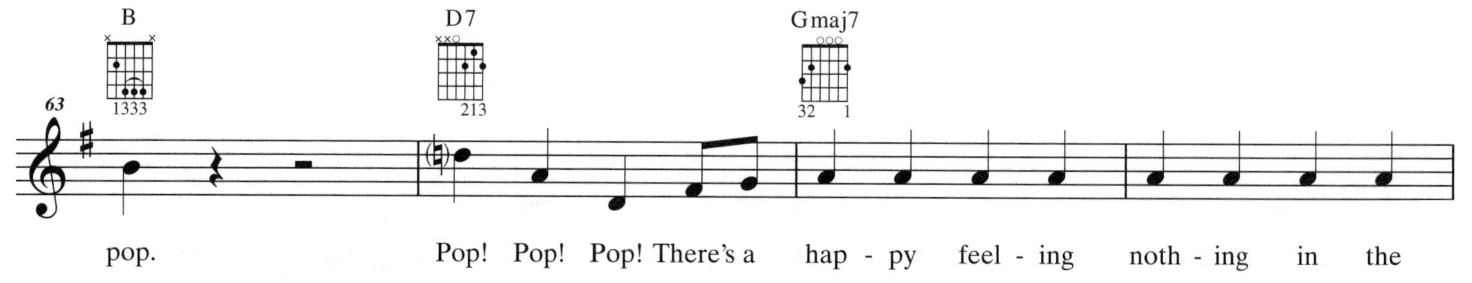

67
world can buy, when they pass a - round the cof - fee and the
G6
G♯dim7
Am7
A♯dim7
71
pump - kin pie. It - 'll near - ly be like a pic - ture print by
G/B
B7
Em
Am7/D
5fr.
75
Cur - ri - er and Ives. These won-der - ful things are the things we re -
79
mem-ber all through our lives! These won-der - ful things are the things we'll re -
D.S. 𝄋 al Coda
Coda
G
83
mem-ber all through our lives! Just hear those
85
you.

# Stand Beneath the Mistletoe

Words and Music by
LOUIS HOLLINGSWORTH

**Brightly**

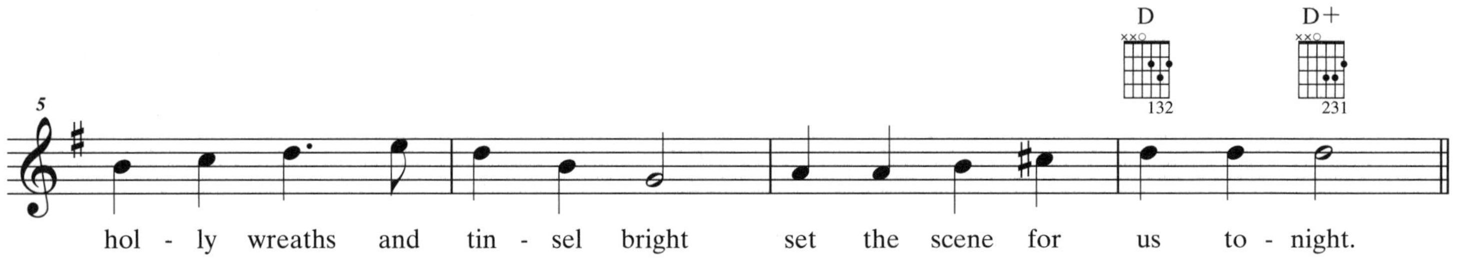


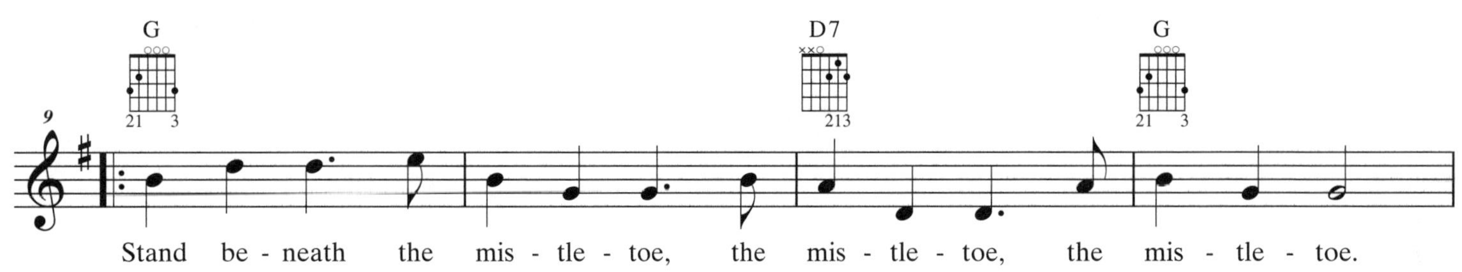


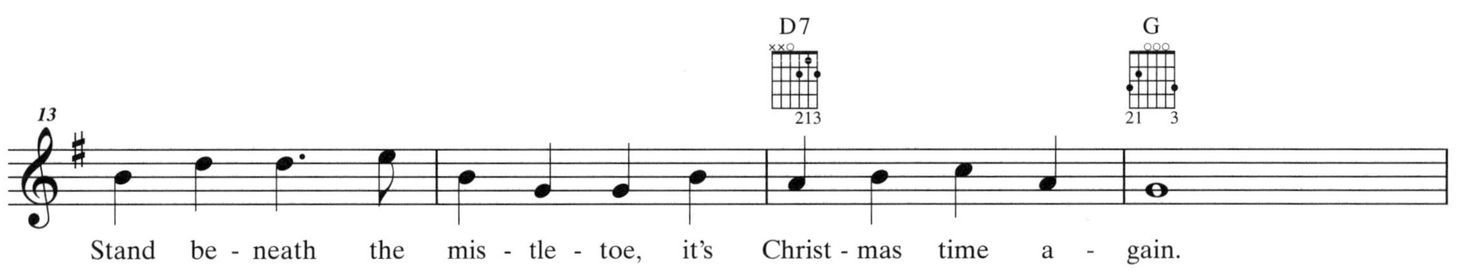


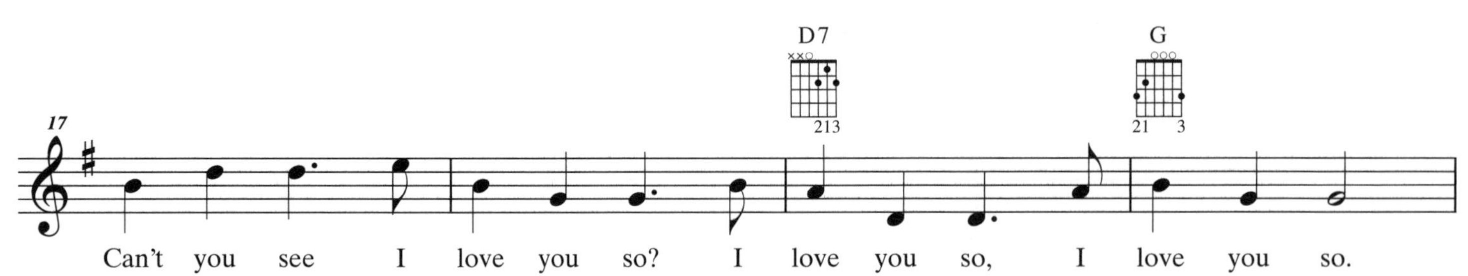

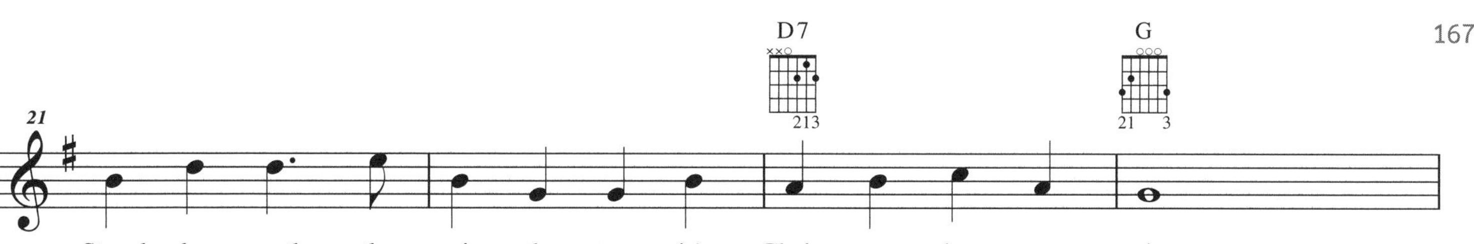
D7
G
21
Stand be - neath the mis - tle - toe, it's Christ - mas time a - gain.

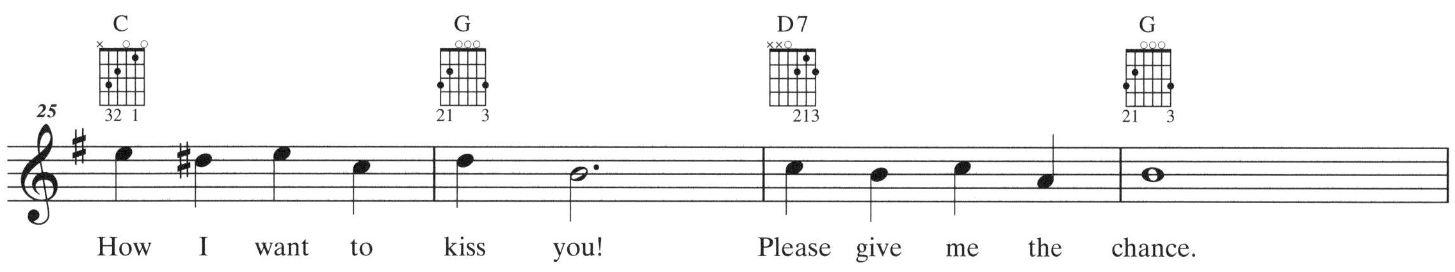
C
G
D7
G
25
How I want to kiss you! Please give me the chance.

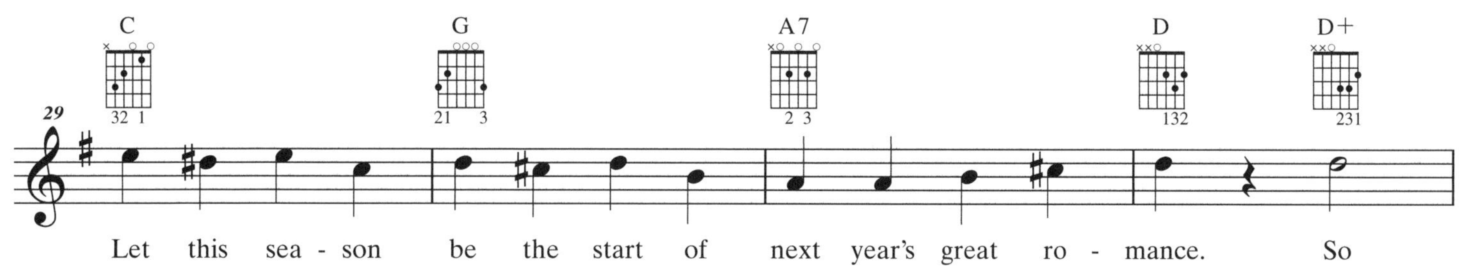
C
G
A7
D
D+
29
Let this sea - son be the start of next year's great ro - mance. So

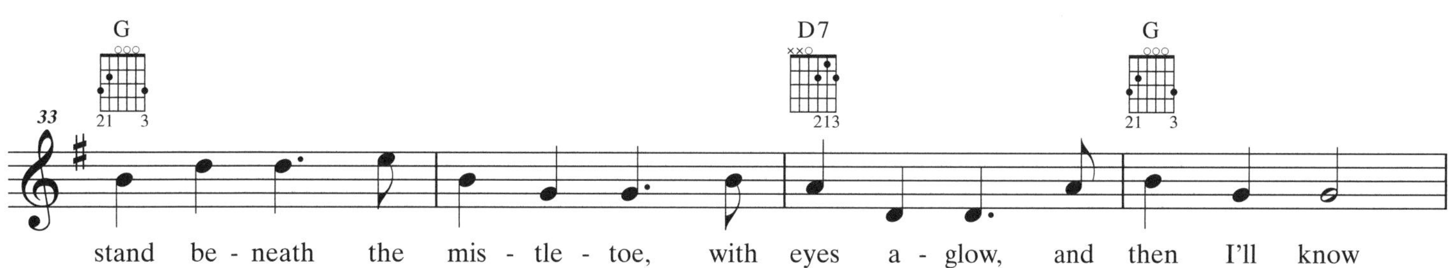
G
D7
G
33
stand be - neath the mis - tle - toe, with eyes a - glow, and then I'll know

1.
2.
D7
G
D+
G
37
we don't need the mis - tle - toe when it's Christ - mas time a - gain. gain.

# The Twelve Days of Christmas

Traditional English Carol

G C G D7
three French_ hens, two tur - tle doves, and a par - tridge_ in a pear
Verse 5:
G D G Em Am D7 G
tree. On the fifth day of Christ - mas my true love sent to me
C♯dim7 3fr. D7 G Em C
five gold - en rings, four_ call - ing birds, three French hens,
D7 G C G D7 G
two_ tur - tle doves, and a par - tridge_ in a pear tree. On the
Verses 6–12:
G Em Am D7 G D7
Repeat as necessary
sixth
sev - enth
eight
ninth
tenth
e - lev - enth
twelfth
day of Christ - mas my true love sent to me
six geese a lay - ing,
sev - en swans a swim - ming,
eight maids a milk - ing,
nine la - dies danc - ing,
ten lords a leap - ing,
e - lev - en pi - pers pip - ing,
twelve drum - mers drum - ming,
C C♯dim7 3fr. D7 G Em C
five gold - en rings, four_ call - ing birds, three French hens,
1.-6. D.S. 7.
D7 G C G D7 G G
two_ tur - tle doves, and a par - tridge_ in a pear tree. 7.–12. On the tree.

# Up on the House Top

Traditional

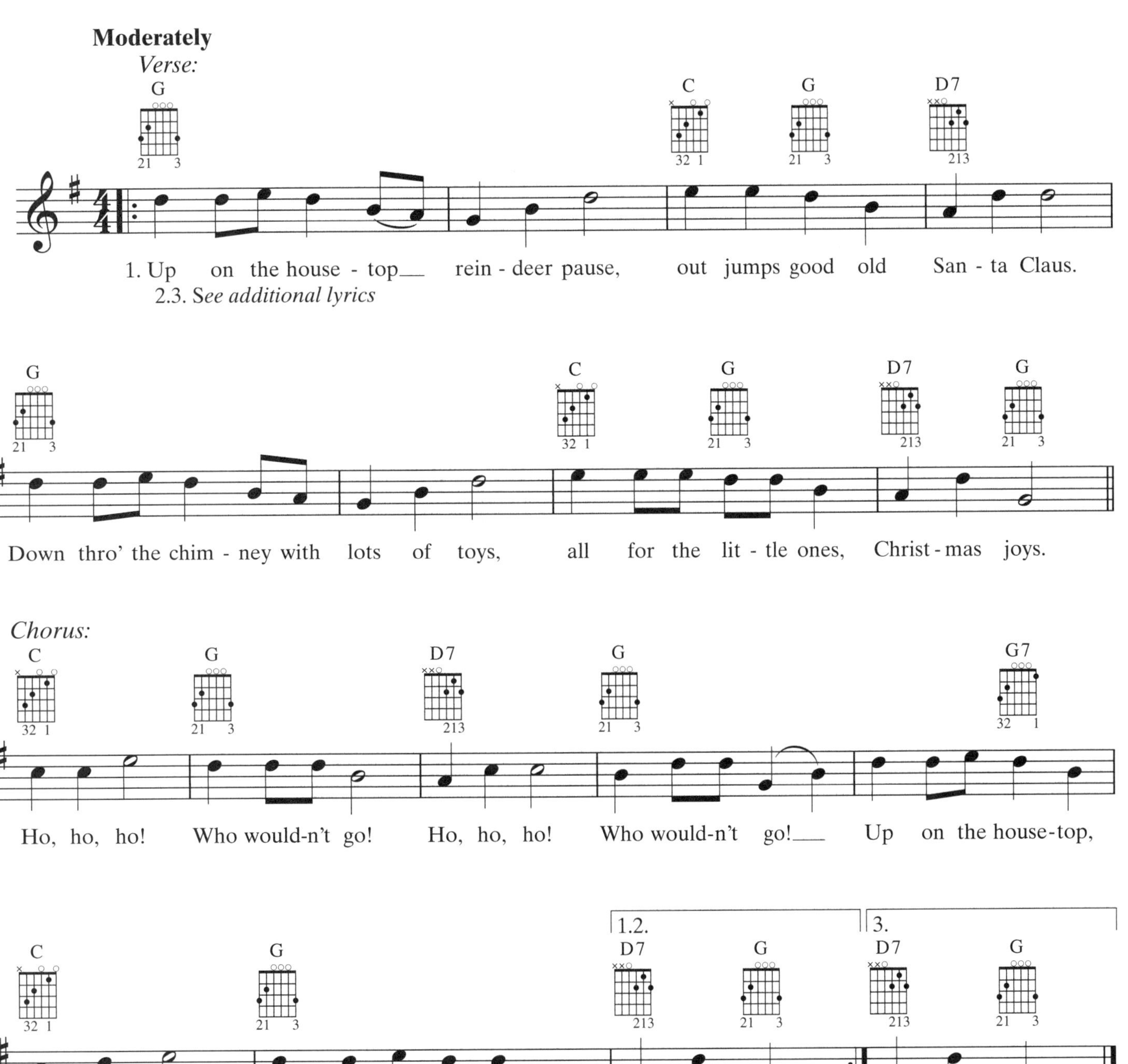


*Verse 2:*
First come the stocking of little Nell.
Oh, dear Santa, fill it well.
Give her a dolly that laughs and cries.
One that can open and shut its eyes.

*Verse 3:*
Look in the stocking of little Bill;
Oh, just see that glorious fill!
Here is a hammer and lots of tacks,
Whistle and ball and a set of jacks.

# We Three Kings of Orient Are

*Verse 3:*
Frankincense to offer have I,
Incense owns a deity nigh.
Prayer and praising, all men raising,
Worship Him, God most high.
*(To Chorus:)*

*Verse 4:*
Myrrh is mine: its bitter perfume
Breathes of life of gathering gloom;
Sorrowing, sighing, bleeding, dying,
Sealed in the stone cold tomb.
*(To Chorus:)*

*Verse 5:*
Glorious now behold Him arise;
King and God and sacrifice.
Alleluia, alleluia,
Earth to heaven replies.
*(To Chorus:)*

# We Wish You a Merry Christmas

# Welcome Christmas

(from *How the Grinch Stole Christmas!*)

Lyrics by
DR. SEUSS

Music by
ALBERT HAGUE

# What Child Is This?

Old English Air

By
WILLIAM C. DIX

# You're a Mean One, Mr. Grinch

(from *How the Grinch Stole Christmas!*)

Lyrics by
DR. SEUSS

Music by
ALBERT HAGUE

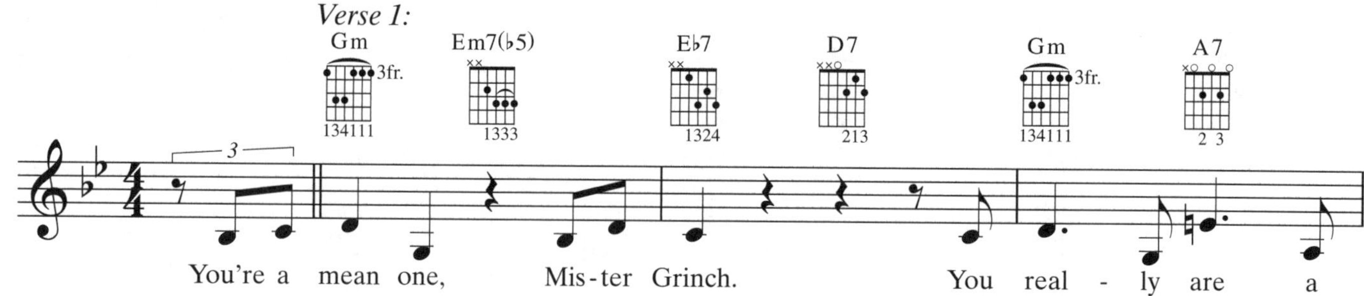


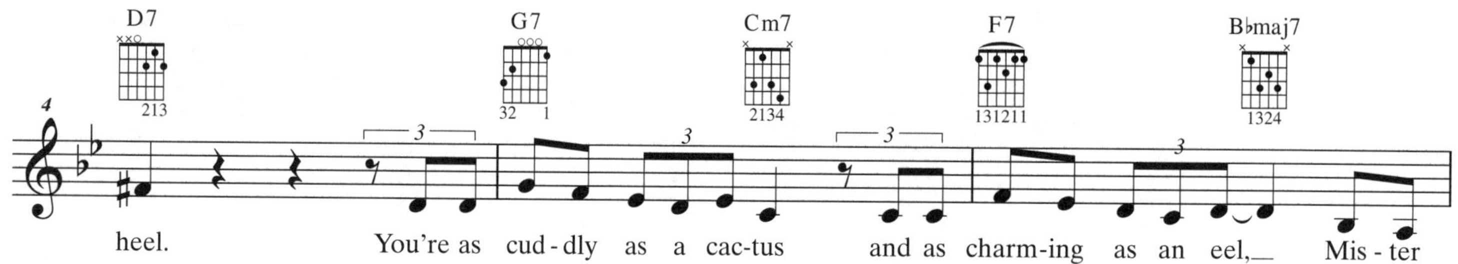

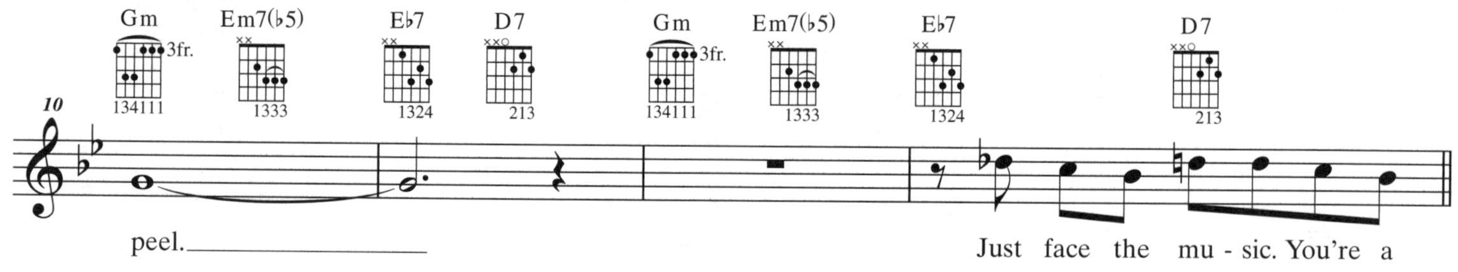


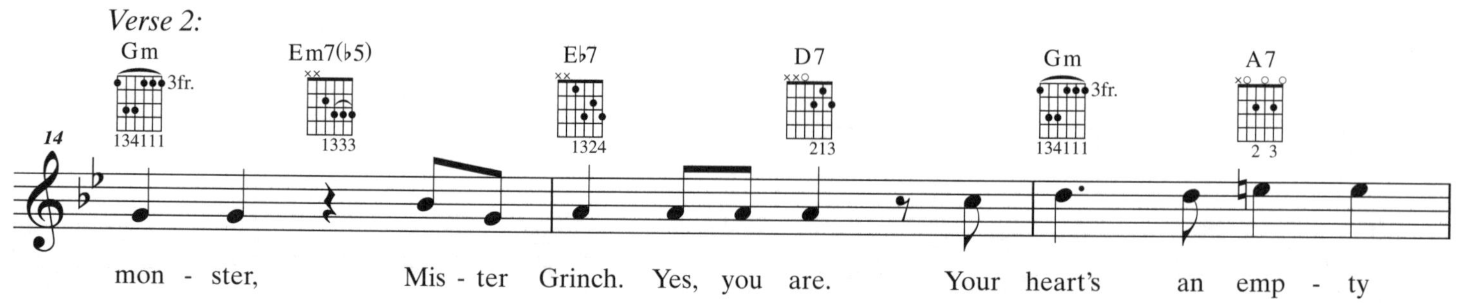

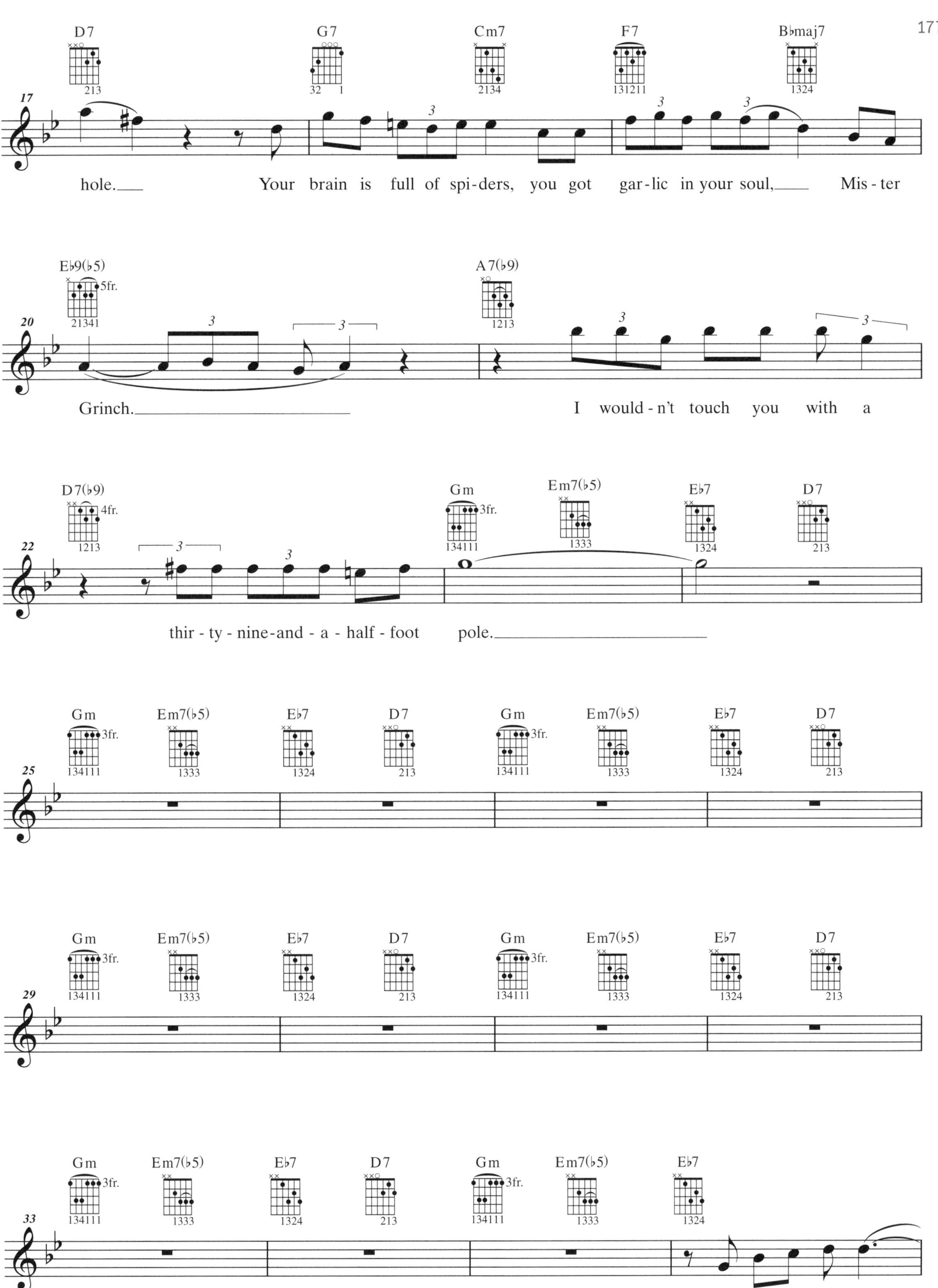
D7 G7 Cm7 F7 B♭maj7
17
hole.___ Your brain is full of spi-ders, you got gar-lic in your soul,___ Mis-ter
E♭9(♭5) A7(♭9)
20
Grinch.___ I would-n't touch you with a
D7(♭9) Gm Em7(♭5) E♭7 D7
22
thir-ty-nine-and-a-half-foot pole.___
Gm Em7(♭5) E♭7 D7 Gm Em7(♭5) E♭7 D7
25
Gm Em7(♭5) E♭7 D7 Gm Em7(♭5) E♭7 D7
29
Gm Em7(♭5) E♭7 D7 Gm Em7(♭5) E♭7
33
No one's de-ny-in'.___

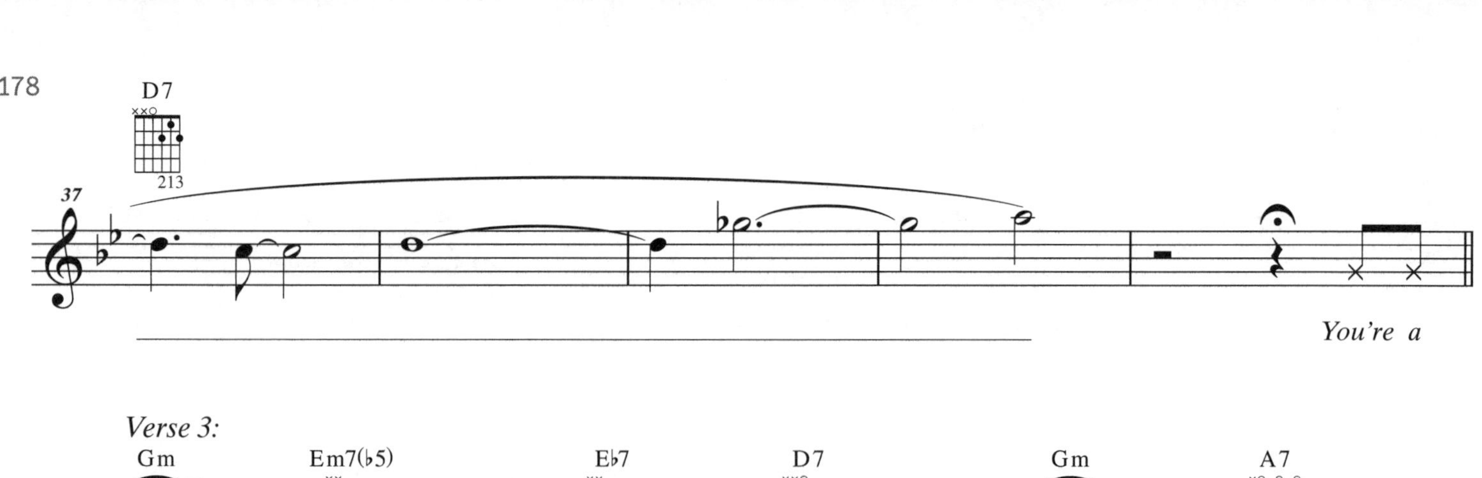
D7
213
37
You're a

Verse 3:

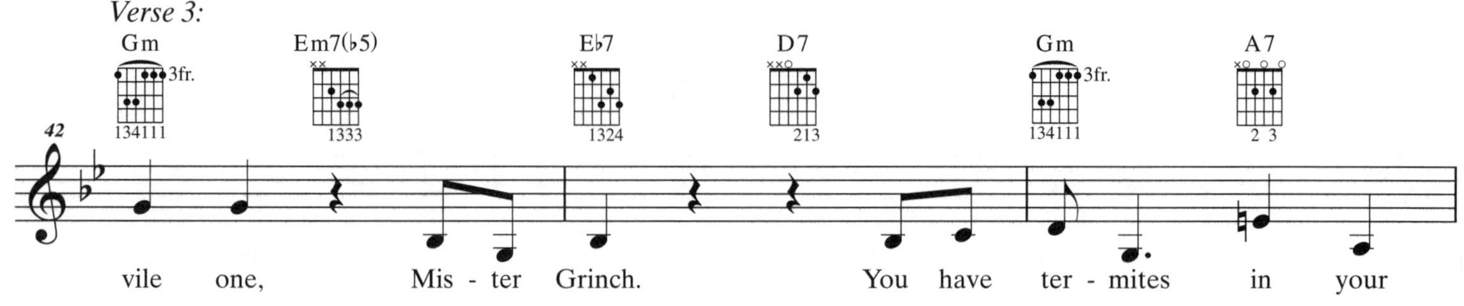
Gm
Em7(♭5)
E♭7
D7
Gm
A7
42
vile one, Mis - ter Grinch. You have ter - mites in your

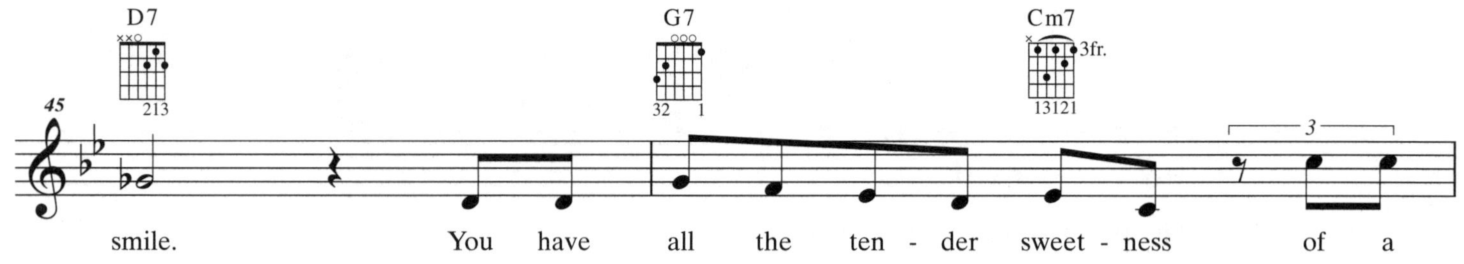
D7
G7
Cm7
45
smile. You have all the ten - der sweet - ness of a

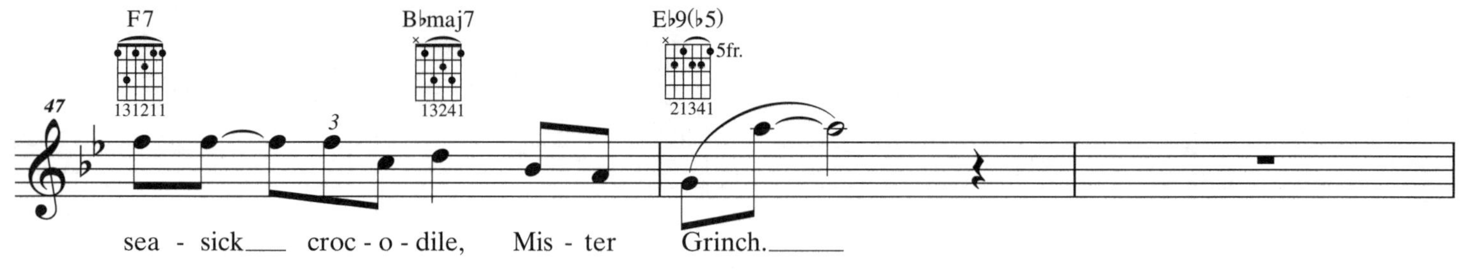
F7
B♭maj7
E♭9(♭5)
47
sea - sick croc - o - dile, Mis - ter Grinch.

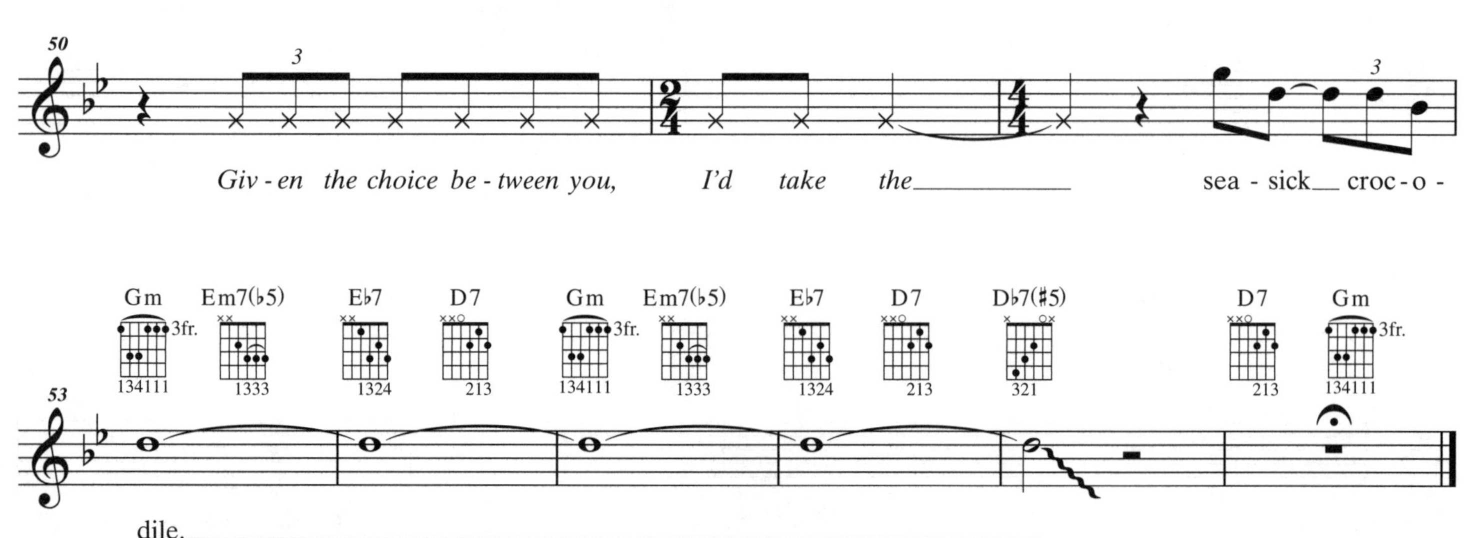
50
Giv - en the choice be - tween you, I'd take the sea - sick croc - o -
Gm
Em7(♭5)
E♭7
D7
Gm
Em7(♭5)
E♭7
D7
D♭7(♯5)
D7
Gm
53
dile.

# When Christmas Comes to Town

(from *The Polar Express*)

Words by
GLEN BALLARD

Music by
ALAN SILVESTRI

Dsus D Em7 A7
18
hard to be a - lone. Put - ting up the Christ - mas tree with
D D/F♯ G D/F♯ Em7 A7sus
20
friends who come a - round, it's so much fun when Christ - mas comes to
Dsus D B♭ C/B♭
22
town. Pres - ents for the chil - dren
Am7 Dm B♭ C/B♭
24
wrapped in red and green; all the things I've heard a - bout but
Am7 Dm Em7(♭5) A7
26
nev - er real - ly seen. No one will be sleep - ing on the
To Coda
Dm Dm/C♯ F/C Fm7 B♭7 Em7 A7sus A7
28
night of Christ-mas Eve hop - ing San - ta's on his way.
D Dsus D Dsus D Dsus D Dsus D
31

D.S. al Coda
Em7 A7 D D/F♯ G D/F♯ Em7 A7sus Dsus D
Coda
Em7 A7sus A7 D Dsus D
way. When San - ta's sleigh - bells ring I
Dsus D Dsus D
lis - ten all a - round. The her - ald an - gels sing; I
Dsus D Em7 A7
nev - er hear a sound. And all the dreams of chil - dren once
D D/F♯ G D/F♯ Em7 A7sus A♯dim7
lost will all be found. That's all I want when Christ - mas comes to
Bm E7
town. That's
Em7 A7sus D Dsus D
all I want when Christ - mas comes to town.

# 'Zat You, Santa Claus?

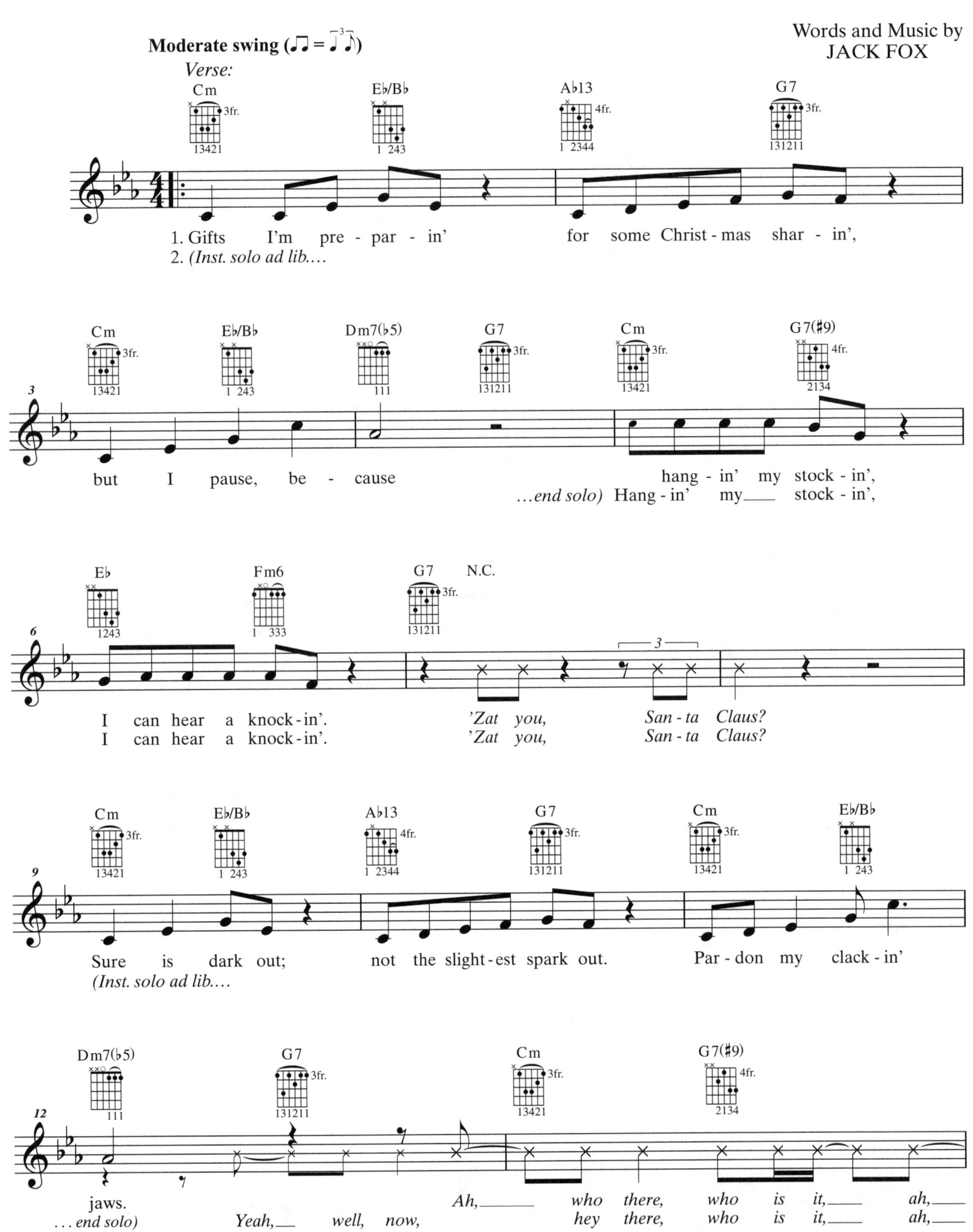

Eb
Fm6
G7
N.C.
3fr.
14
stop-pin' for a vis-it?
'Zat you, San-ta Claus?
stop-pin' for a vis-it?
'Zat you, San-ta Claus?
Bridge:
C
C7
Fm
17
1. Are you bring-in' a pre-sent for me,
something pleas-ant-ly
2. Whoa there, San-ta, you gave me a scare.
Now, stop teas-in', 'cause
Gm7(b5)
Ab7/Eb
20
pleas-ant for me?
That's what I've been wait-in' for.
I know you're there.
We don't be-lieve in no gob-lins to-day.
But,
G7/D
Cm
Eb/Bb
23
Would you mind slip-pin' it un-der the door?
Four winds are howl-in', oh,
I can't ex-plain why I'm shak-in' this way.
Well, I see ol'
Ab13
4fr.
26
or may-be that'd be growl-in'.
My legs feel like
San-ta in the key-hole.
I'll give to the
1.
Dm7(b5)
G7(#9)
28
straws.
Oh, my, my, me my.
Kind-ly would you re-ply?

2.
G7
N.C.
Dm7(♭5)
G7
31
'Zat you, San - ta Claus?
cause.
Cm
G7(♯9)
E♭
N.C.
34
One peek, and I'll try there. Uh - oh, there's an eye there.
Cm
E♭
F7
A♭7
36
'Zat you, San-ta Claus?
G7
N.C.
Fm6
N.C.
G7sus
40
Please, please; I pit - y my knees. Say that's you,
G7(♯5)
Cm
E♭/B♭
F7/A
A♭7
43
San - ta Claus.
Cm
G7
Cm
G7
D♭7(♭5)
Cm
46
That's him, all right.

# SOLO GUITAR
## ARRANGEMENTS

# Angels We Have Heard on High

Traditional Carol

**Moderately**

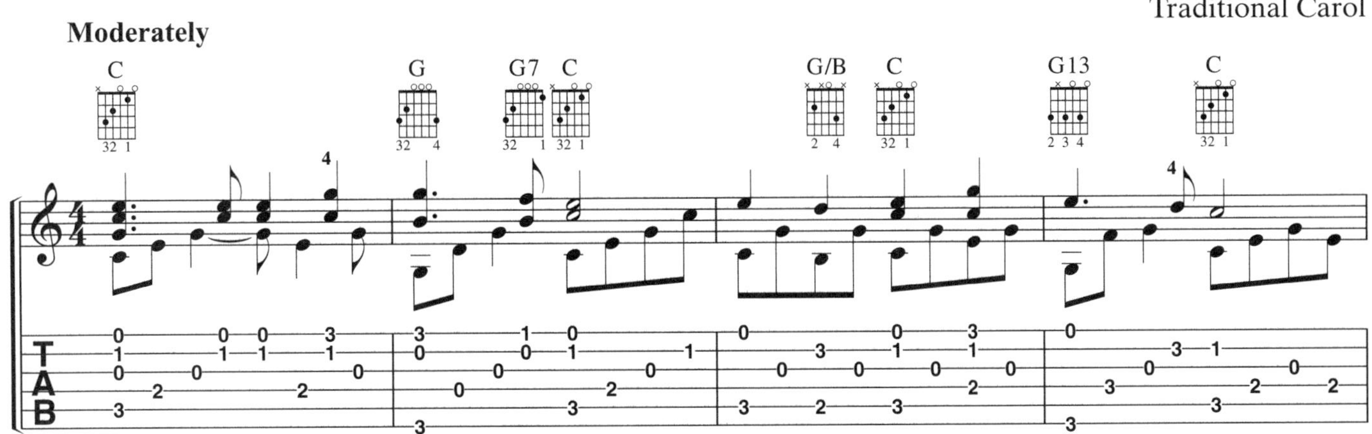


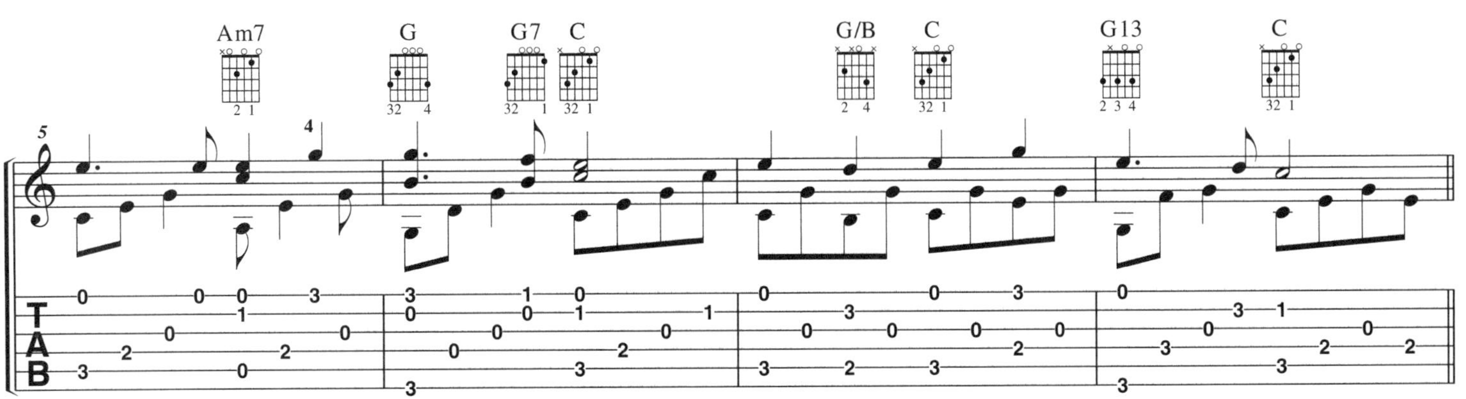


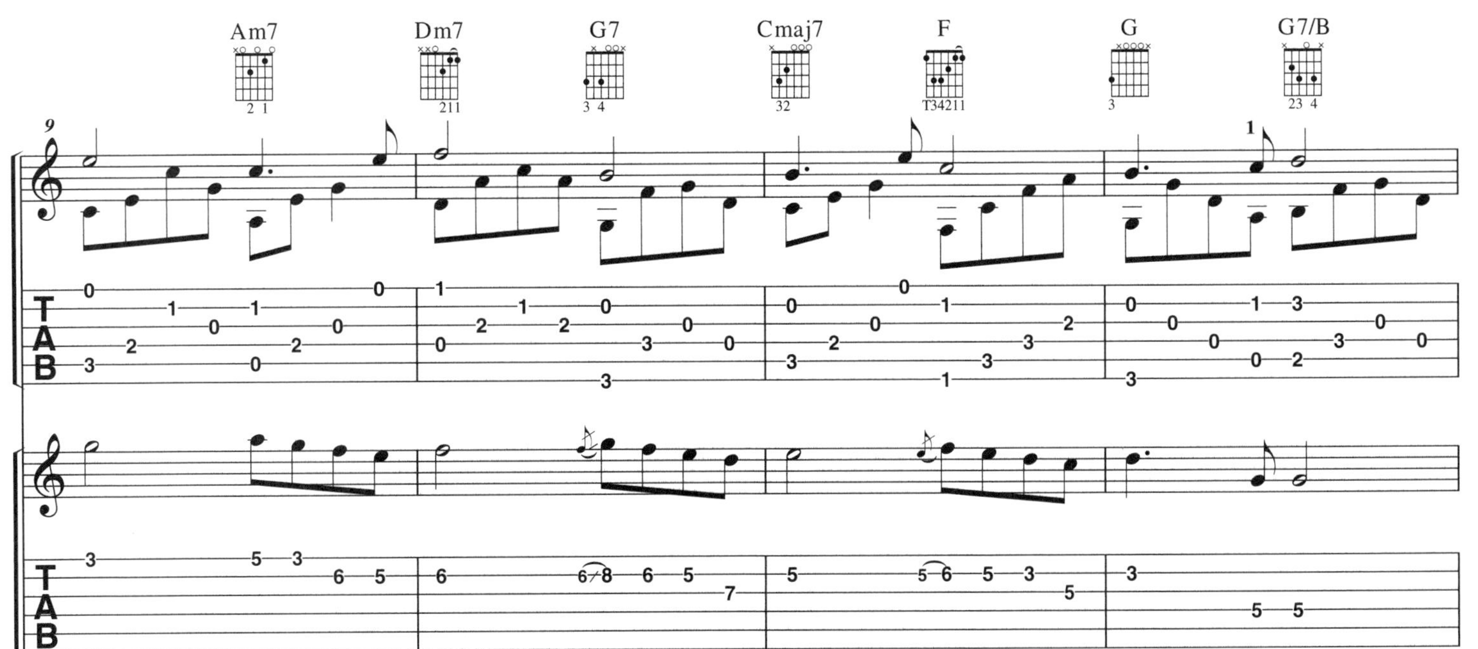

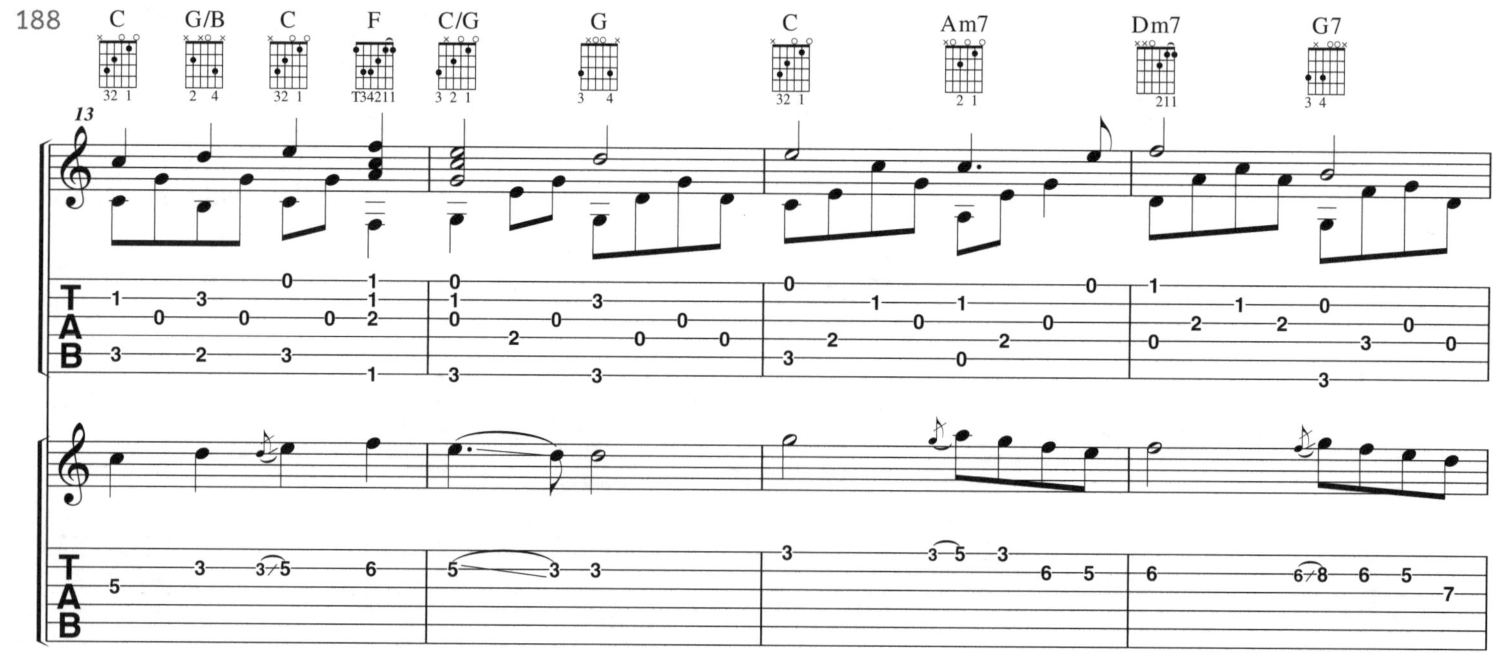
C
G/B
C
F
C/G
G
C
Am7
Dm7
G7
TAB

Cmaj7
F
G
G7/B
C
G/B
C
F
C/G
G
C
TAB

TAB

26
30
C
Am7
Dm7
G7
Cmaj7
F
33
G
G7/B
C
G/B
C
F
C/G
G

C
Am7
Dm7
G7
Cmaj7
F
36

G
G7/B
C
G/B
C
F
C/G
G7
C
39

# Away in a Manger

Music by
JAMES R. MURRAY
*Arranged by*
*CRAIG B. DOBBINS*

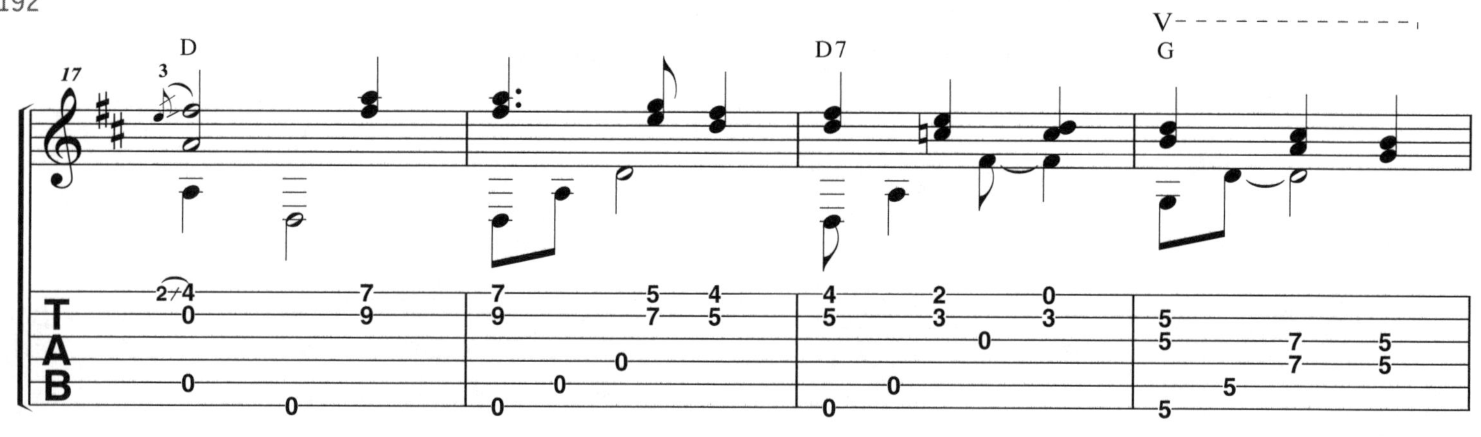
D
D7
G
V

D
A7
D
G
A7
V

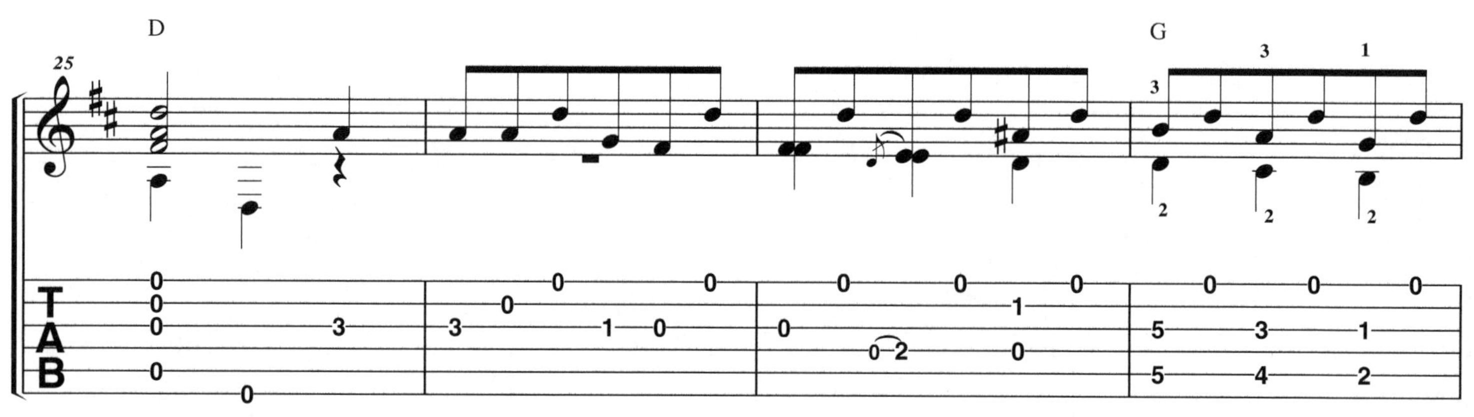
D
G

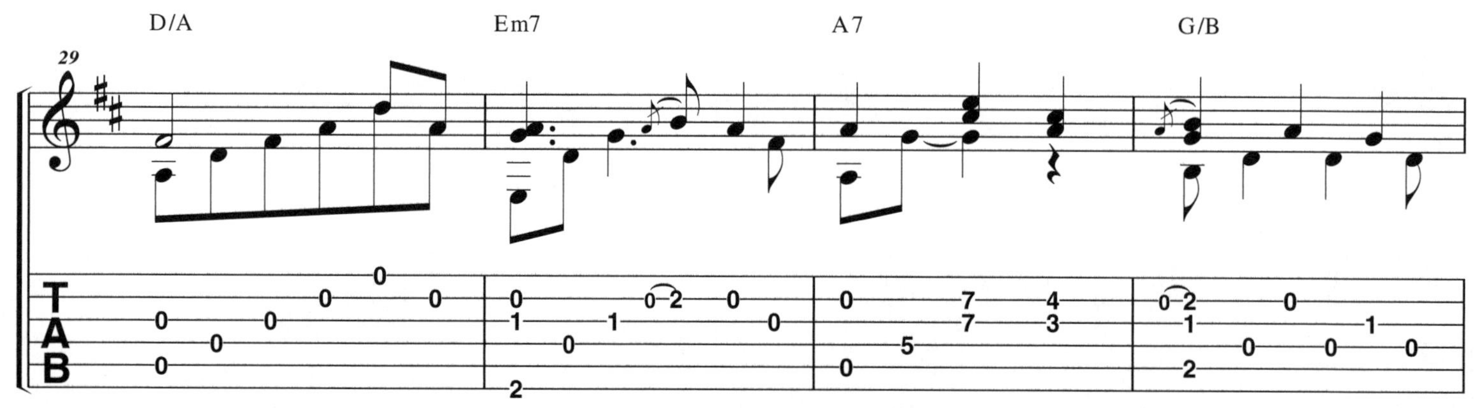
D/A
Em7
A7
G/B

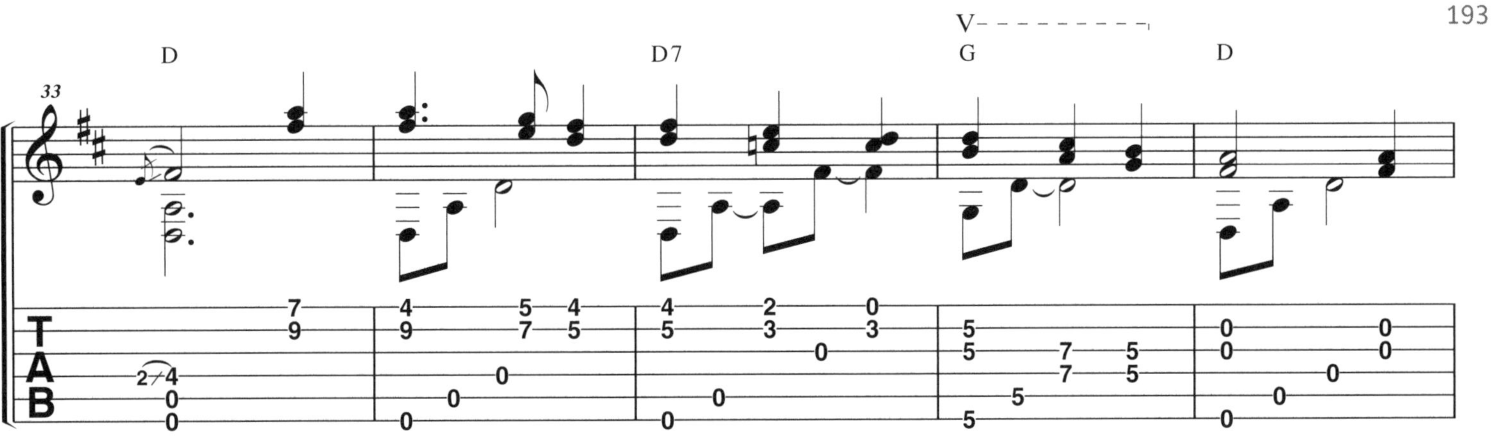
V
33
D
D7
G
D

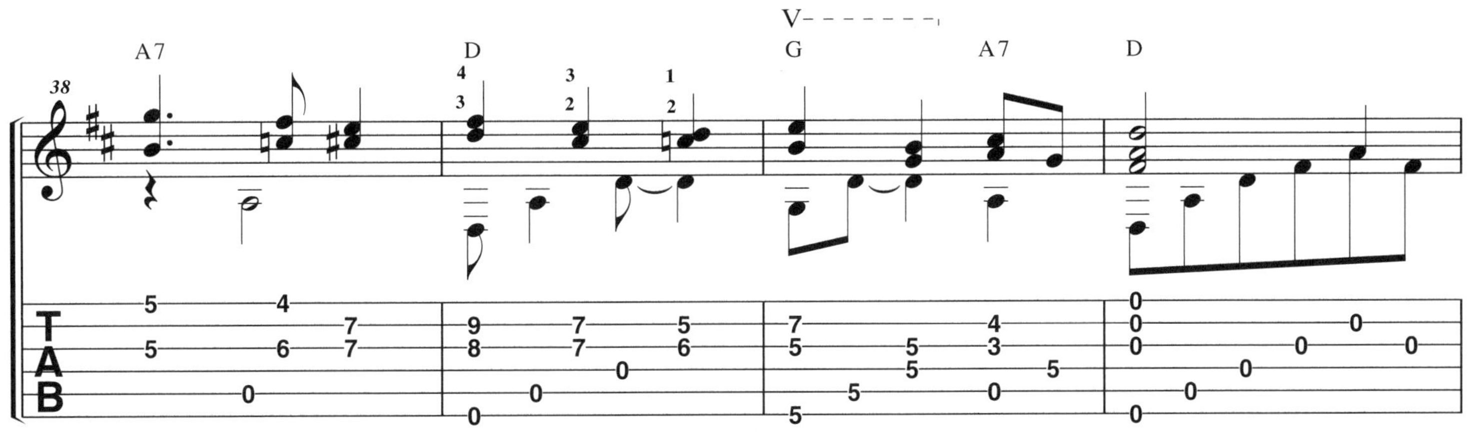
V
38
A7
D
G
A7
D

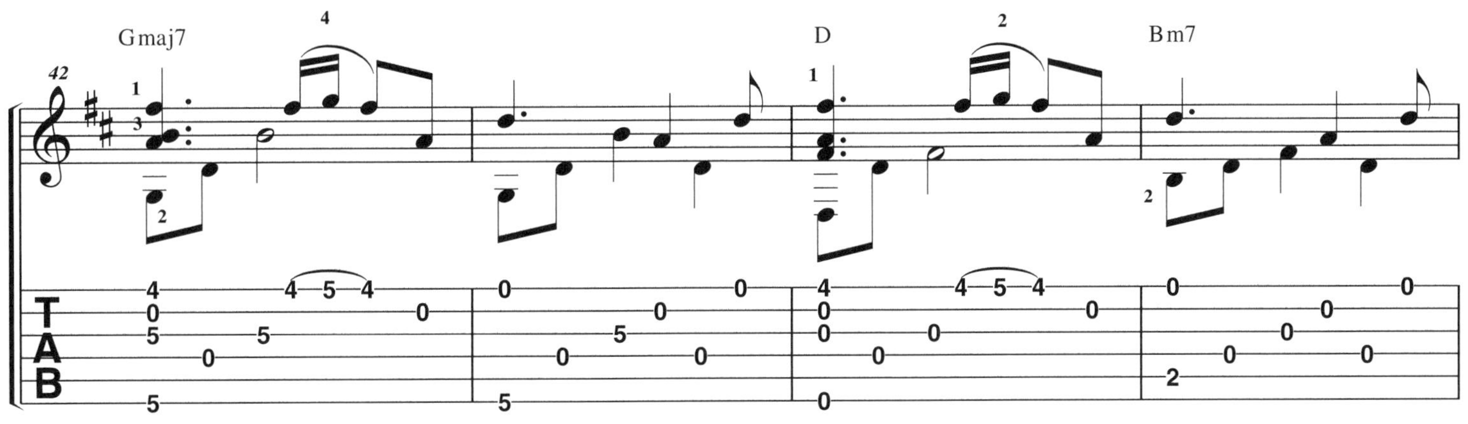
42
Gmaj7
D
Bm7

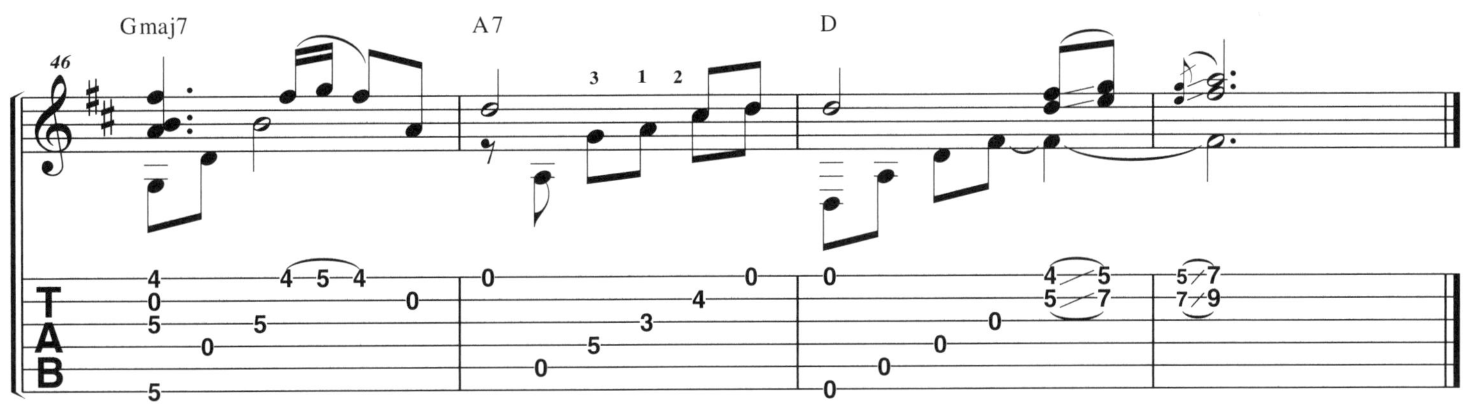
46
Gmaj7
A7
D

# Deck the Halls

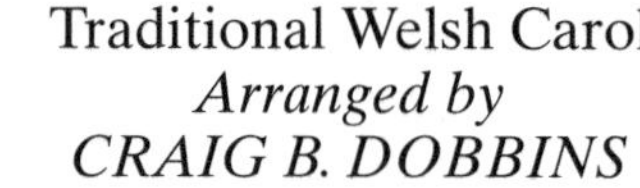
Traditional Welsh Carol
*Arranged by*
*CRAIG B. DOBBINS*

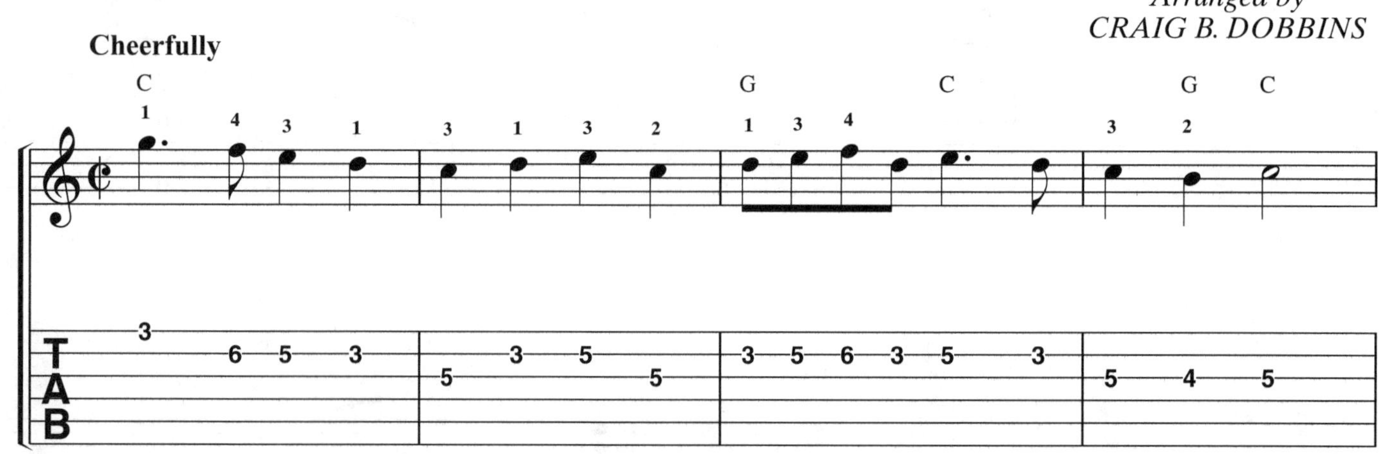


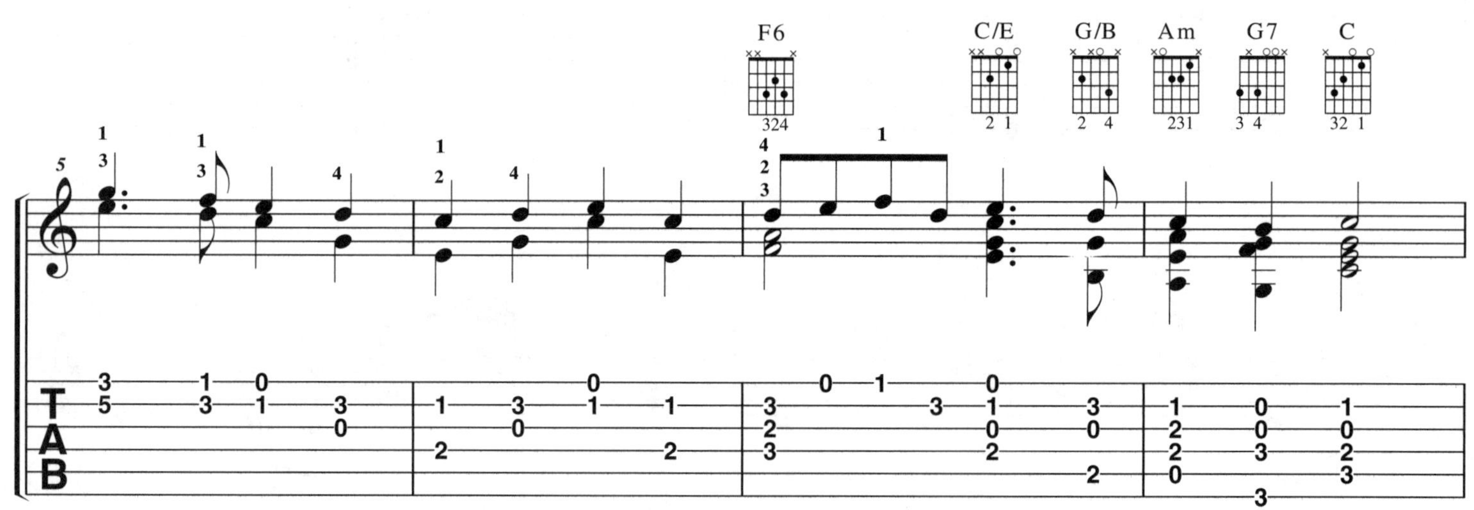


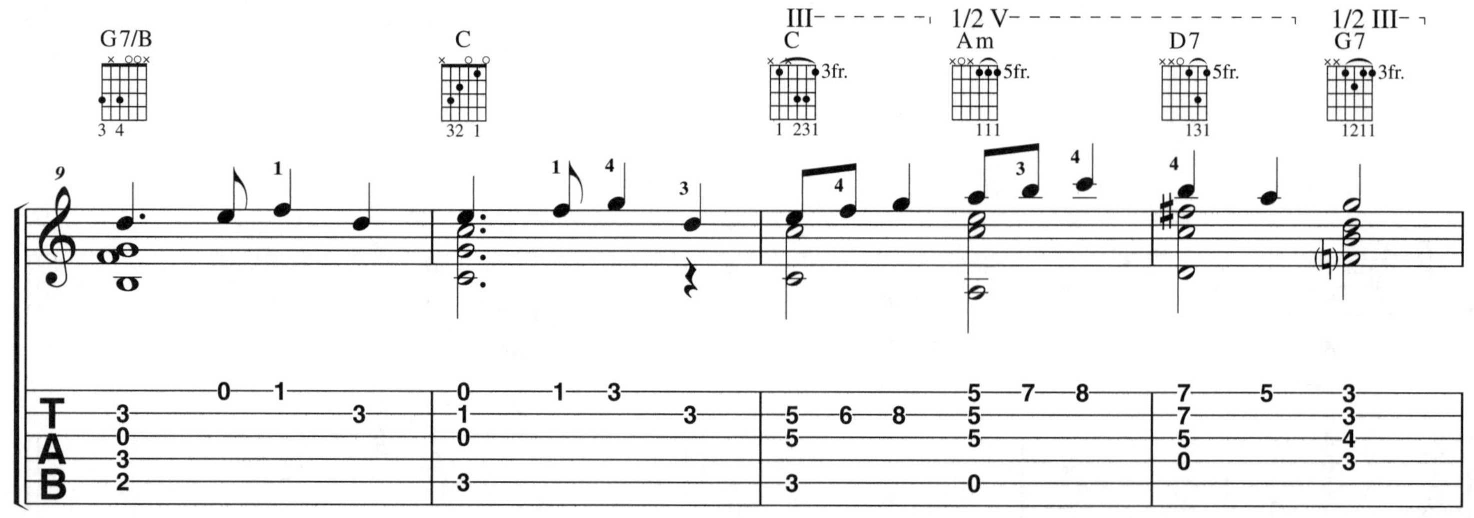

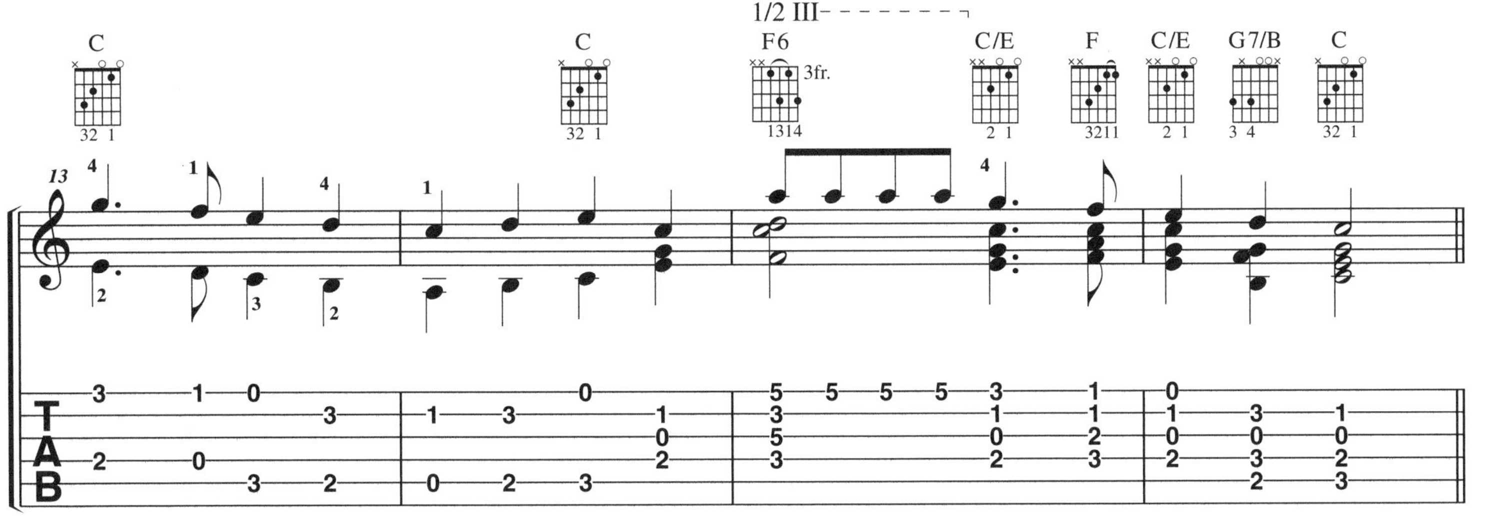
1/2 III
C
C
F6
3fr.
C/E
F
C/E
G7/B
C
13

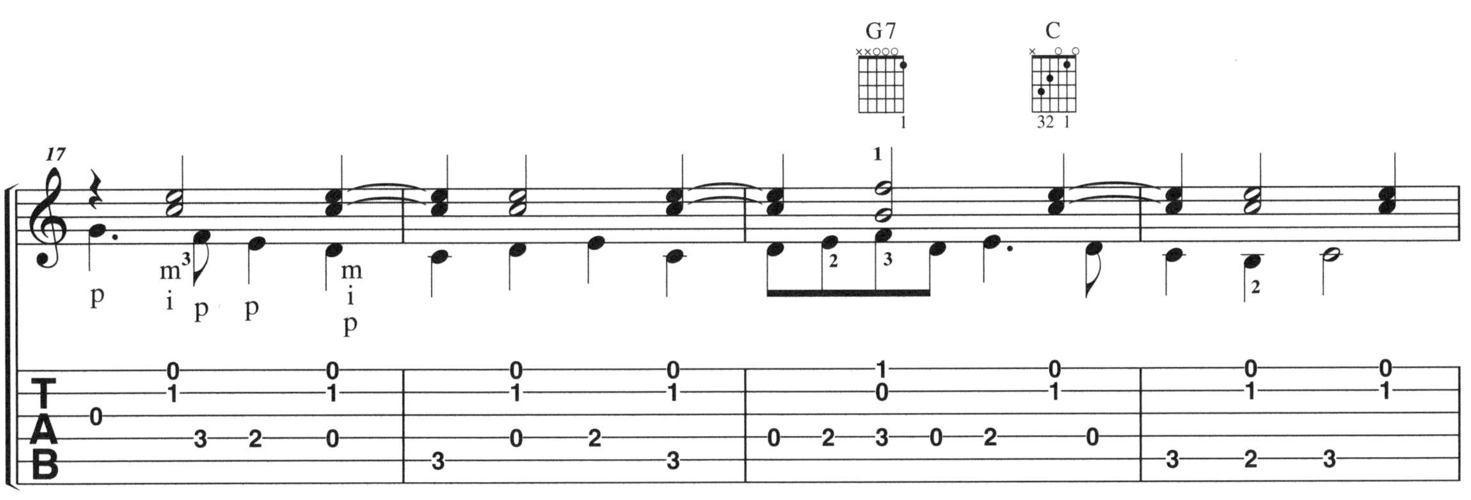
G7
C
17

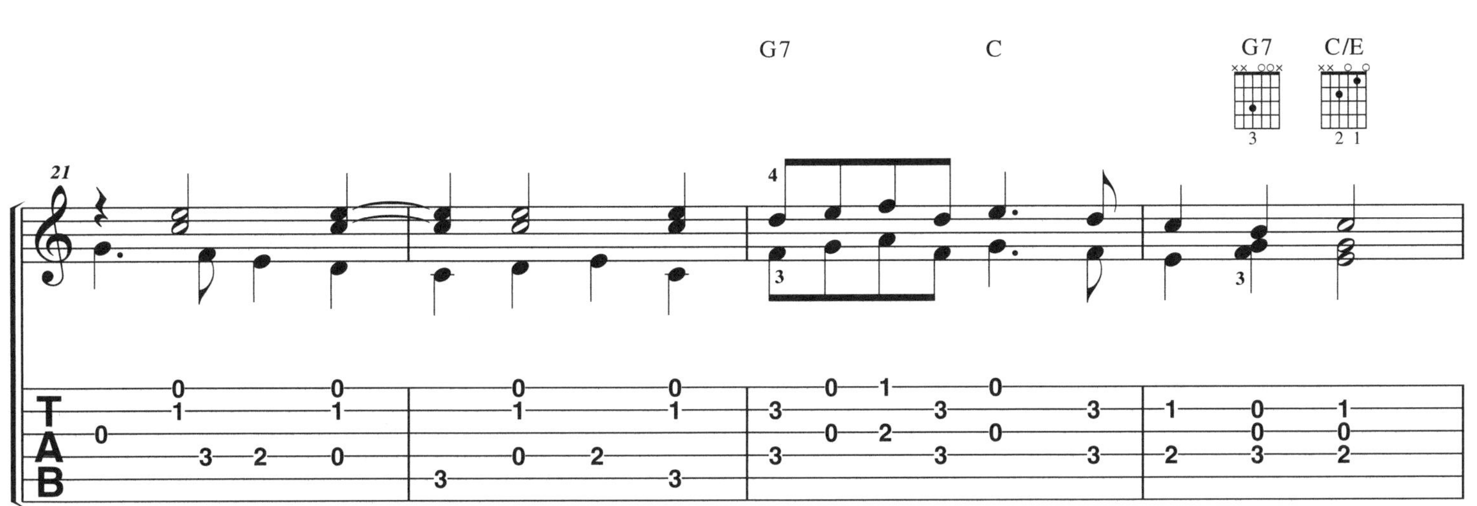
G7
C
G7
C/E
21

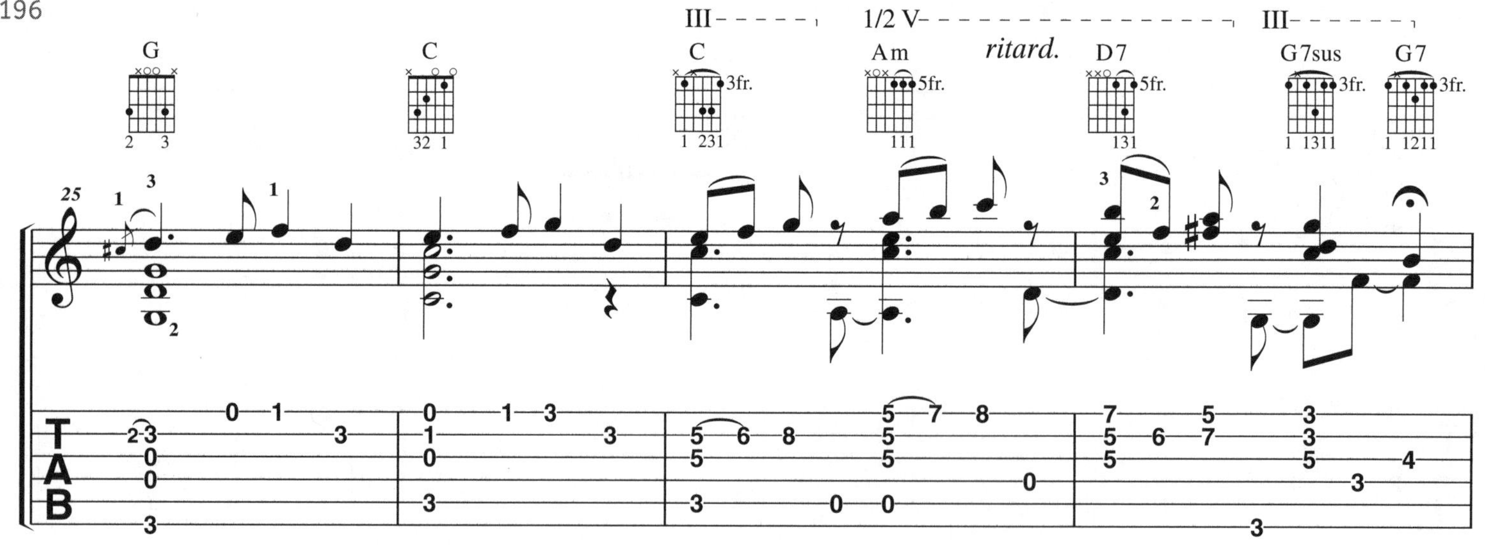


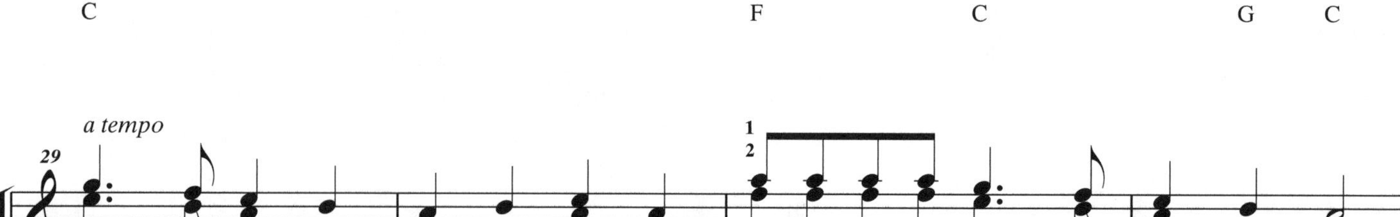

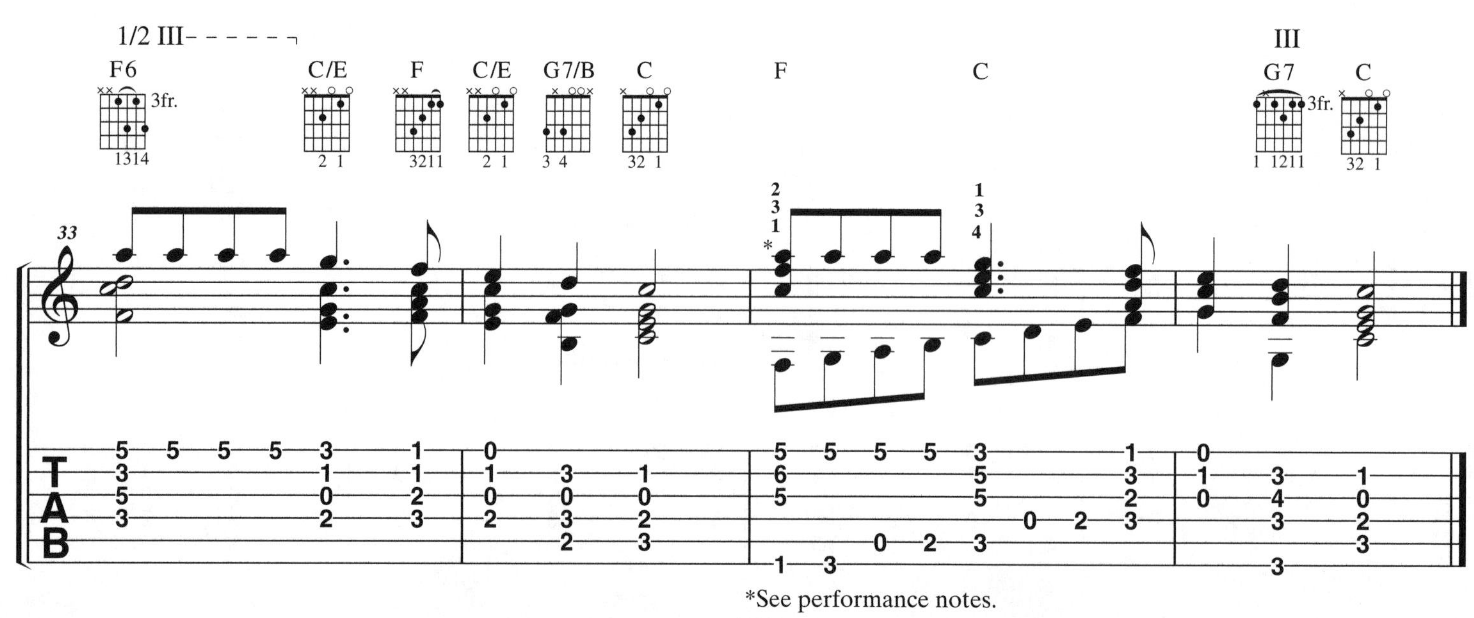


*See performance notes.

# The First Noel

Traditional English Carol
*Arranged by VINCENT J. CARROLA*

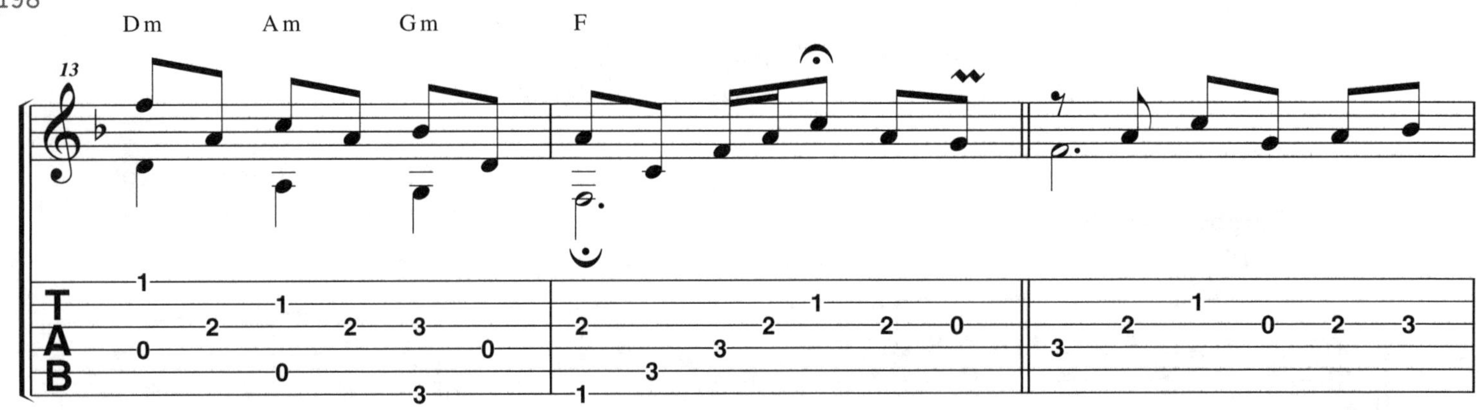
Dm
Am
Gm
F
13
TAB

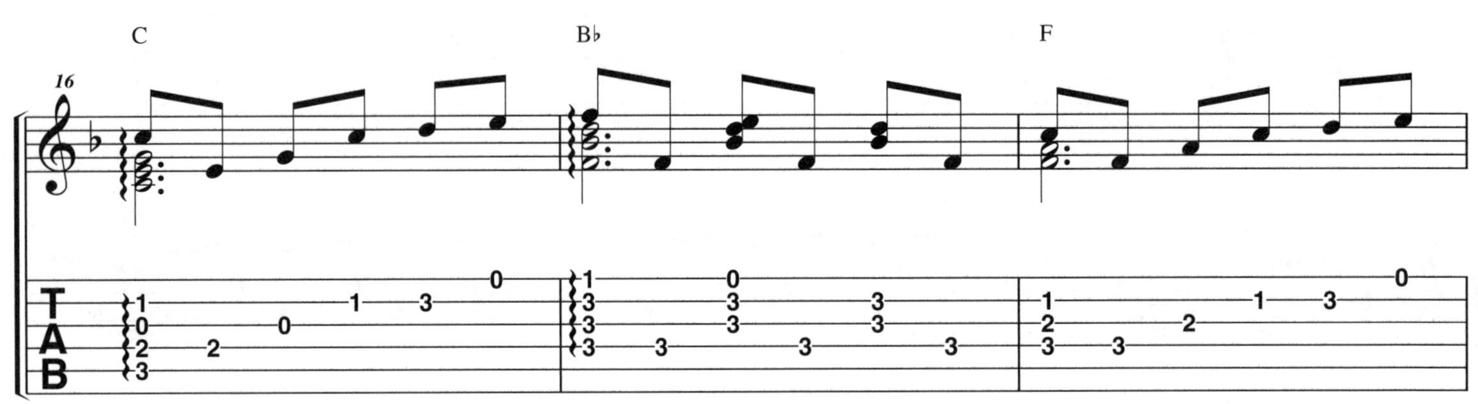
C
B♭
F
16
TAB

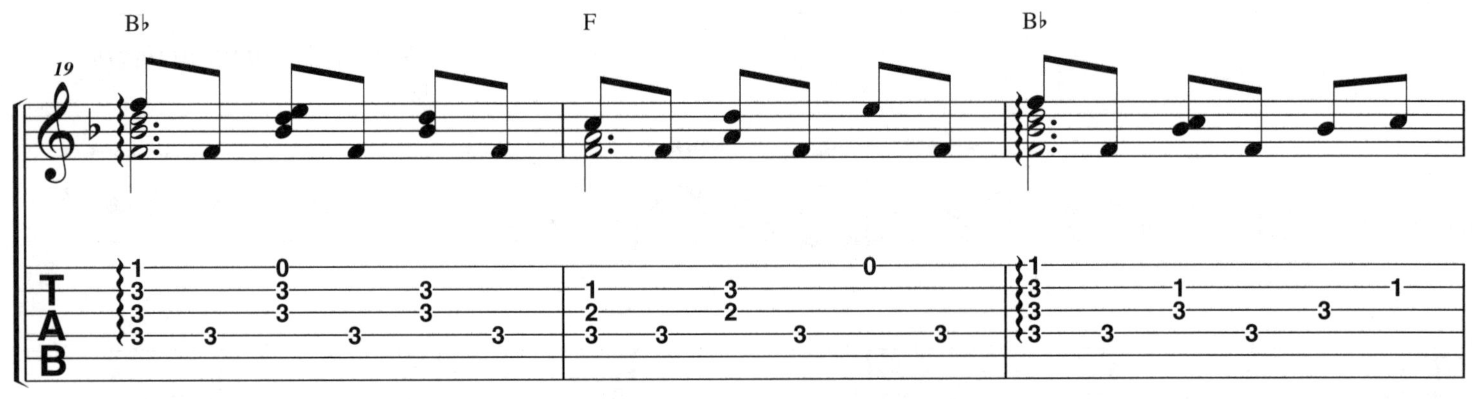
B♭
F
B♭
19
TAB

F
Am
22
f
TAB

B♭
F
Dm
C
B♭
25
mf

Am
B♭
C
Dm
Am
Gm
F
28

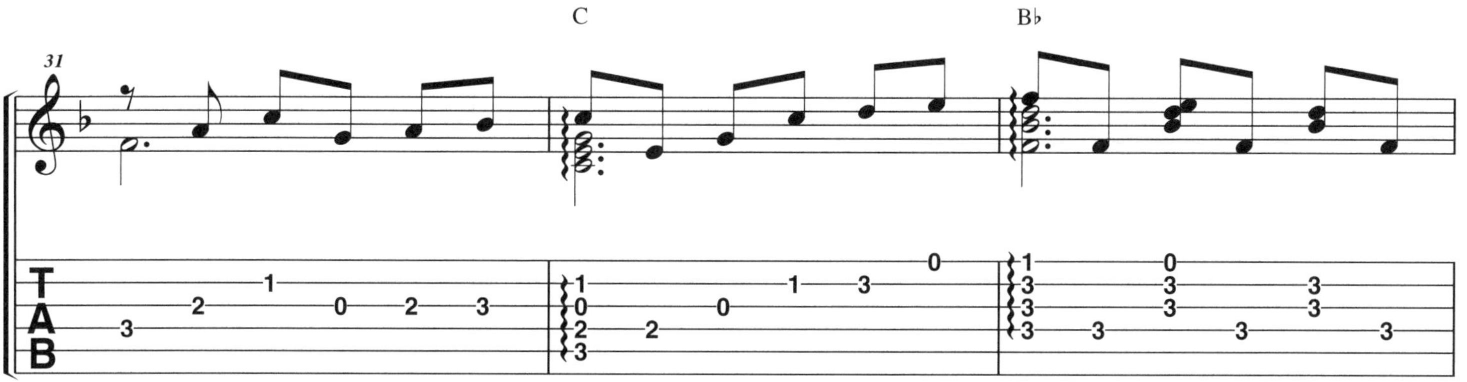
C
B♭
31

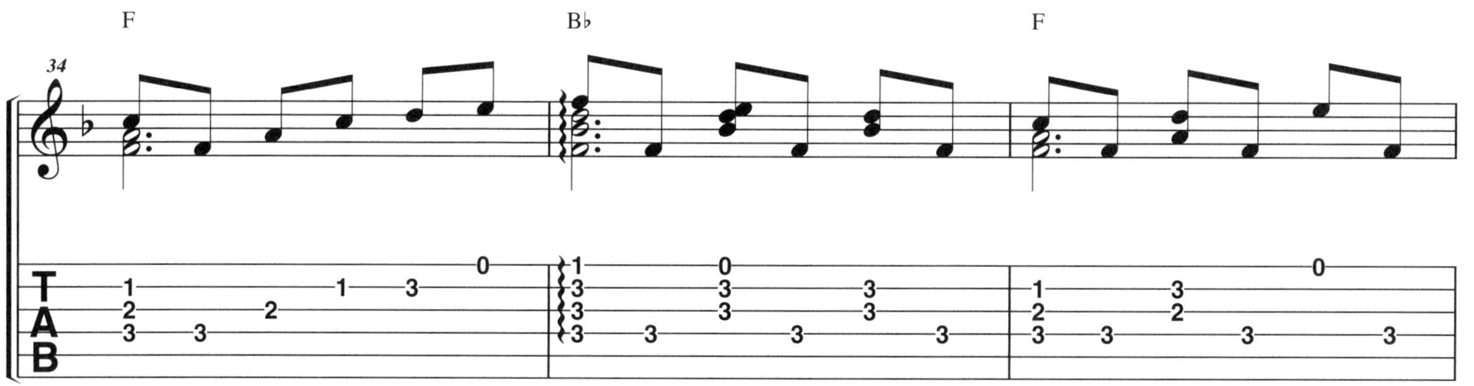
F
B♭
F
34

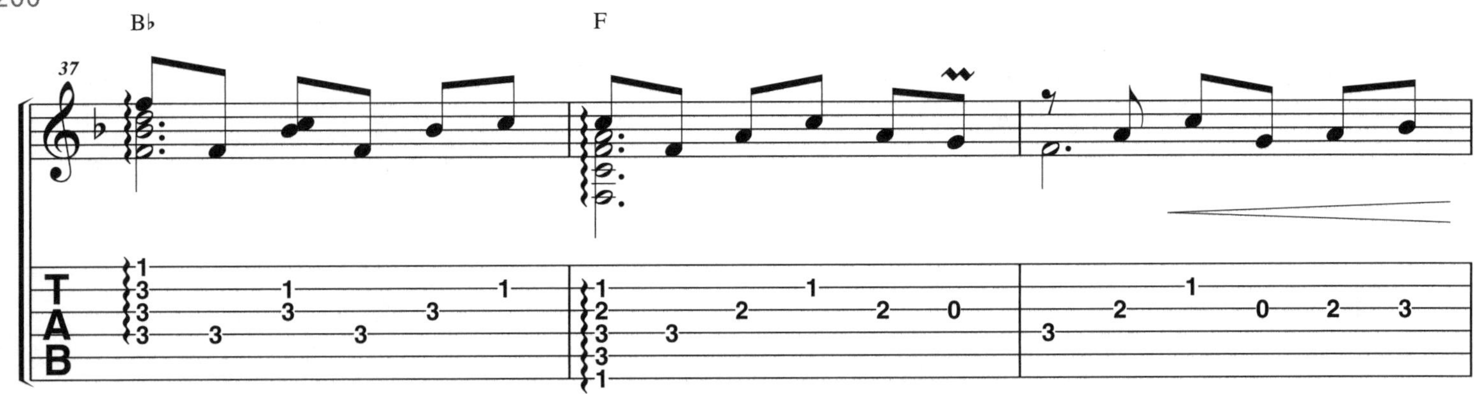
B♭
F
37

Am
B♭
F
40
f
mf

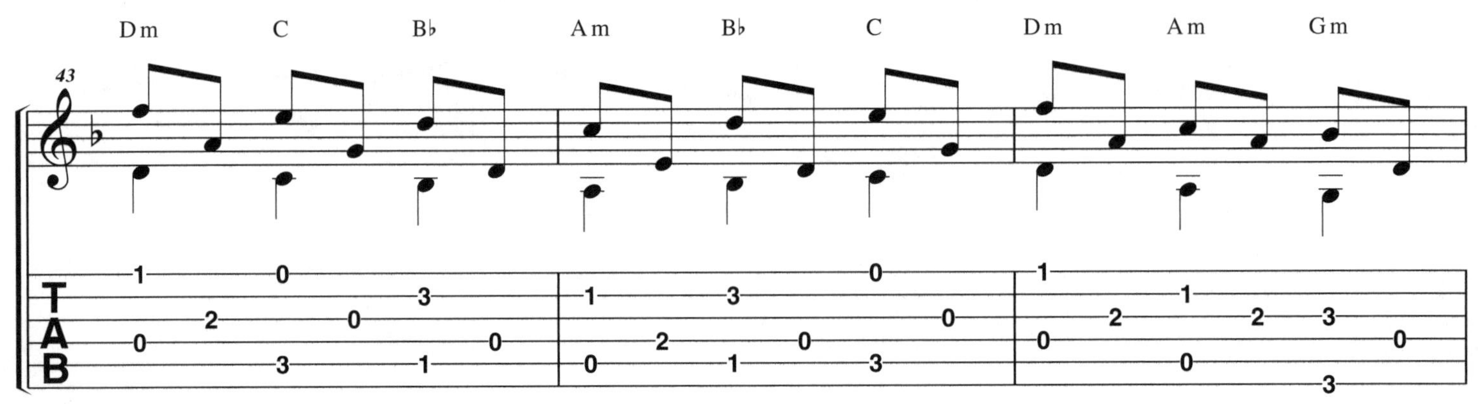
Dm
C
B♭
Am
B♭
C
Dm
Am
Gm
43

F
Dm
Am
46
f

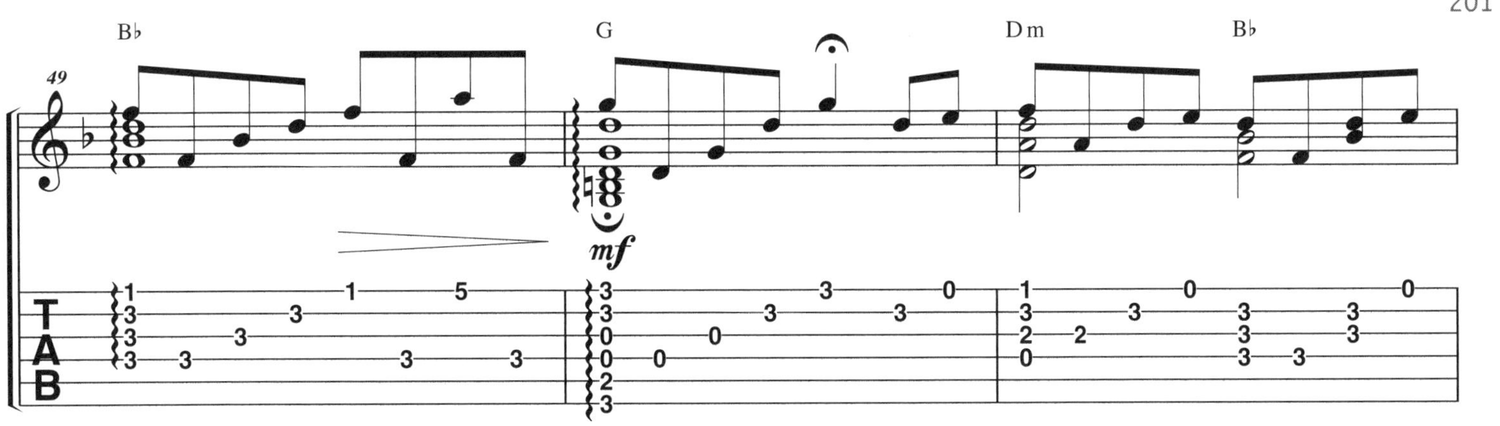

B♭
G
Dm
B♭
49
mf


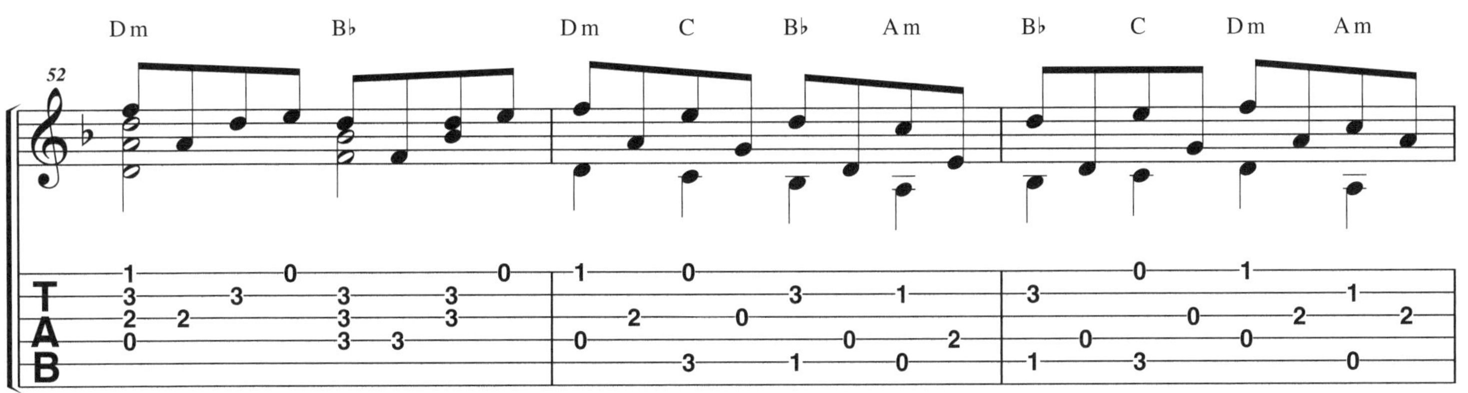

Dm
B♭
Dm
C
B♭
Am
B♭
C
Dm
Am
52

Gm
F
Am
55

very slow and with feeling
BIII④
B♭
F
G
58
f
p

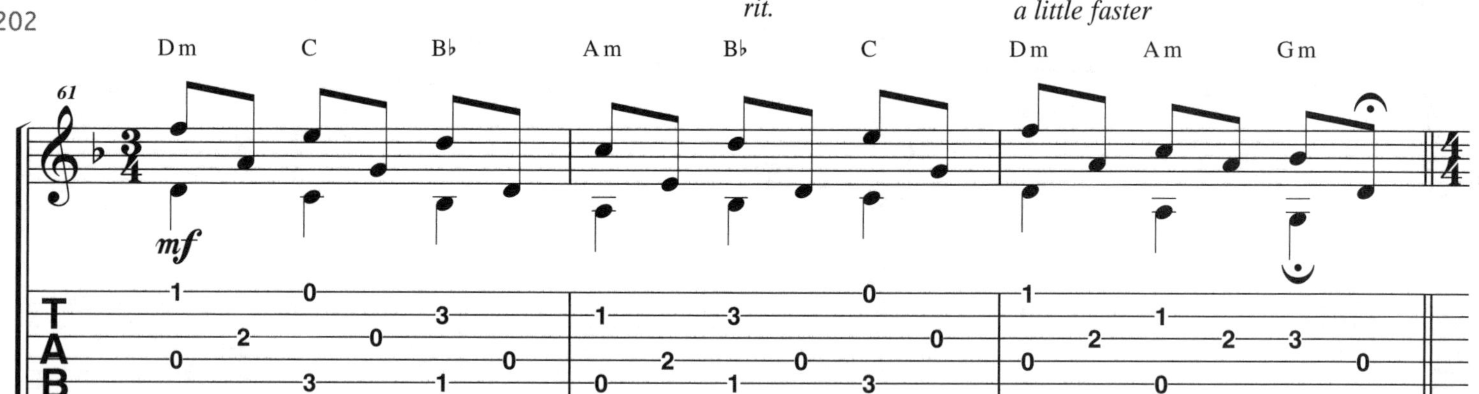
rit.
a little faster
Dm
C
B♭
Am
B♭
C
Dm
Am
Gm
61
mf

**Tempo I**

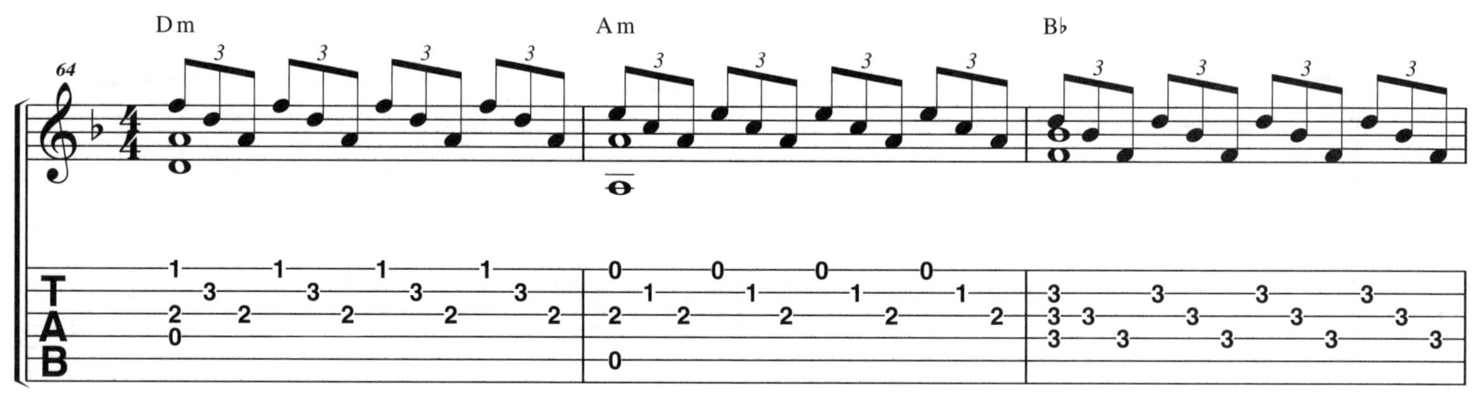
Dm
Am
B♭
64

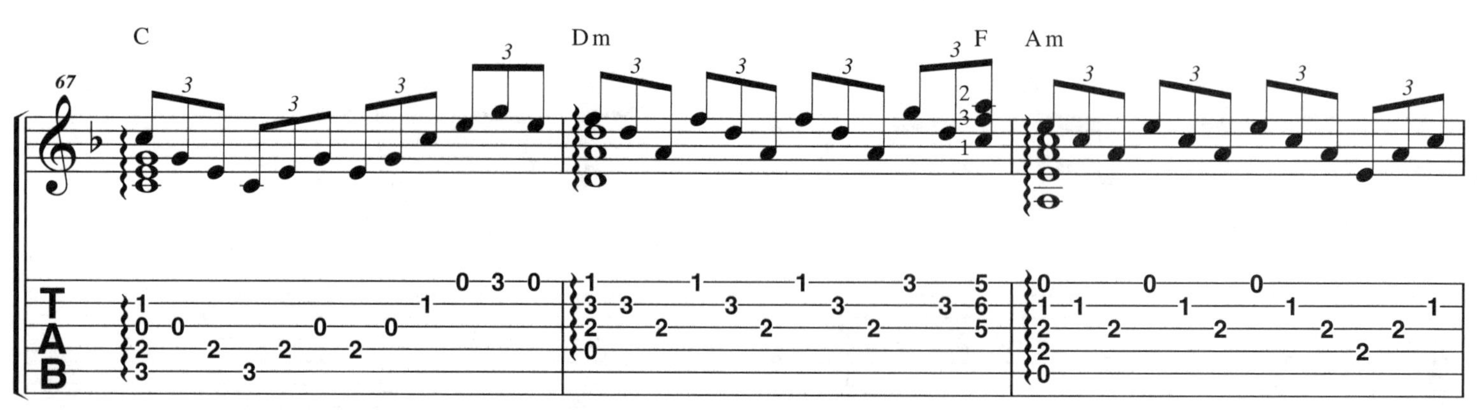
C
Dm
F
Am
67

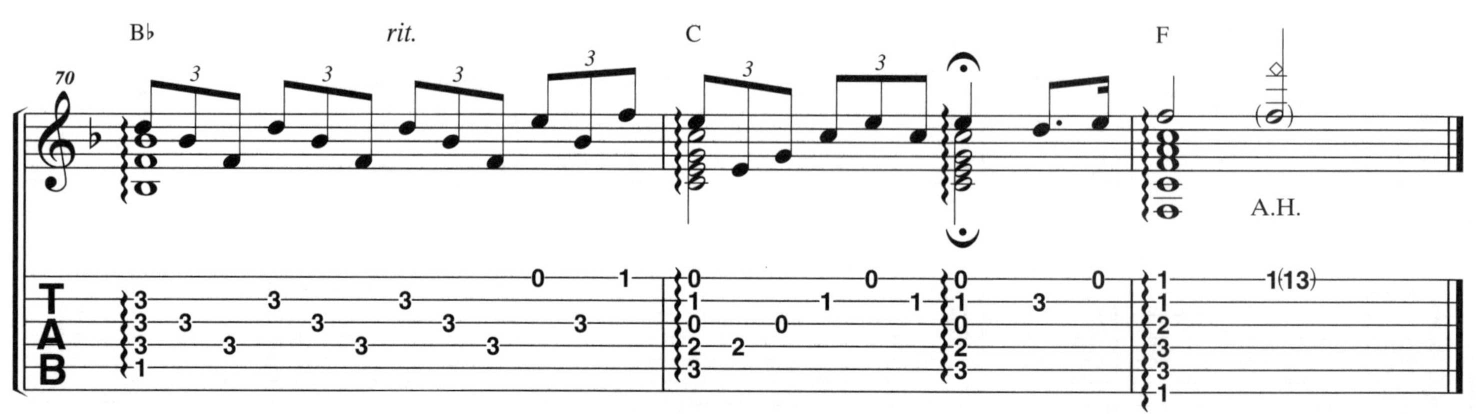
B♭
rit.
C
F
70
A.H.

# Jesu, Joy of Man's Desiring

Composed by
J.S. BACH

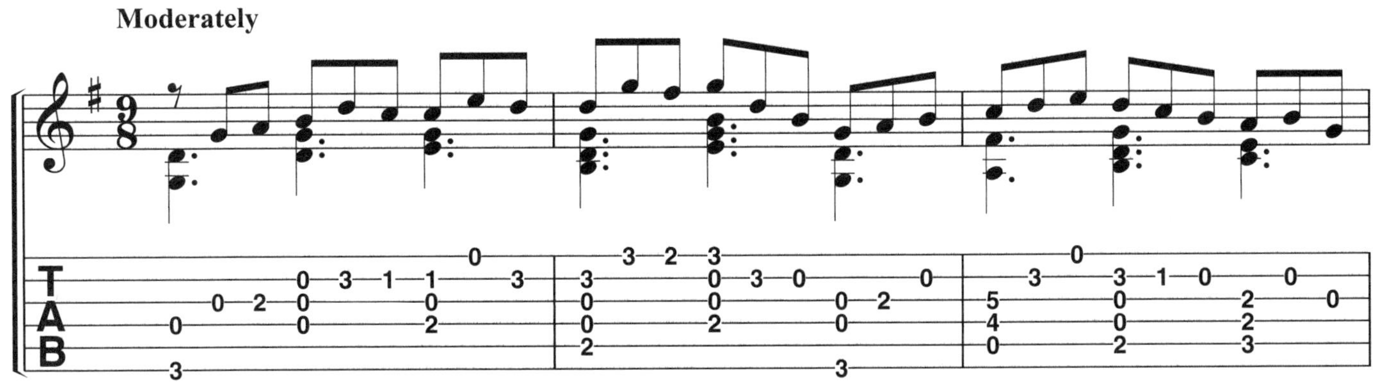

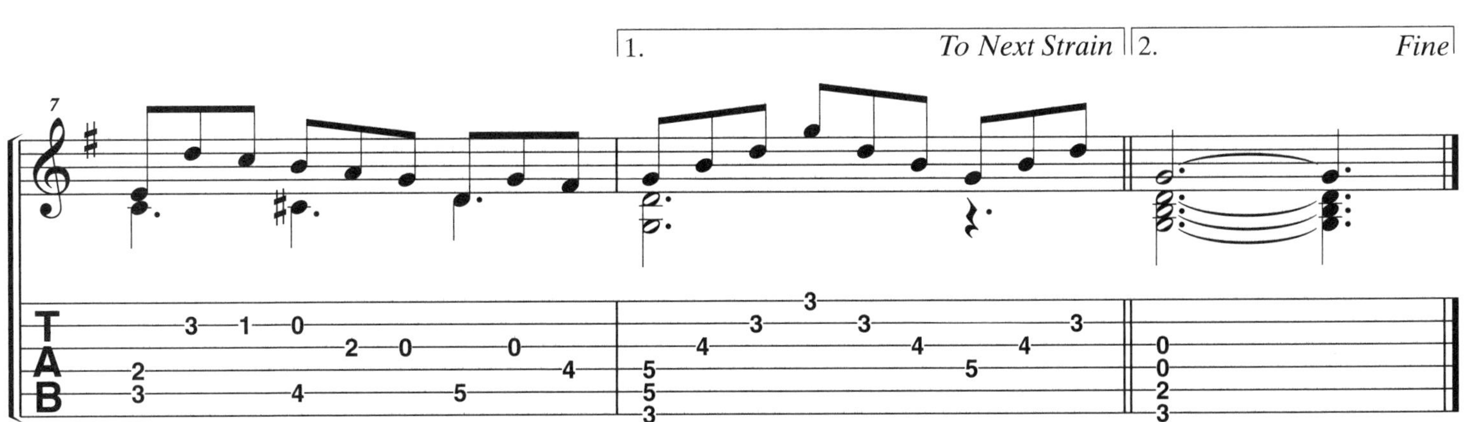

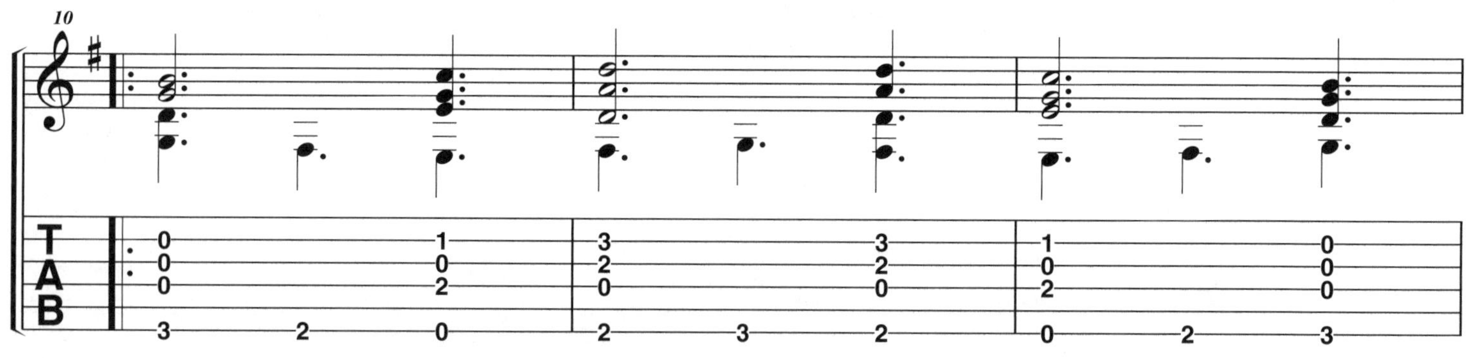
10
T
A
B

13
T
A
B

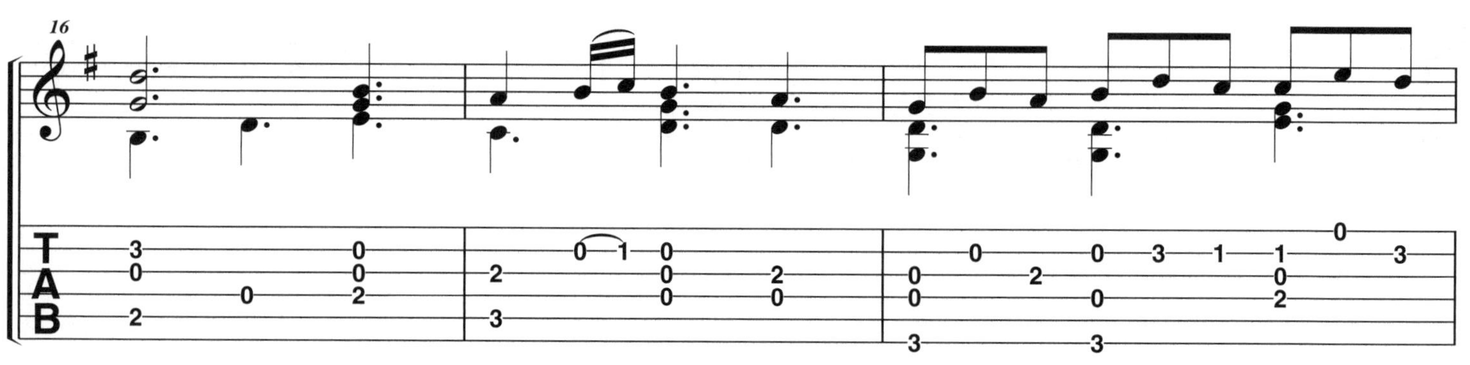
16
T
A
B

19
T
A
B

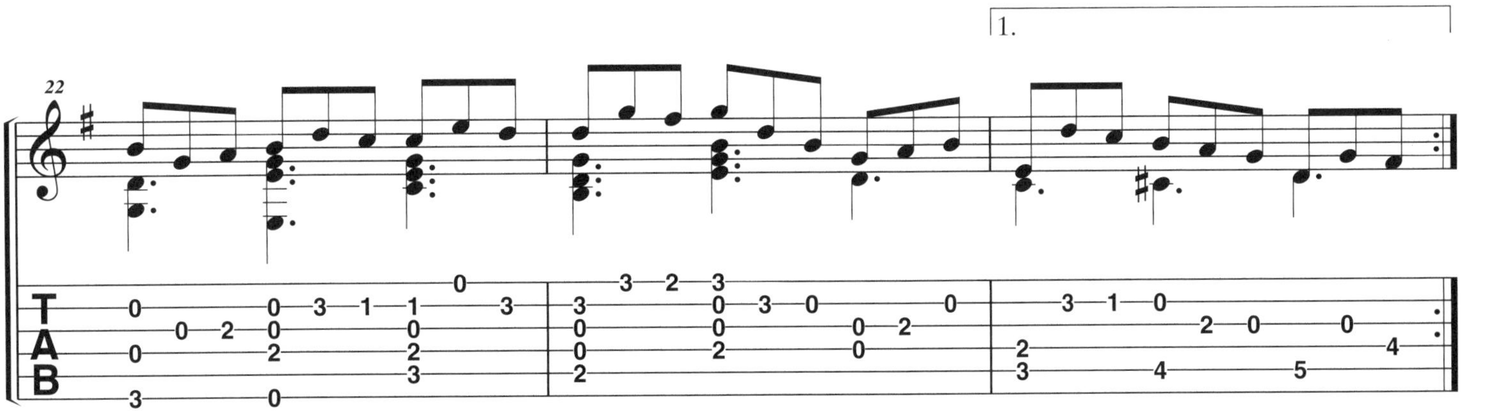
1.
22
T
A
B

2.
25
T
A
B

28
T
A
B

31
T
A
B

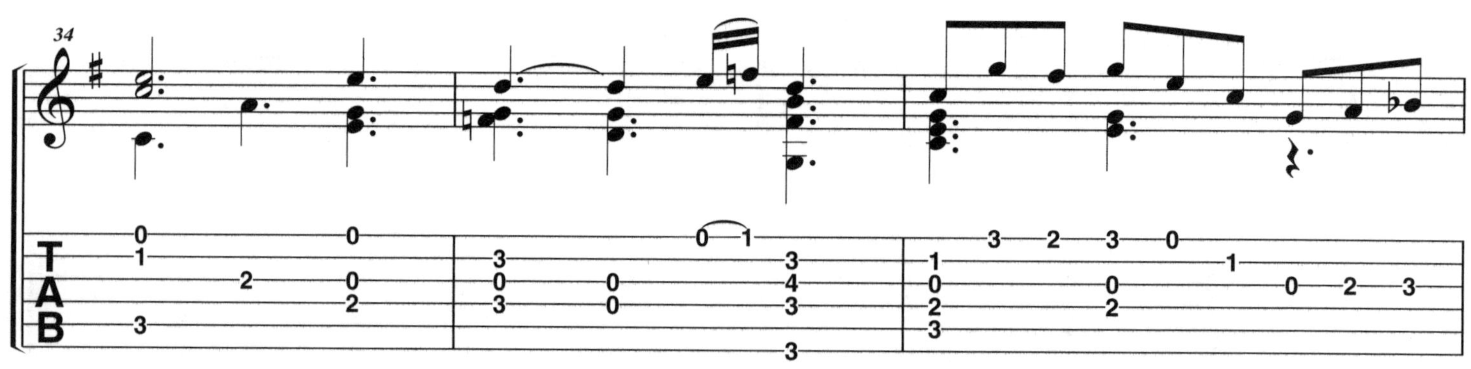

D.C. al Fine

# Joy to the World / It Came Upon the Midnight Clear

Joy to the World:
Music by G. F. HANDEL
Words by ISAAC WATTS

*Arranged by*
CRAIG B. DOBBINS

It Came Upon the Midnight Clear:
Traditional Carol

E
Am
G
D/F♯
G7/B
C
E7
F
B7/F♯
G7
harm.

# O Come, All Ye Faithful

(Adeste Fideles)

Guitar in Drop D tuning:
⑥ = D

English Words by FREDERICK OAKELEY
Latin Words Attributed to JOHN FRANCIS WADE

Music by JOHN READING
*Arranged by VINCENT J. CARROLA*

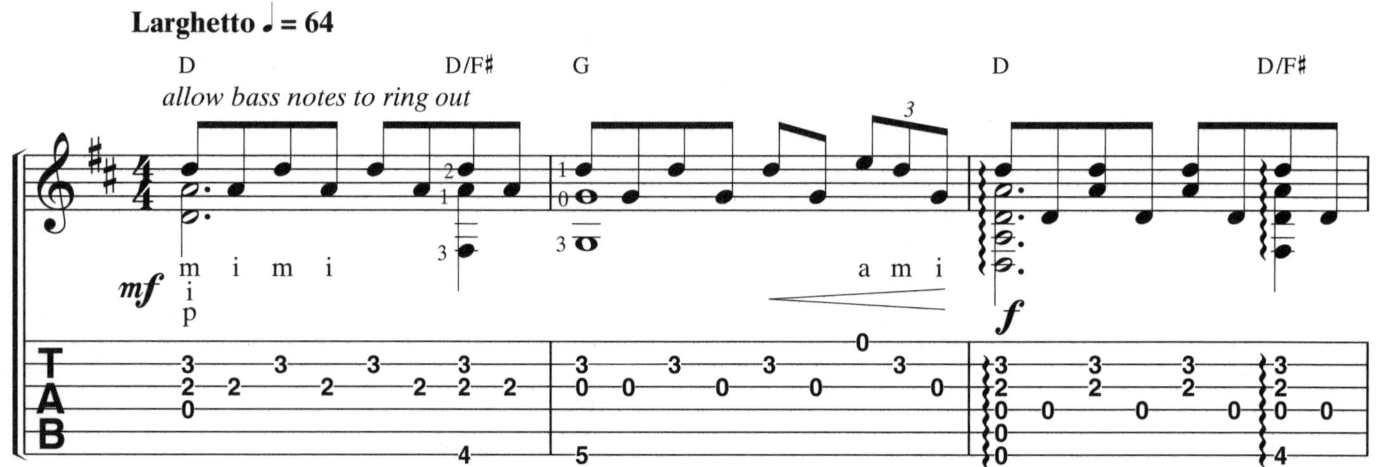


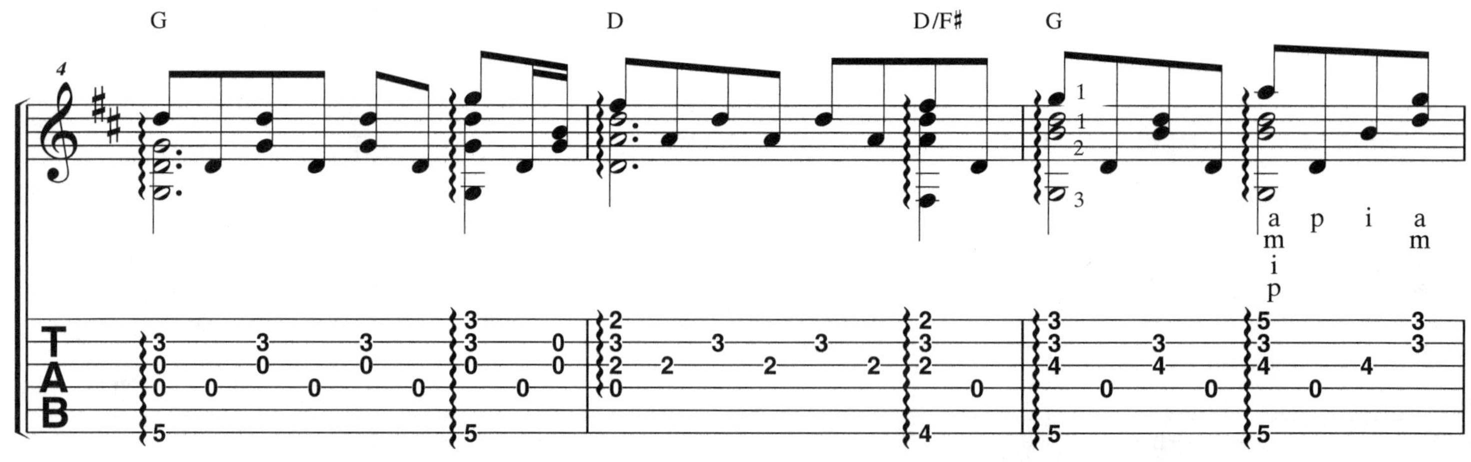


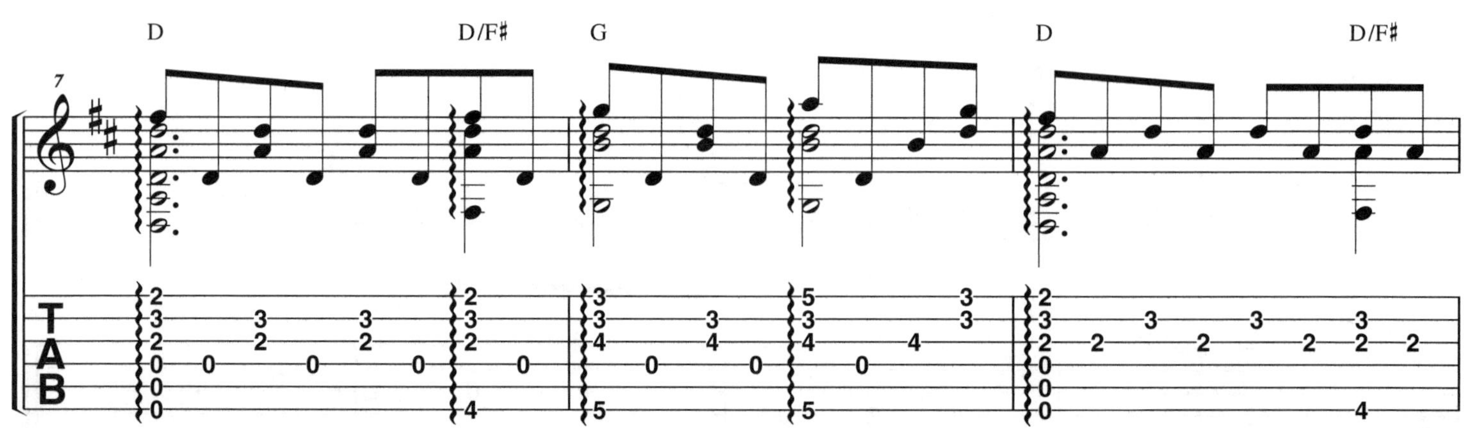

G
A
D
mf
A
D
A
D
G
D
A
Bm
A
E
A
E7
A
D
A
E7
A
D
A7
D
A7
D
f

A
D
Bm
Em
A
D
A
D
A7
D
A
D
A7
D
A
D
A7
D
A
E7
A
D
G
D
A7
D
D/F♯
G
D
D/F♯
mf
3
f

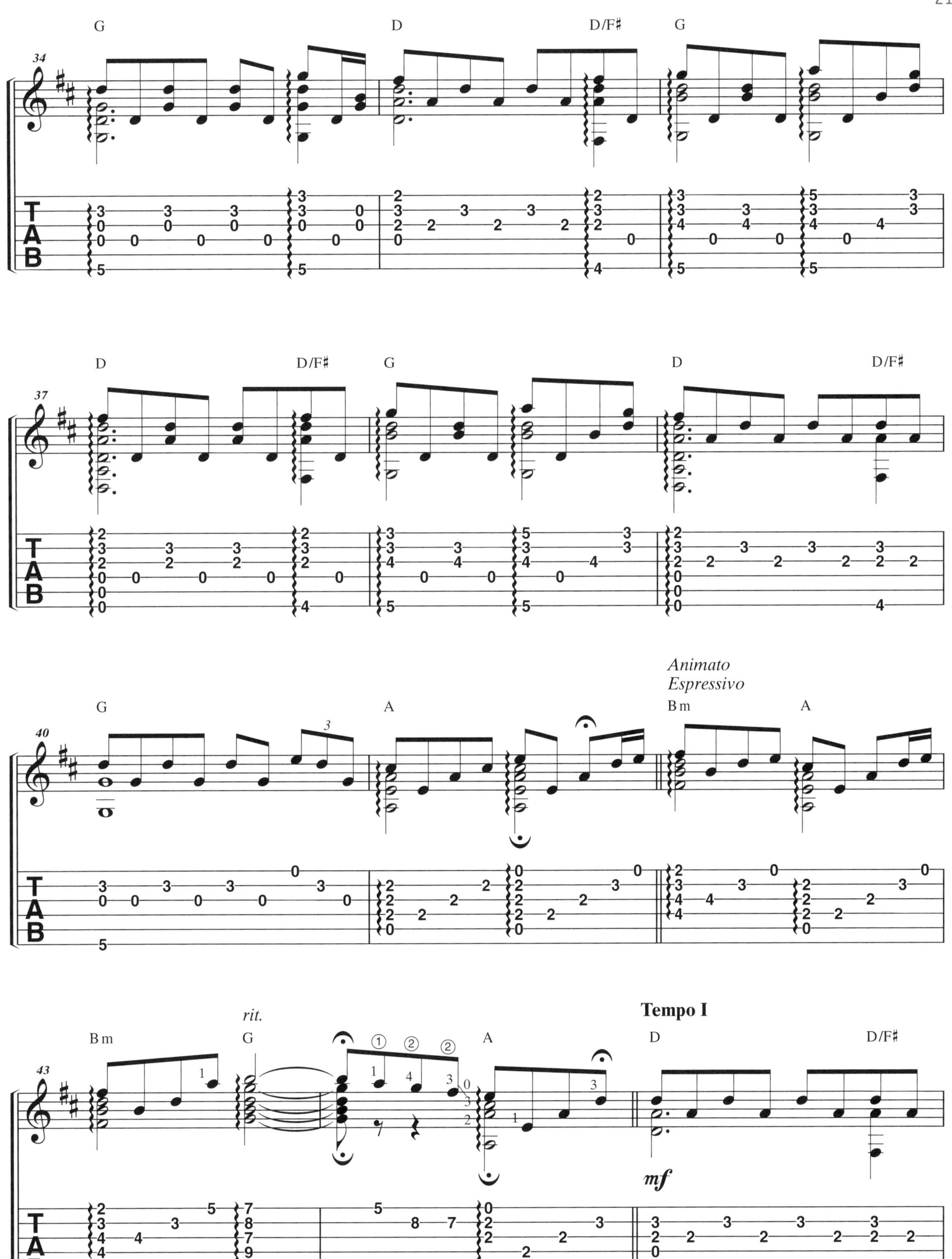
G
D
D/F♯
G
D
D/F♯
G
D
D/F♯
G
A
Animato
Espressivo
Bm
A
Bm
rit.
G
A
Tempo I
D
D/F♯
mf

G
D
D/F♯
G
D
A
D
A7
D
A
D
A7
D
A
D
A7
D
A
E7
A
D
G
D
A7
D
D/F♯
G
rit.
D
A.H.

# O Holy Night

Largo ♩. = 50
with feeling
allow notes ring out
Words and Music by
J.S. DWIGHT and ADOLPHE ADAM
Arranged by VINCENT J. CARROLA
C
C/E
F
C
G7
C
C/E
F
C

C7 BVIII Em/B BVII B7 Em

a tempo

rit. G7 BIII Am7 BV④

G7 C BV④

Am BV③ Em

p i m a m i

*f*

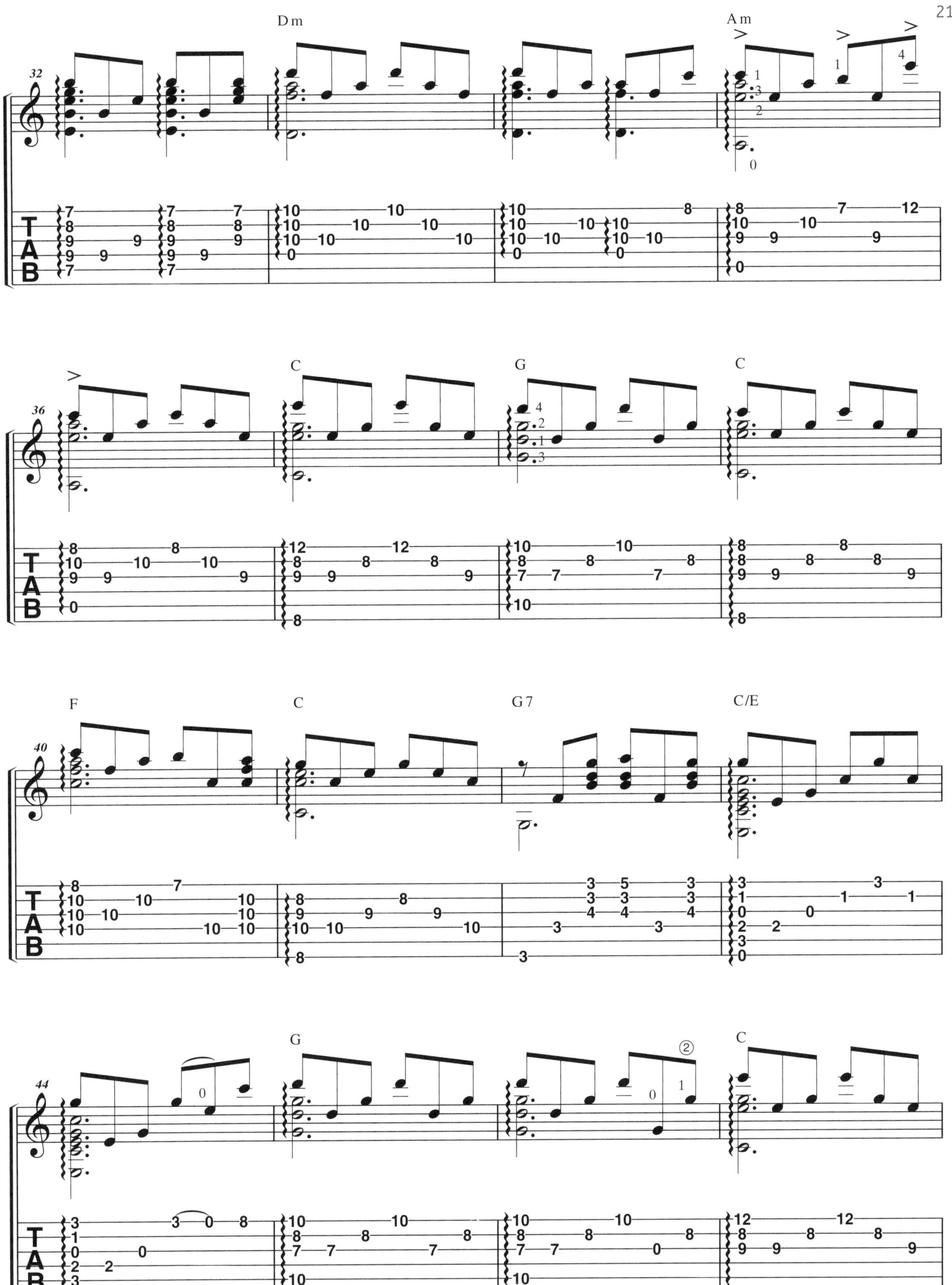
Dm
Am
C
G
C
F
C
G7
C/E
G
C

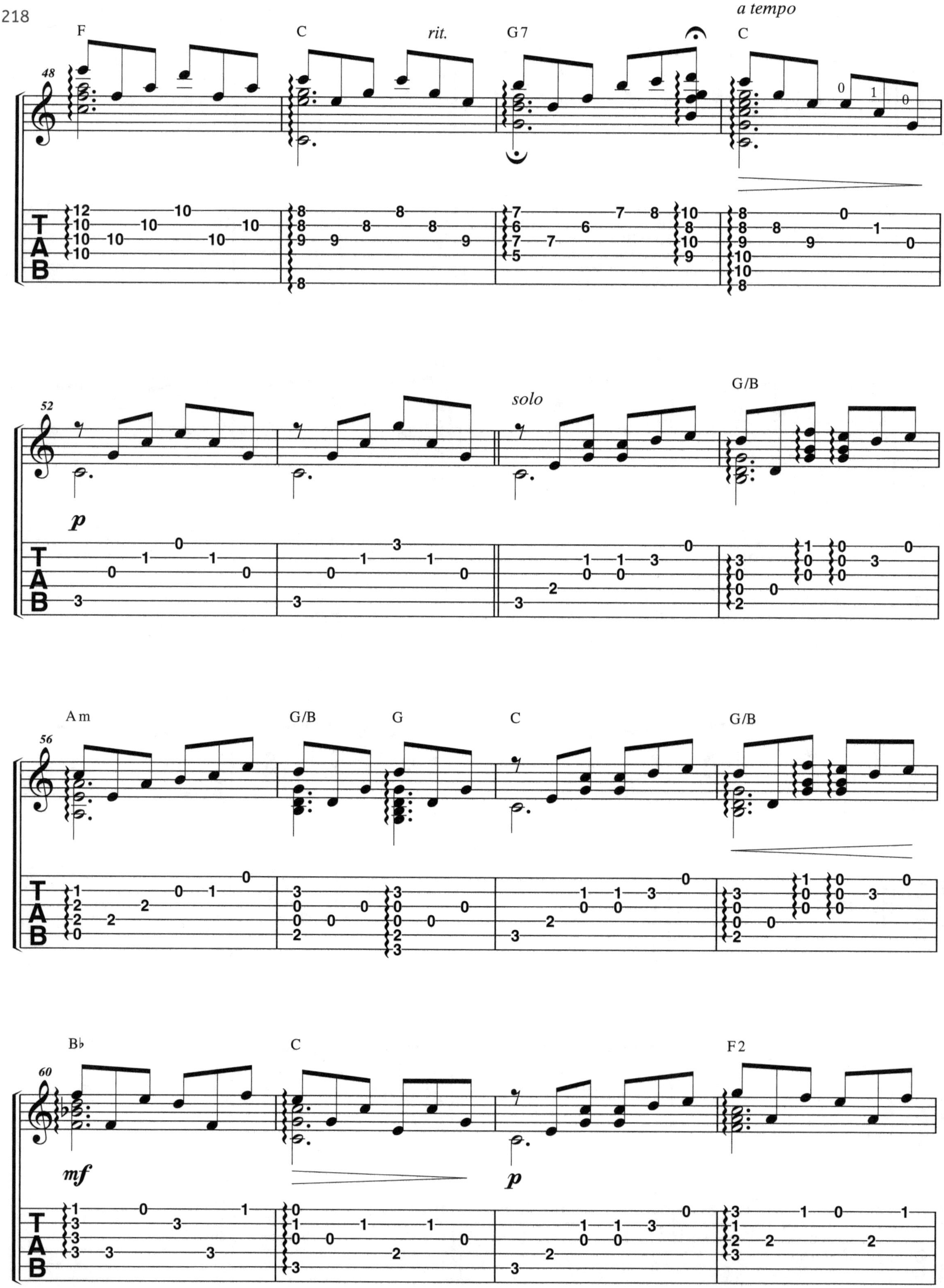

a tempo

F C *rit.* G7 C

48

12 10 10 10 10 10 10 10 10
8 8 9 9 8 8 8 9 8
7 6 7 5 7 6 7 8 10 8 10 9
8 8 9 10 10 8 8 9 0 1 0

52

*p*

solo

G/B

3 0 1 0 1 0
3 0 1 3 1 0
3 2 1 0 1 0 3 0
3 0 0 2 0 1 0 0 0 0 3 0

Am G/B G C G/B

56

1 2 2 0 2 2 0 1 0
3 0 0 2 0 0 3 0 0 2 3 0 0
3 2 1 0 1 0 3 0
3 0 0 2 0 1 0 0 0 0 3 0

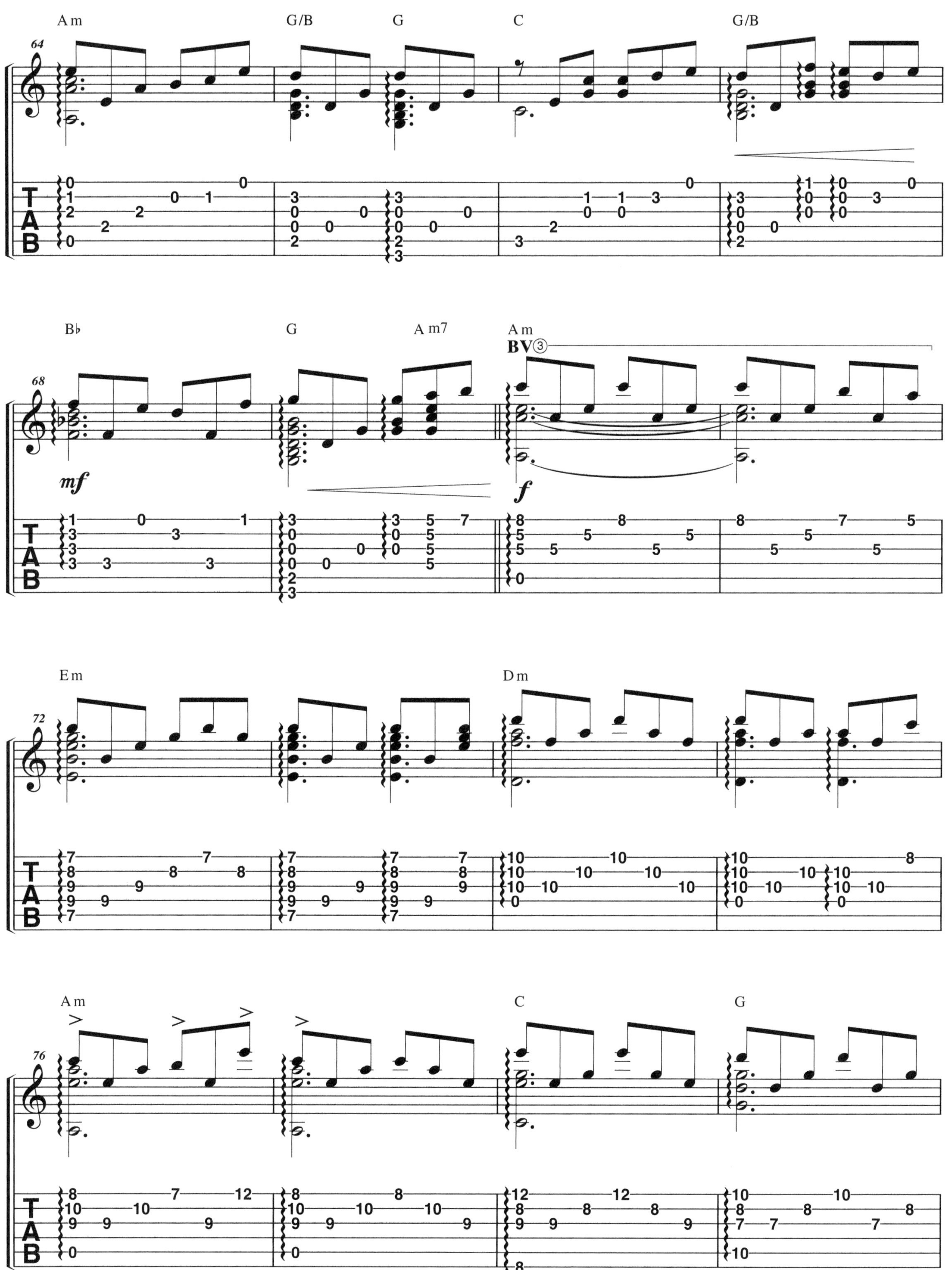
Am
G/B
G
C
G/B
B♭
G
Am7
Am
BV③
mf
f
Em
Dm
Am
C
G

C F C G7

C/E G *rit.*

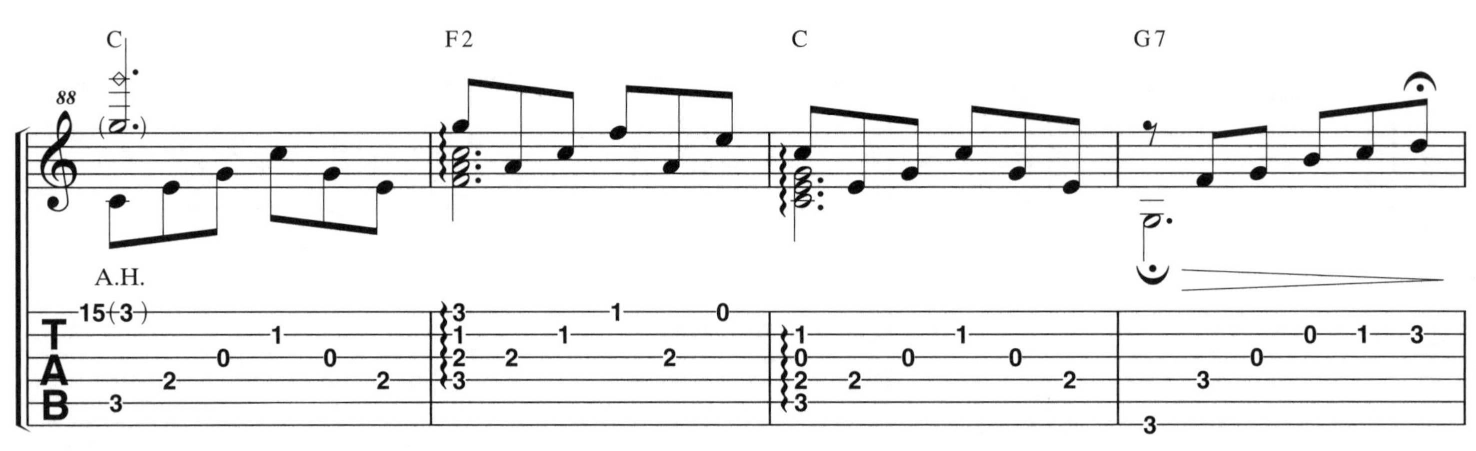


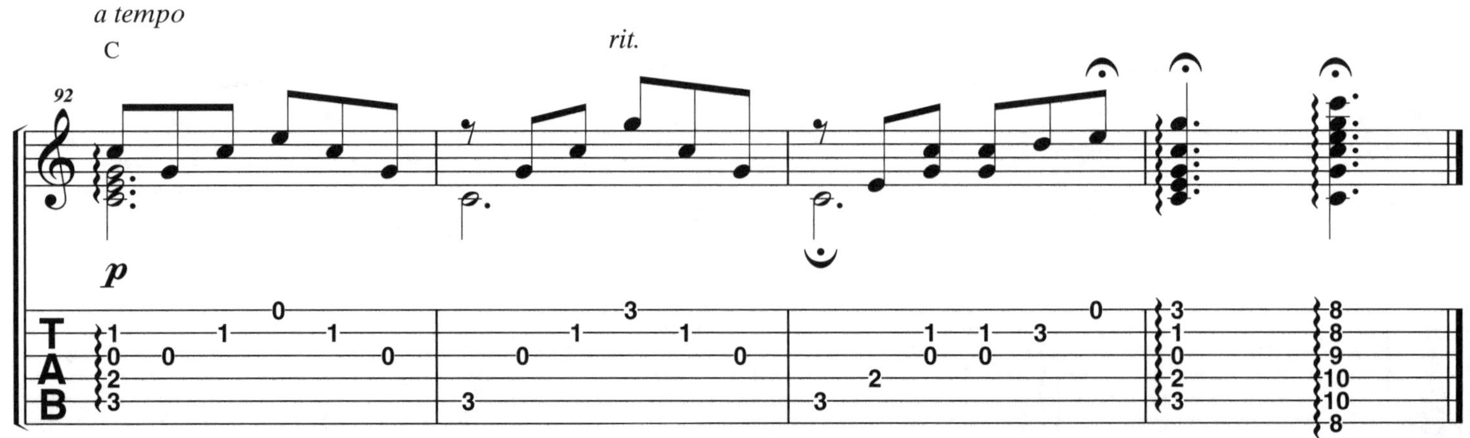

# Silent Night

Words and Music by
JOSEPH MOHR and FRANZ GRUBER
*Arranged by CRAIG B. DOBBINS*

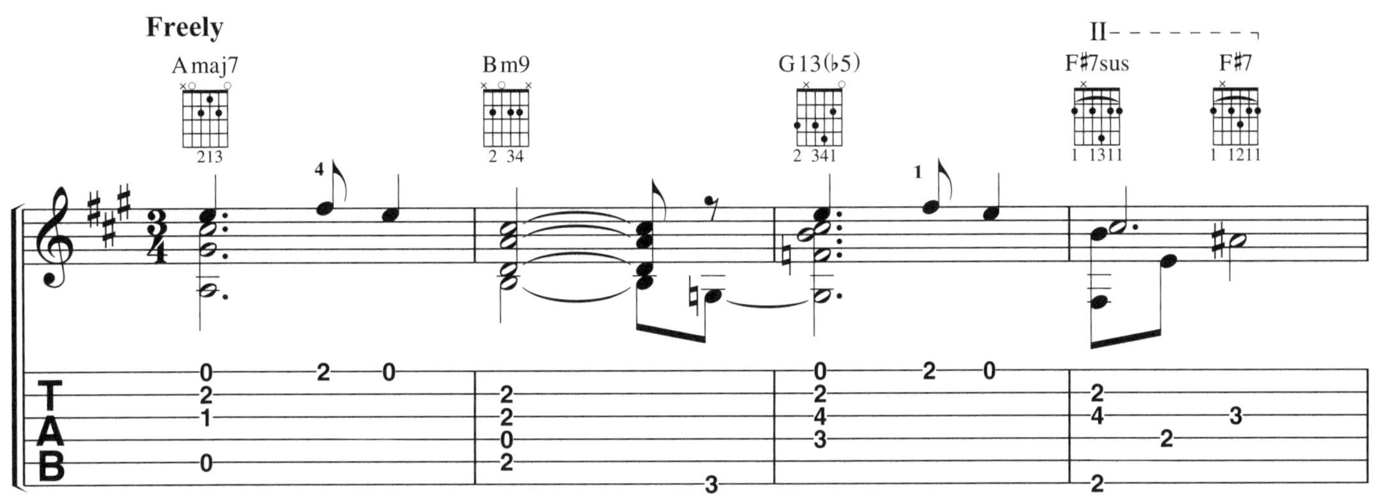


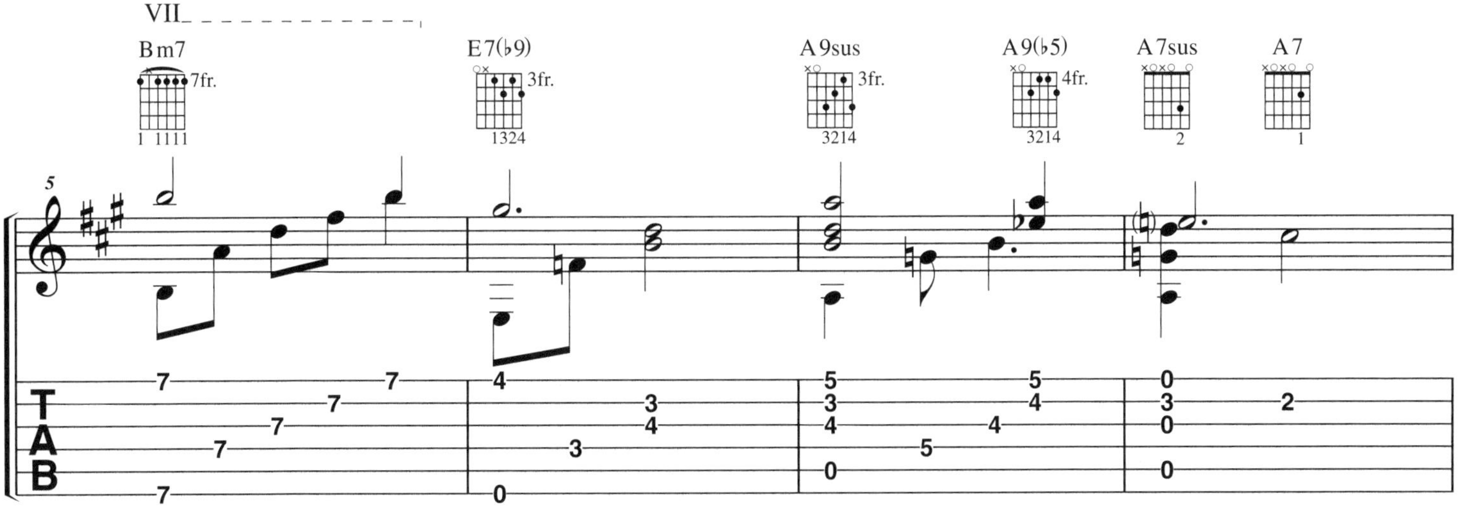


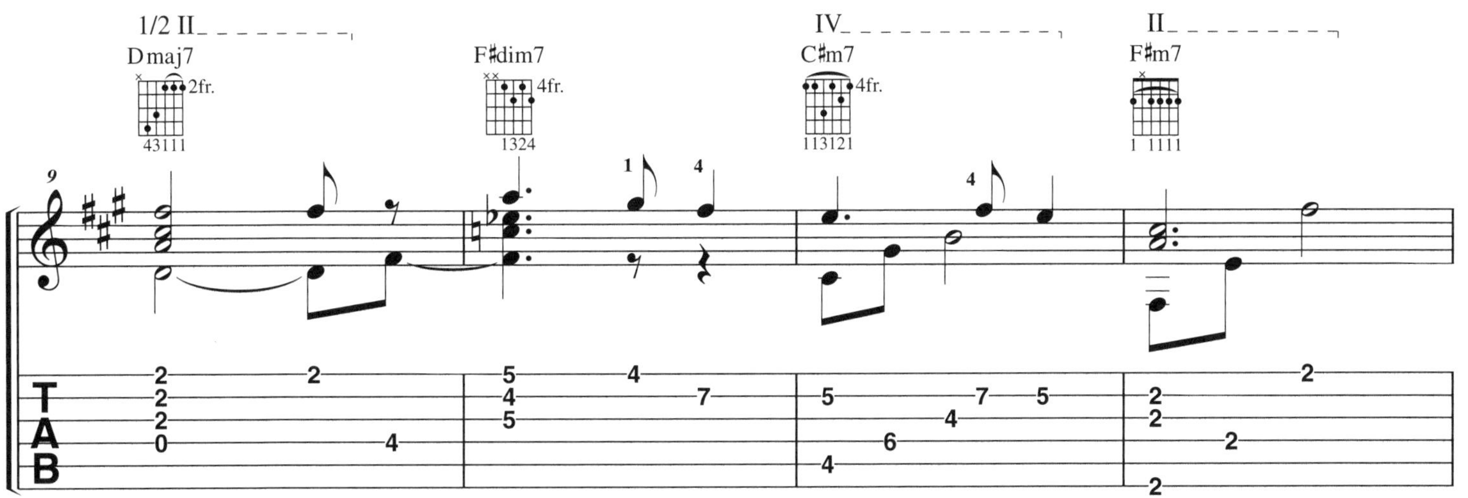

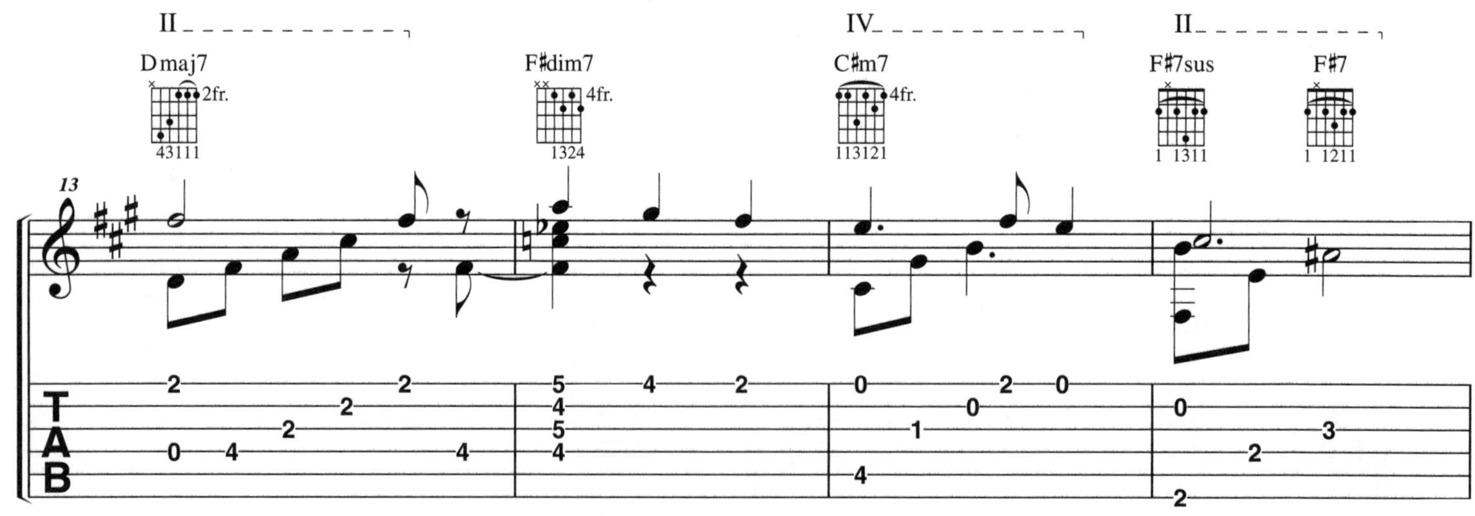
II
IV
II
Dmaj7
2fr.
43111
F♯dim7
4fr.
1324
C♯m7
4fr.
113121
F♯7sus
1 1311
F♯7
1 1211
13

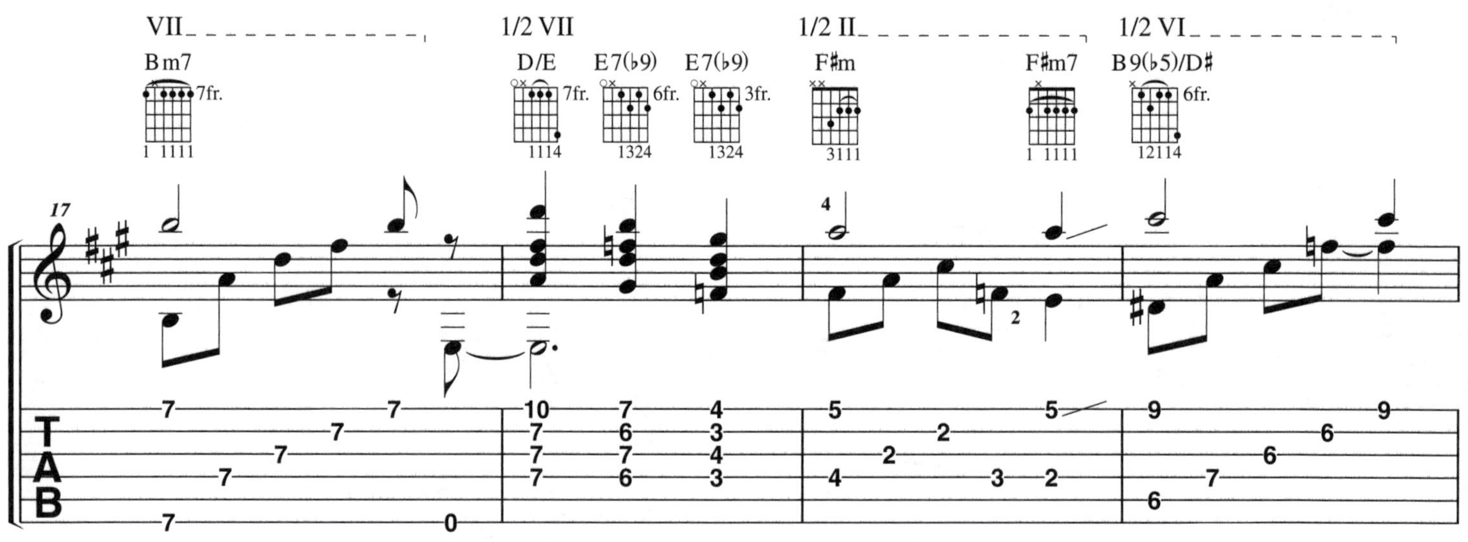
VII
1/2 VII
1/2 II
1/2 VI
Bm7
7fr.
1 1111
D/E
7fr.
1114
E7(♭9)
6fr.
1324
E7(♭9)
3fr.
1324
F♯m
3111
F♯m7
1 1111
B9(♭5)/D♯
6fr.
12114
17

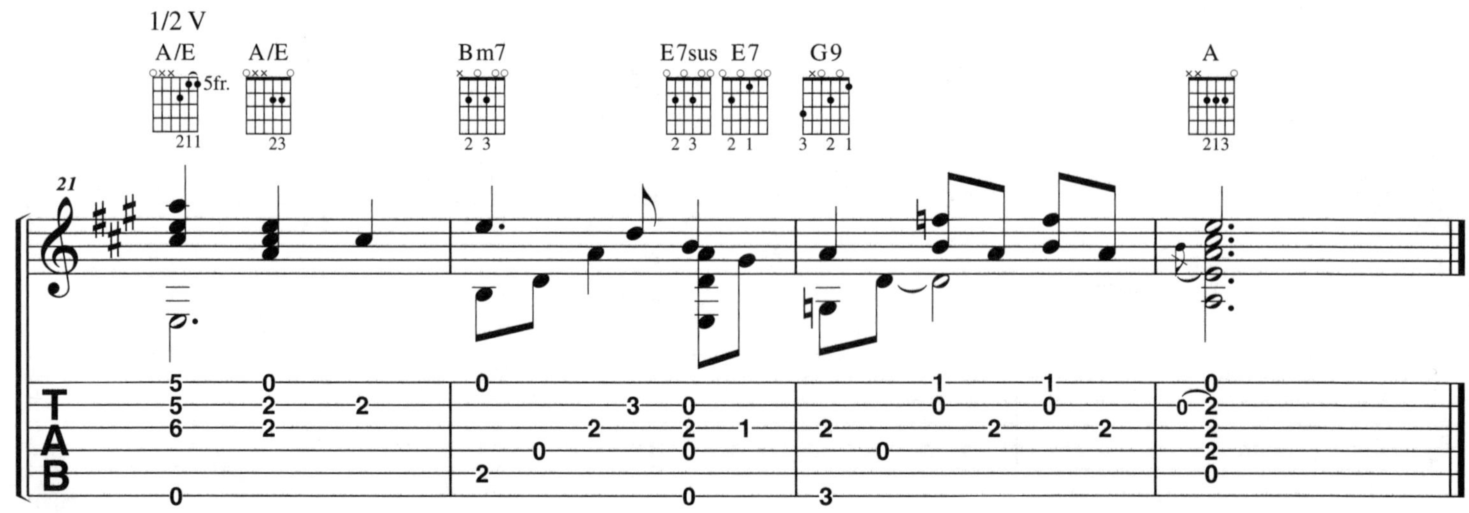
1/2 V
A/E
5fr.
211
A/E
23
Bm7
2 3
E7sus
2 3
E7
2 1
G9
3 2 1
A
213
21

# Ukrainian Carol

Traditional

(Carol of the Bells)

Medium

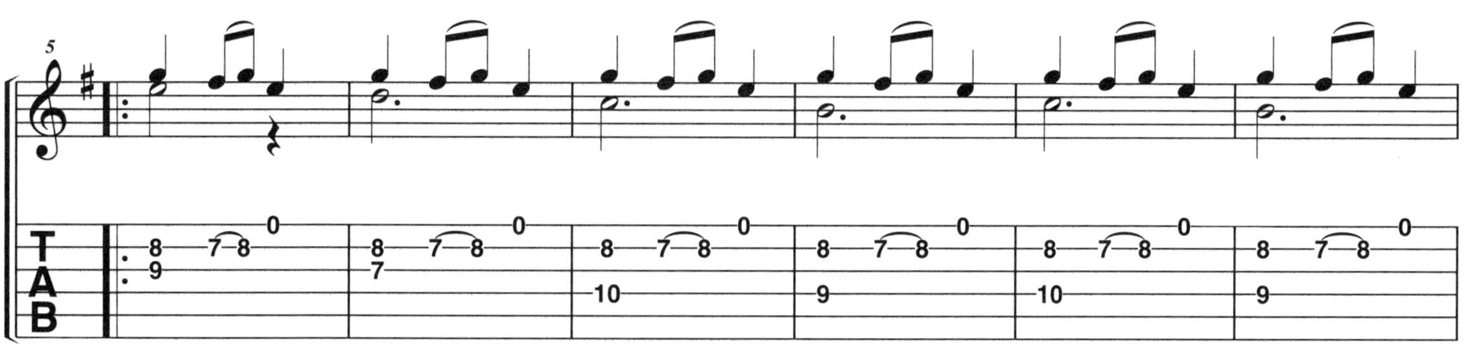
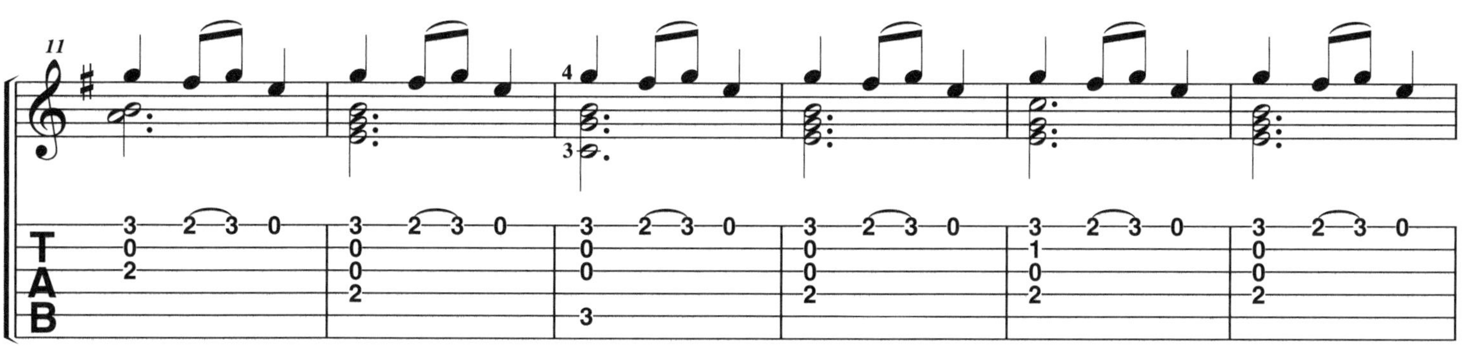
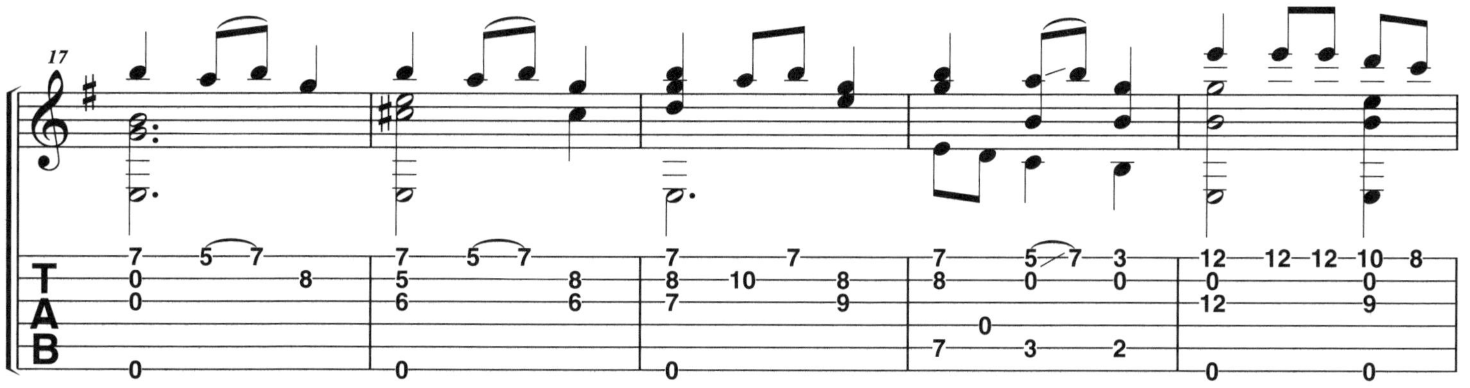

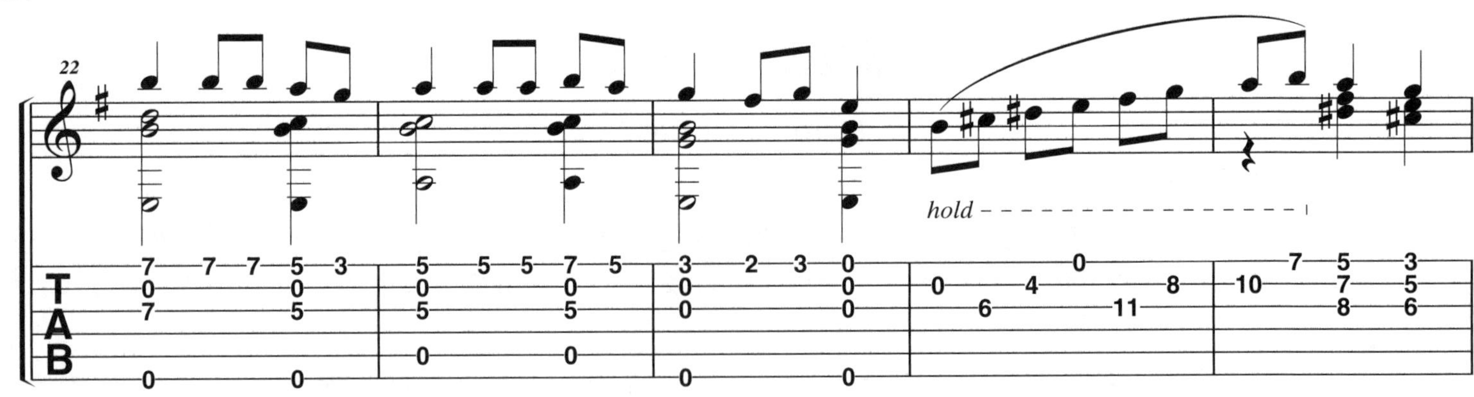
hold

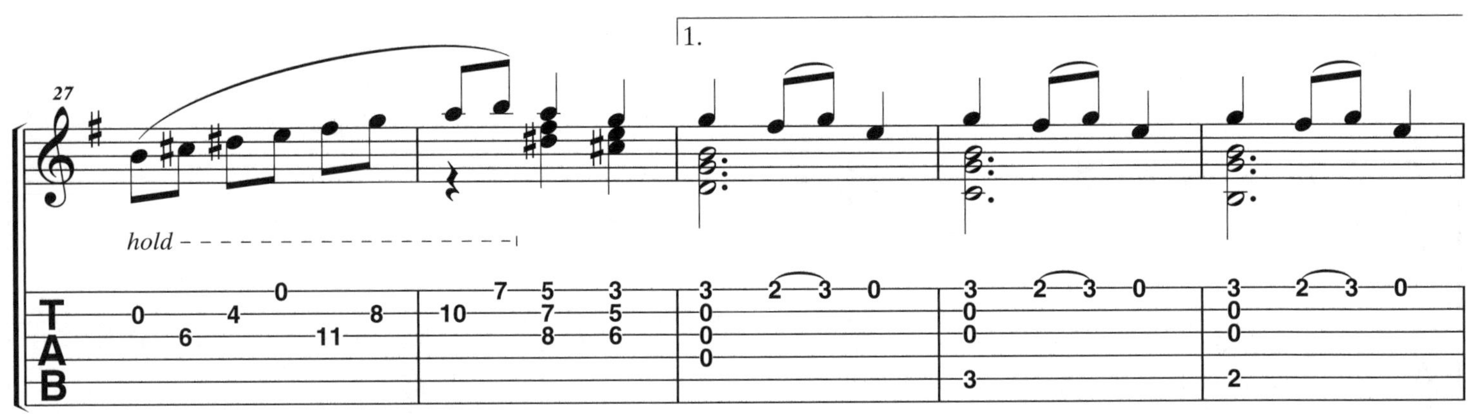
1.
hold

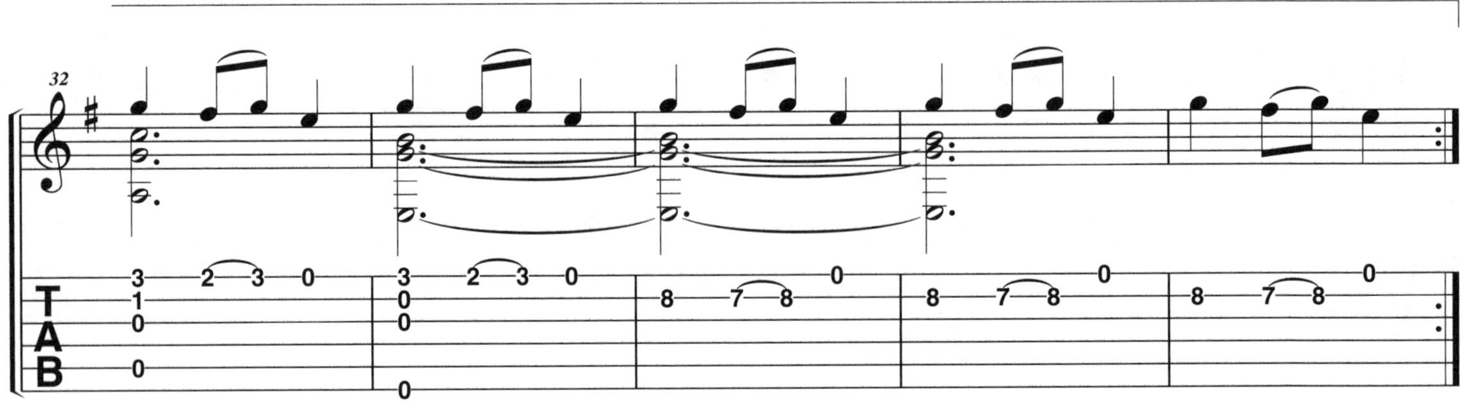

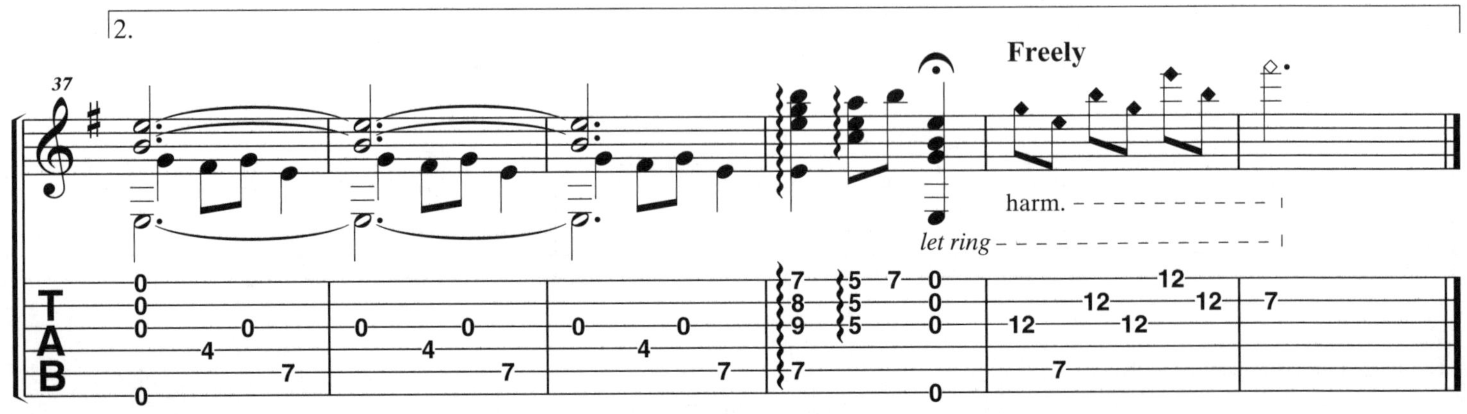
2.
Freely
harm.
let ring

# We Three Kings of Orient Are / God Rest Ye Merry, Gentlemen

"We Three Kings of Orient Are"
Words and Music by
JOHN H. HOPKINS, JR.
*Arranged by VINCENT J. CARROLA*

"God Rest Ye Merry, Gentlemen"
Traditional Carol
*Arranged by VINCENT J. CARROLA*

**Moderato ♩ = 100**
*Mysteriously, allow notes to ring out*

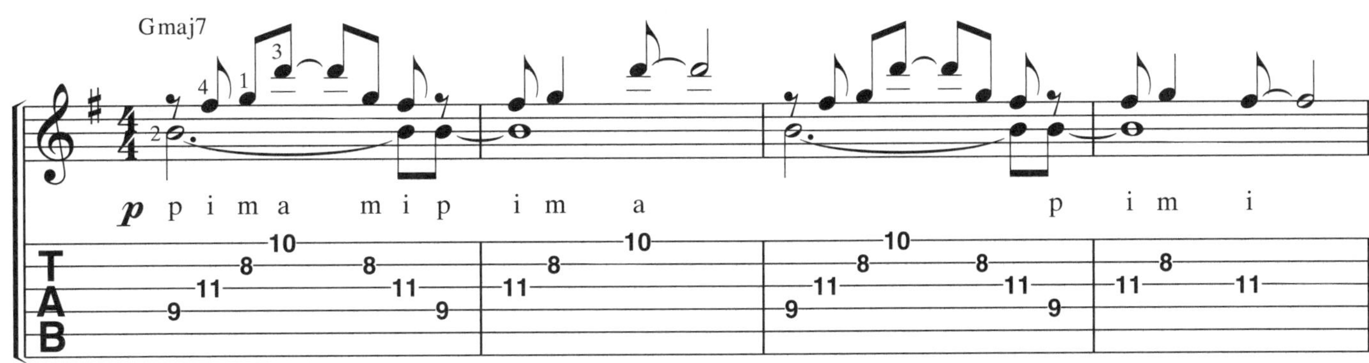


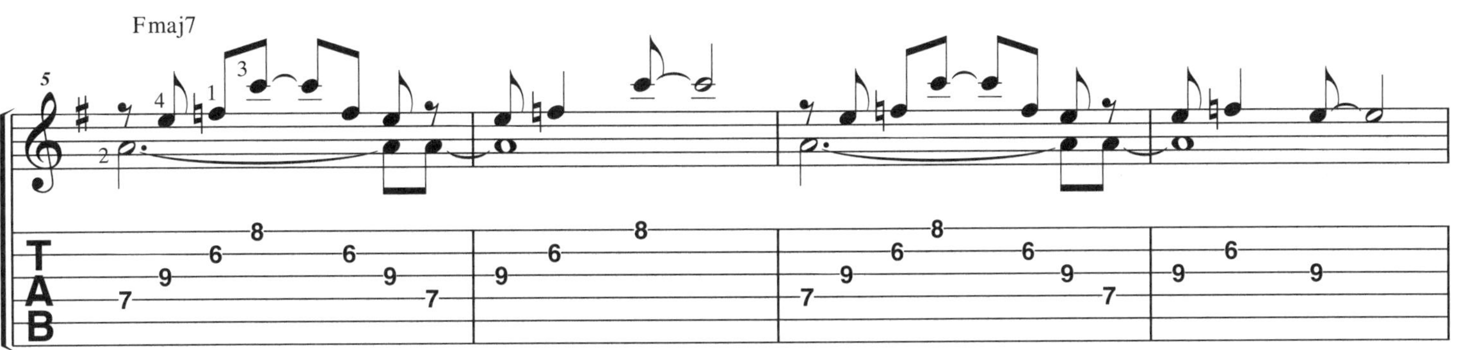

Em
13
mf
G
17
f
Em
G
21
Em
C
25
D
Em
a p i m p a m i a
a i m a p a m i a
m
i
p
m
i
p

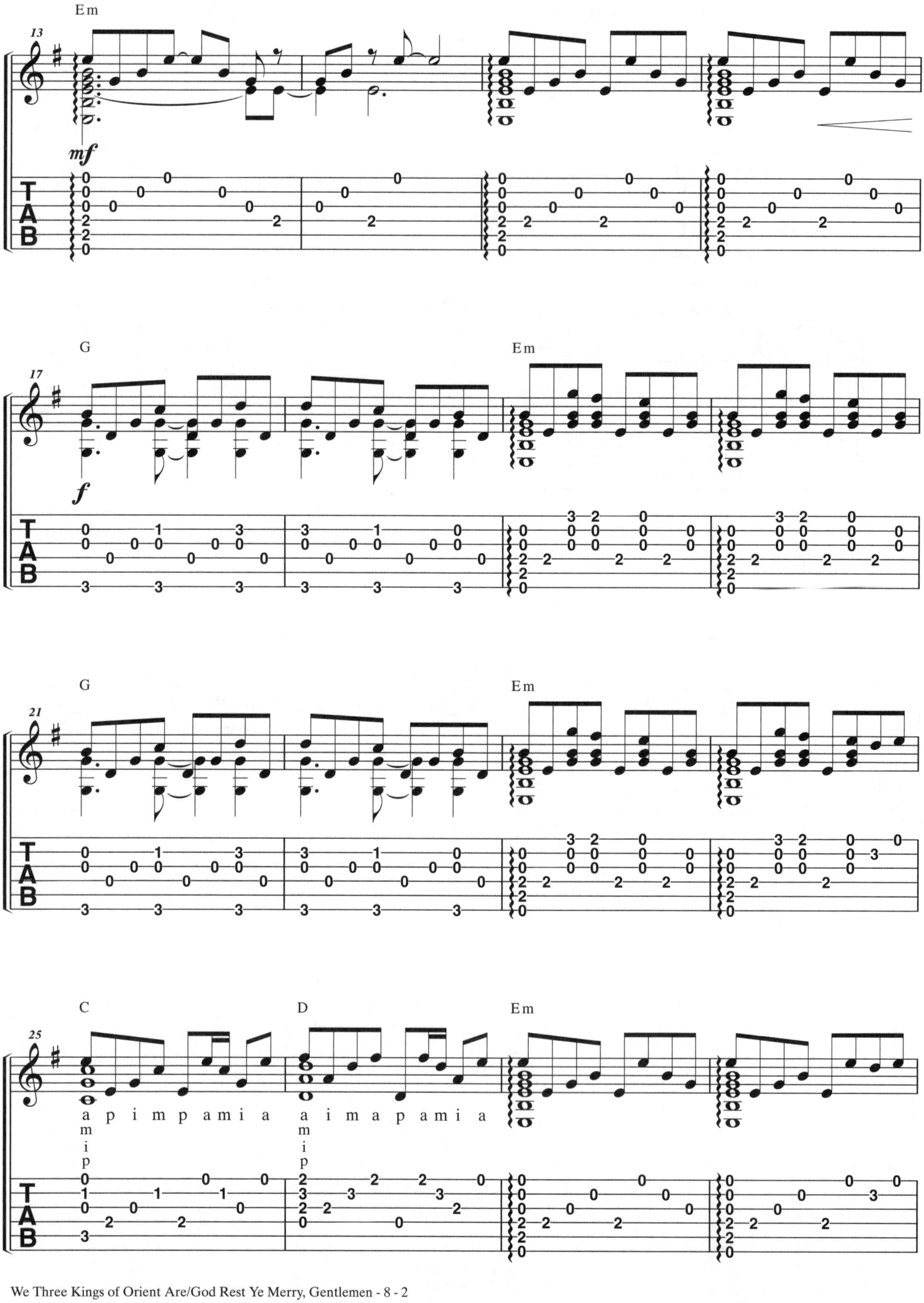

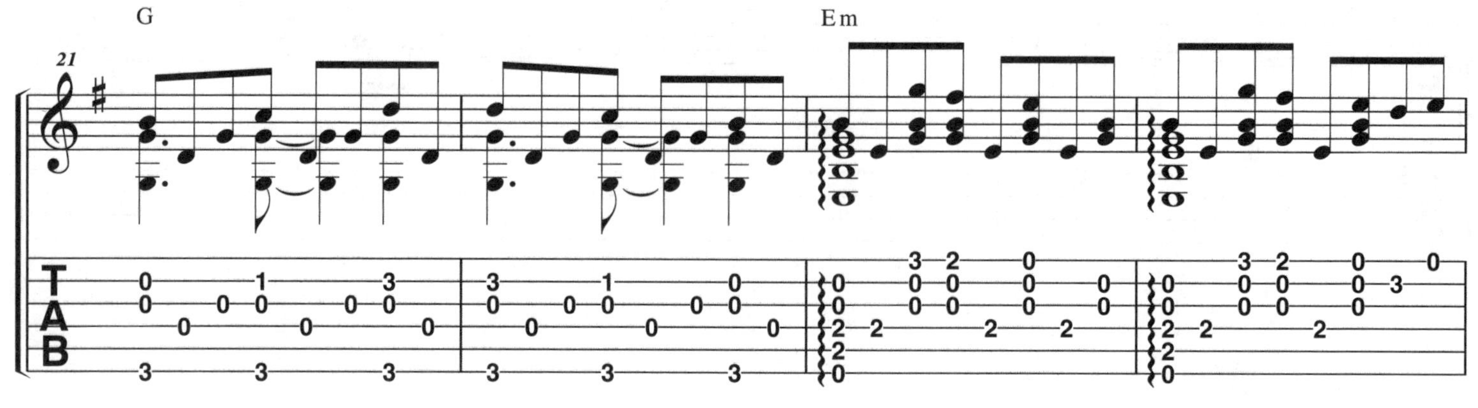

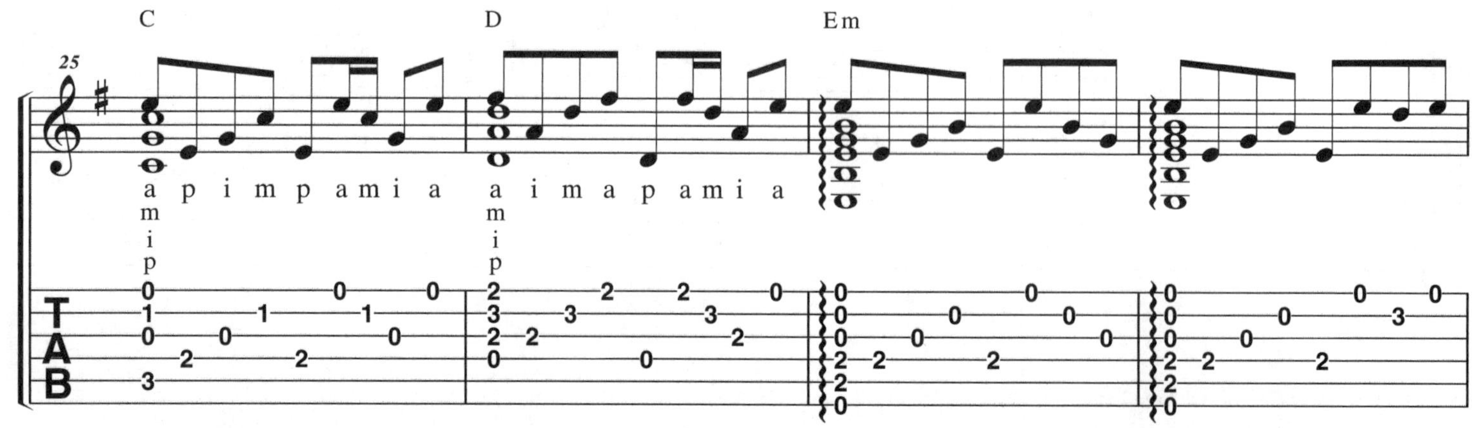

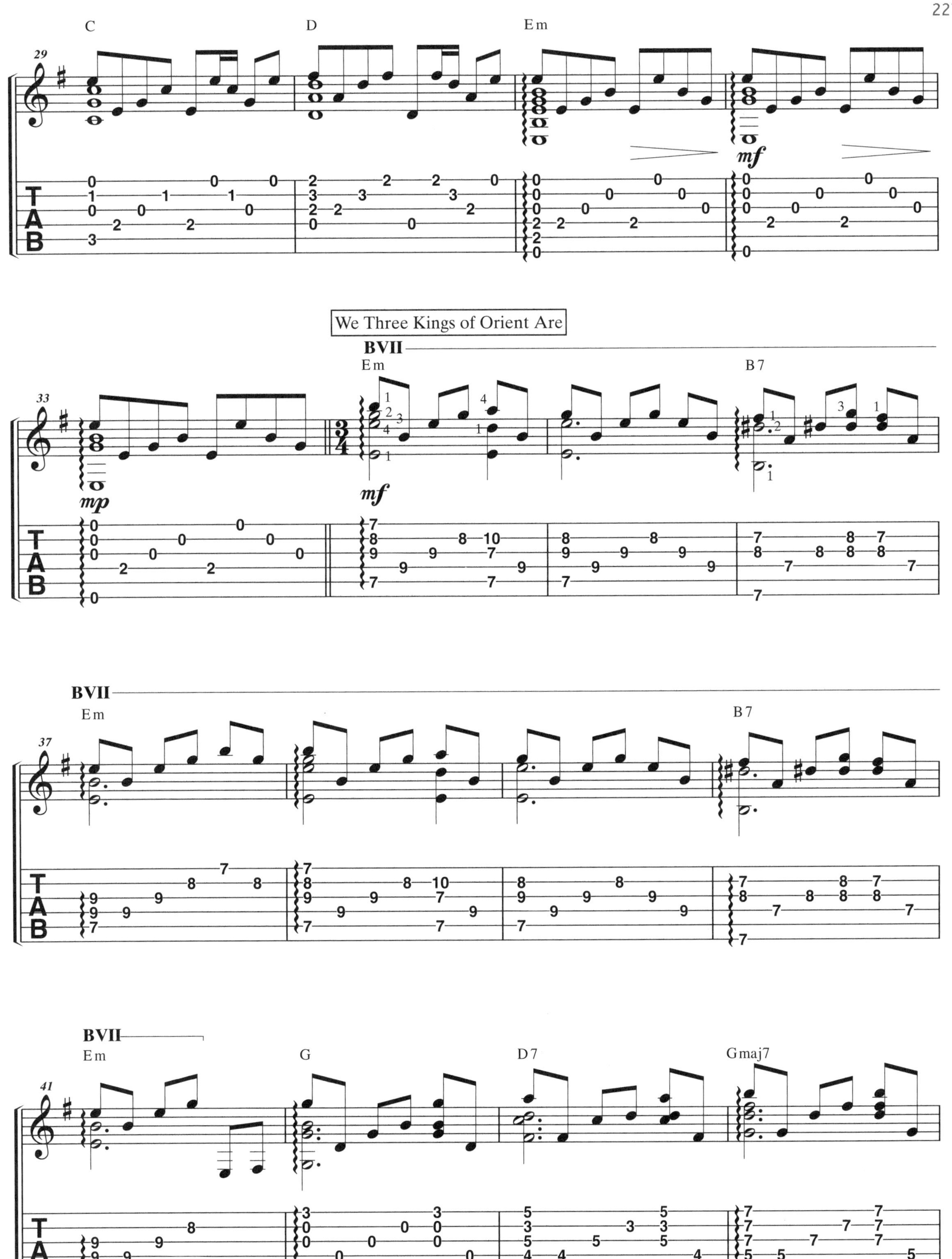
C
D
Em
We Three Kings of Orient Are
BVII
Em
B7
BVII
Em
B7
BVII
Em
G
D7
Gmaj7

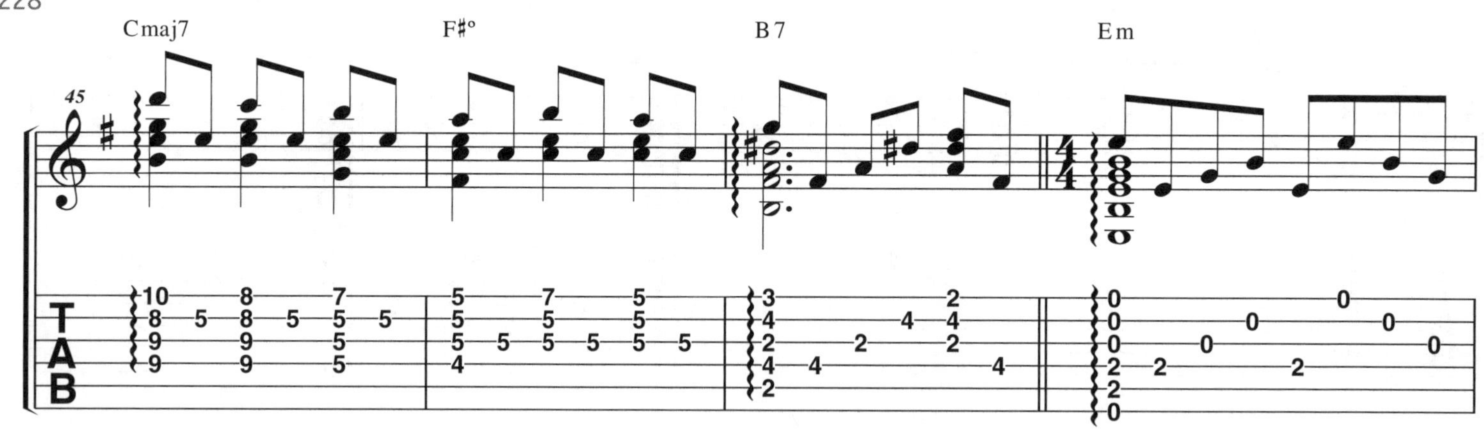
Cmaj7
F♯°
B7
Em
45

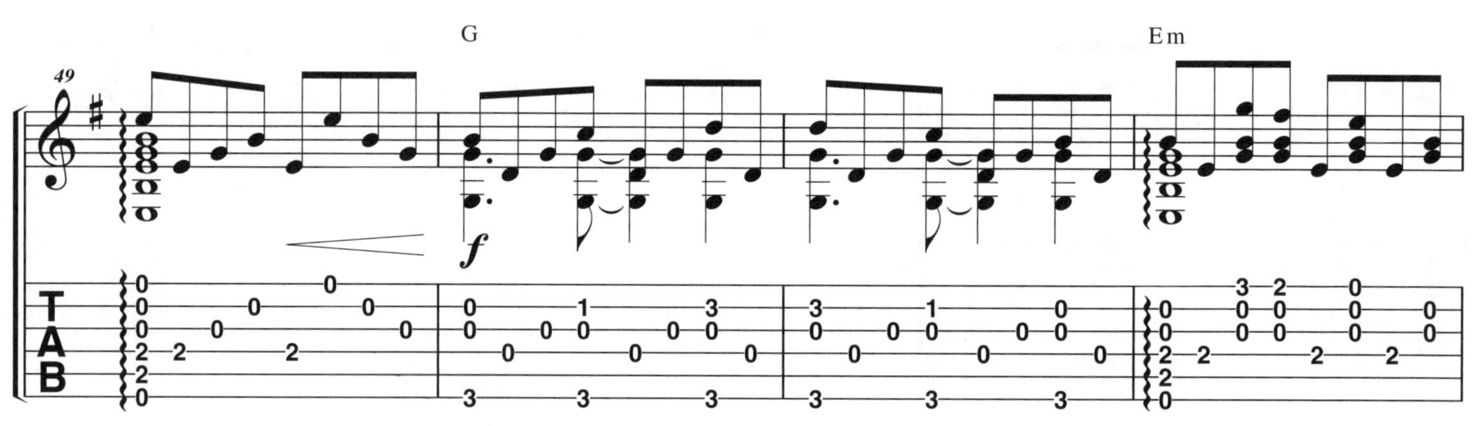
G
Em
49

G
Em
53

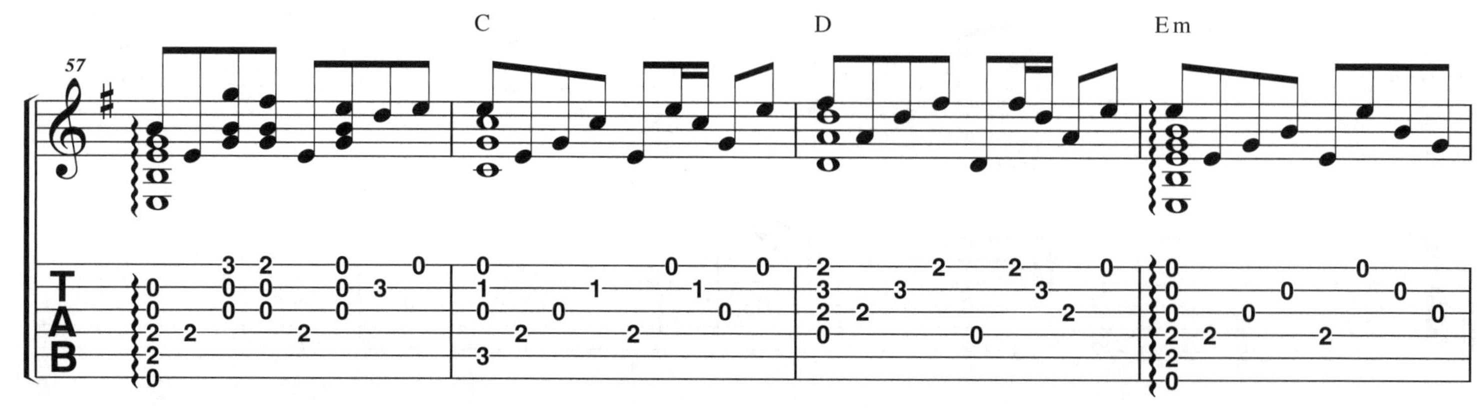
C
D
Em
57

C
D
Em
God Rest Ye Merry, Gentlemen
faster
Em
B7
Em
BVII
mf
mp
mf
C
BVIII
B7
BVII
Em
B7
Em
C
B7
Am7
BV④
G
B7
BIV④

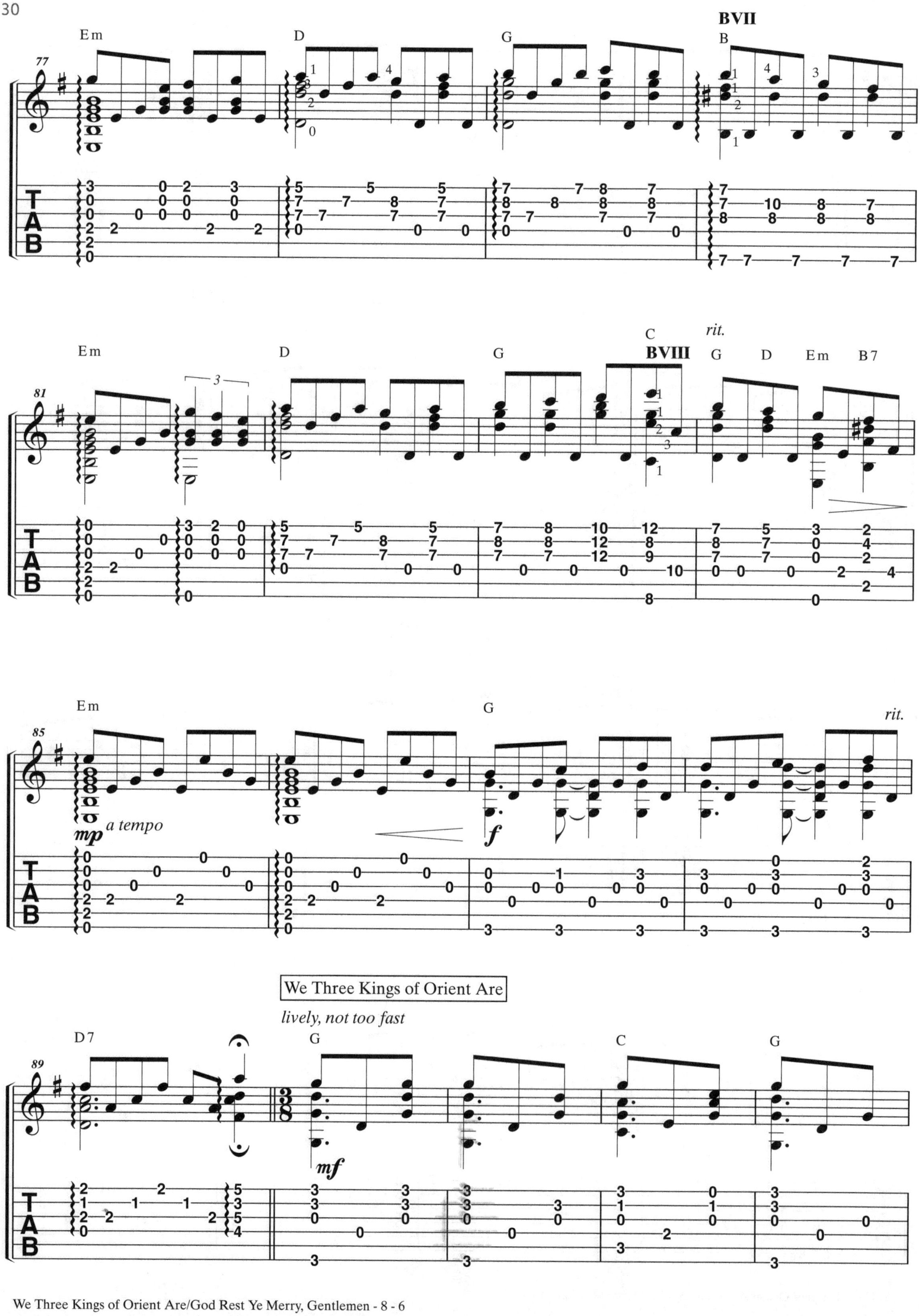

BVII

Em D G B

77

Em D G C BVIII rit. G D Em B7

81

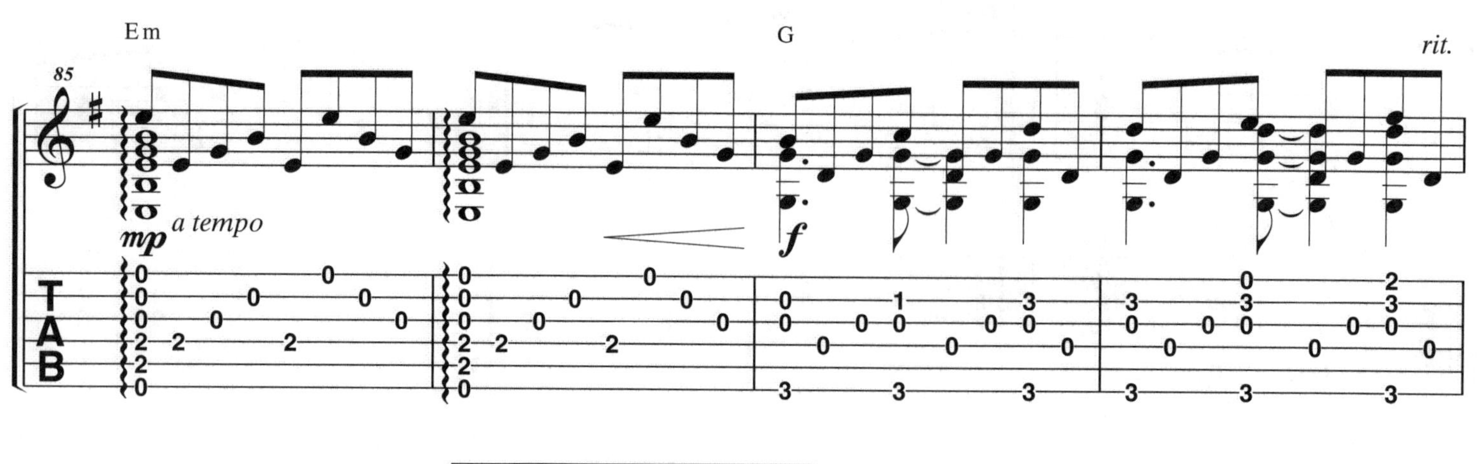


## We Three Kings of Orient Are

*lively, not too fast*

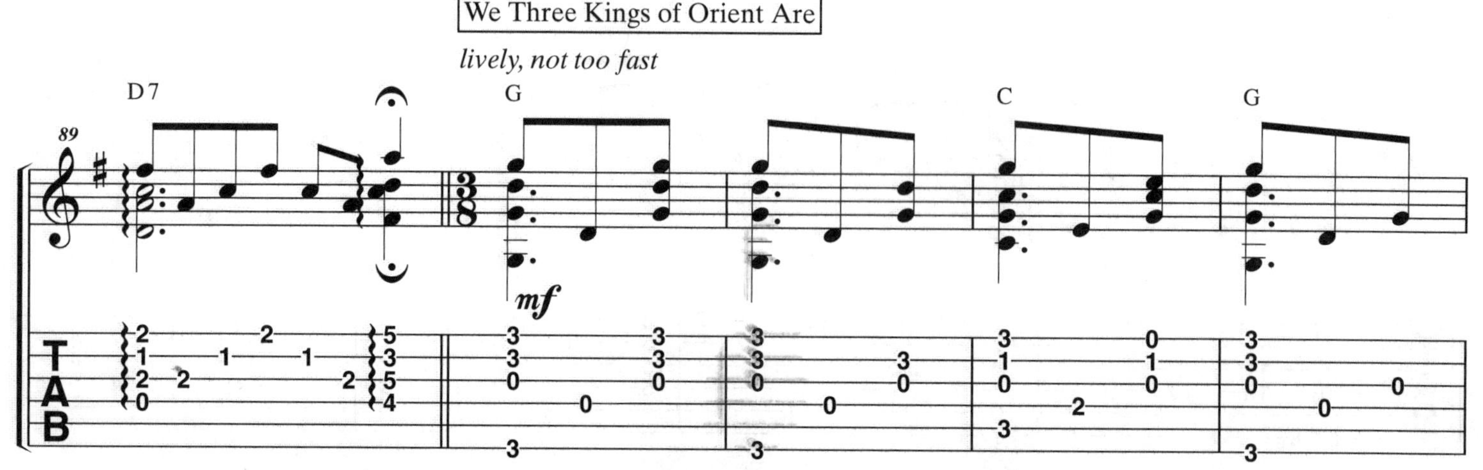

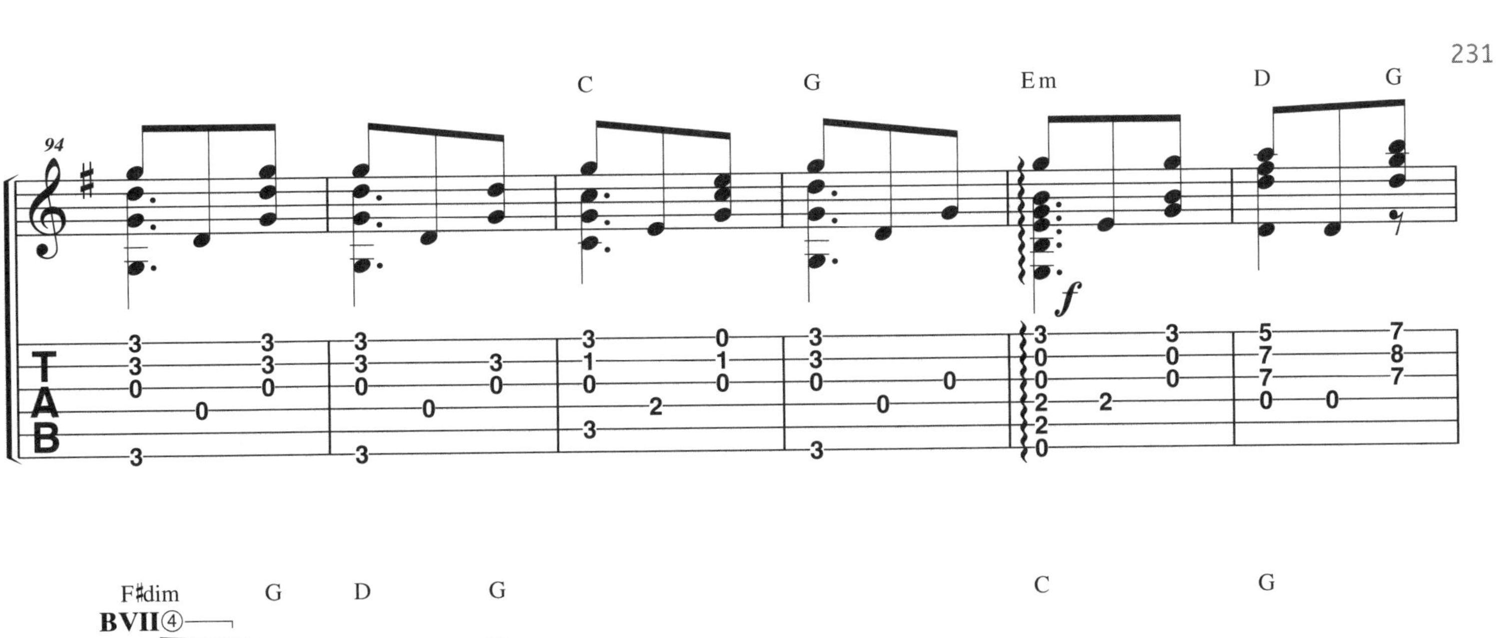
C
G
Em
D
G
94
f

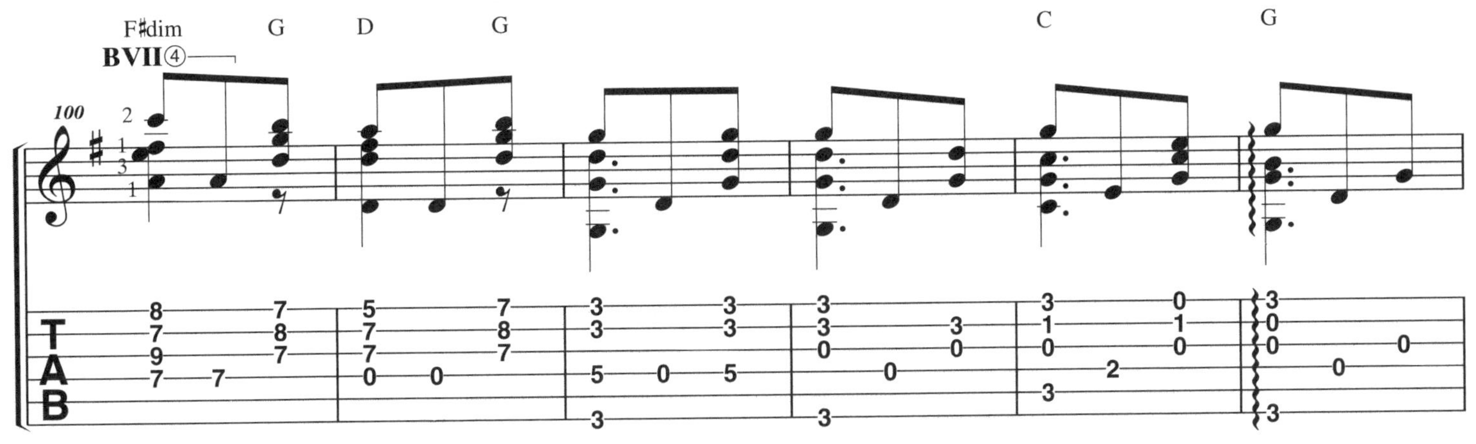
F♯dim
G
D
G
C
G
BVII④
100

Em
106

G
Em
112

ritard heavily
B7
BII⑤
118

Tempo I
Mysteriously, allow notes to ring out
rasq.
C
D
F♯
F♯maj7
124
p i m a m i

fade out
F♯maj7(♯5)
128

# What Child Is This?

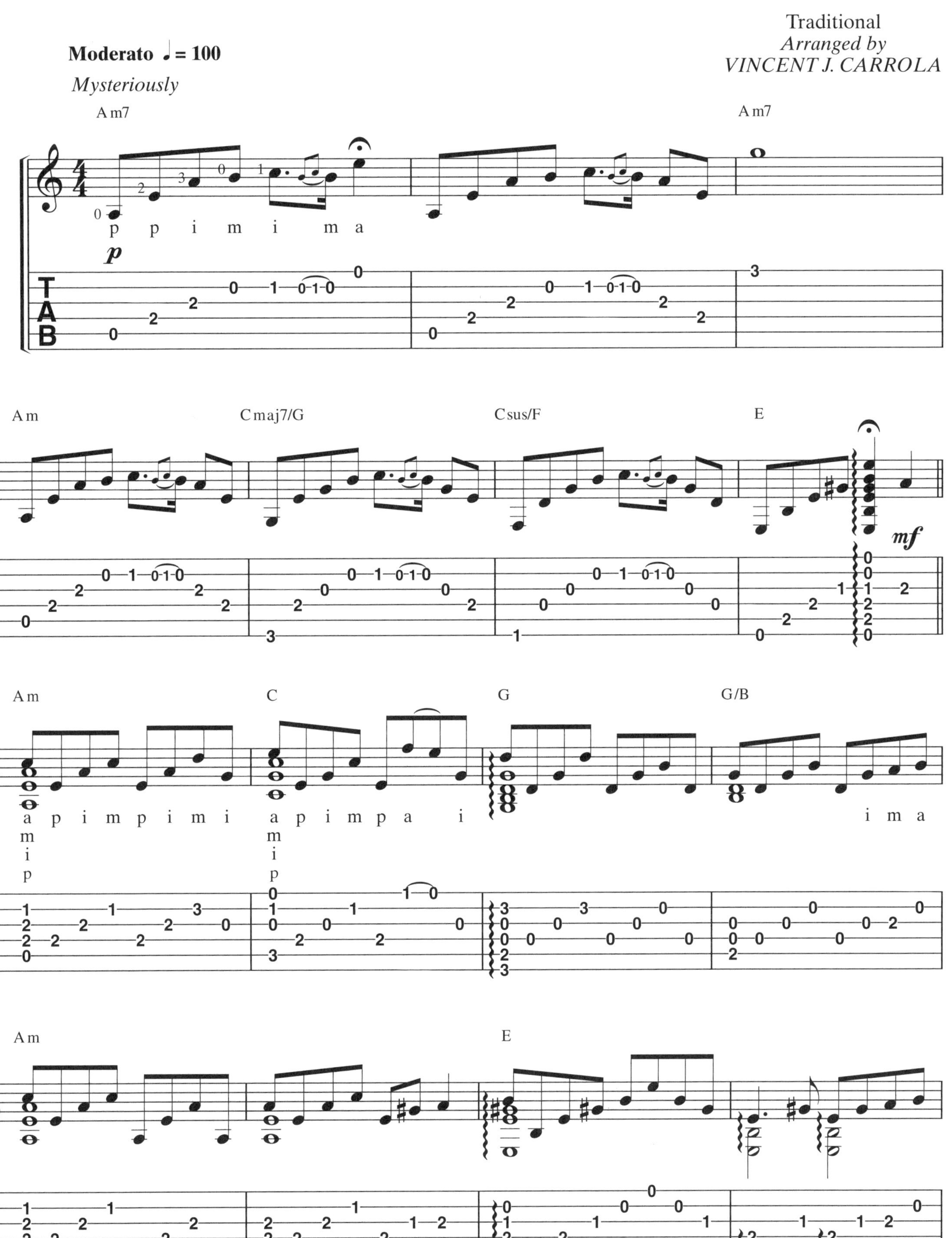

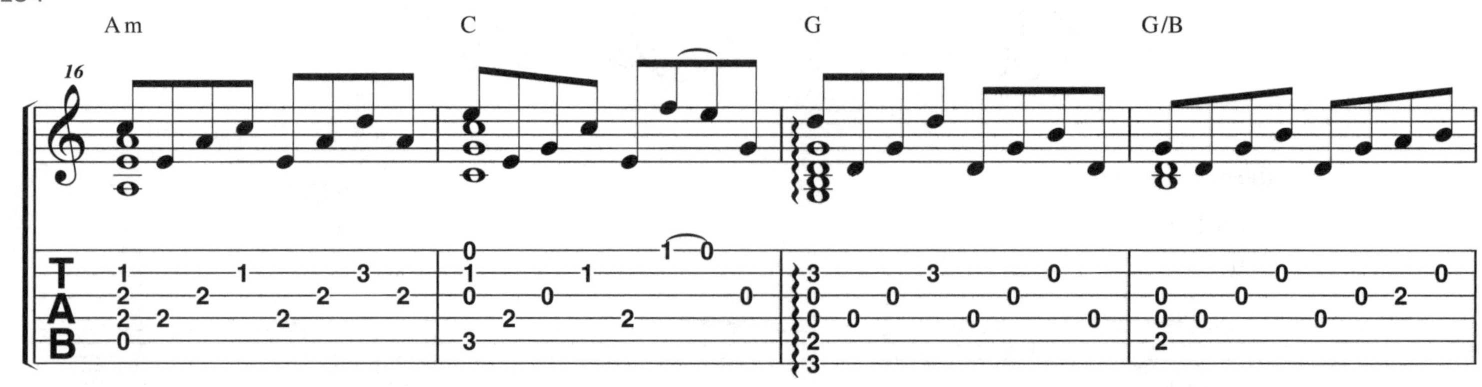
Am
C
G
G/B
16

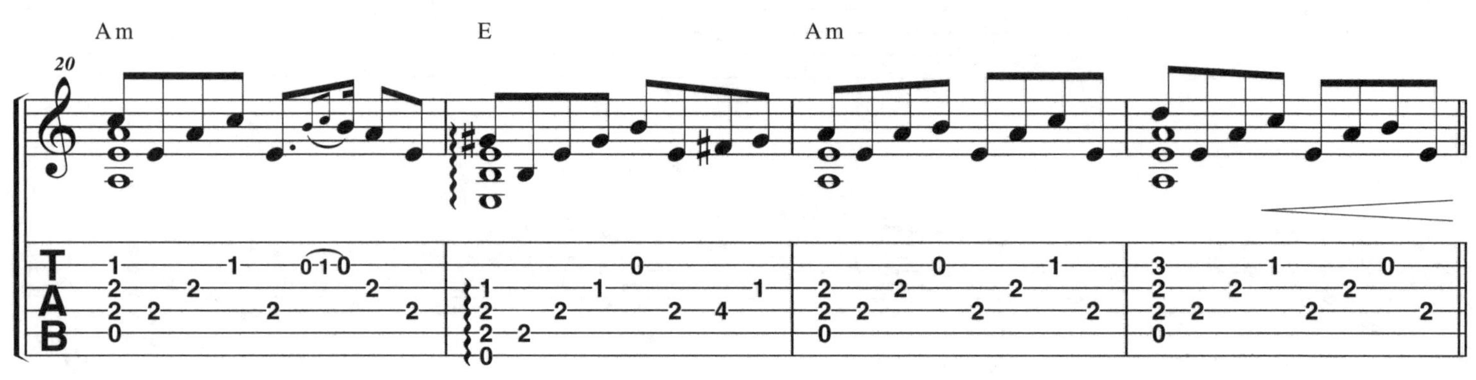
Am
E
Am
20

C
G
G/B
24
f

Am
E
28
mf

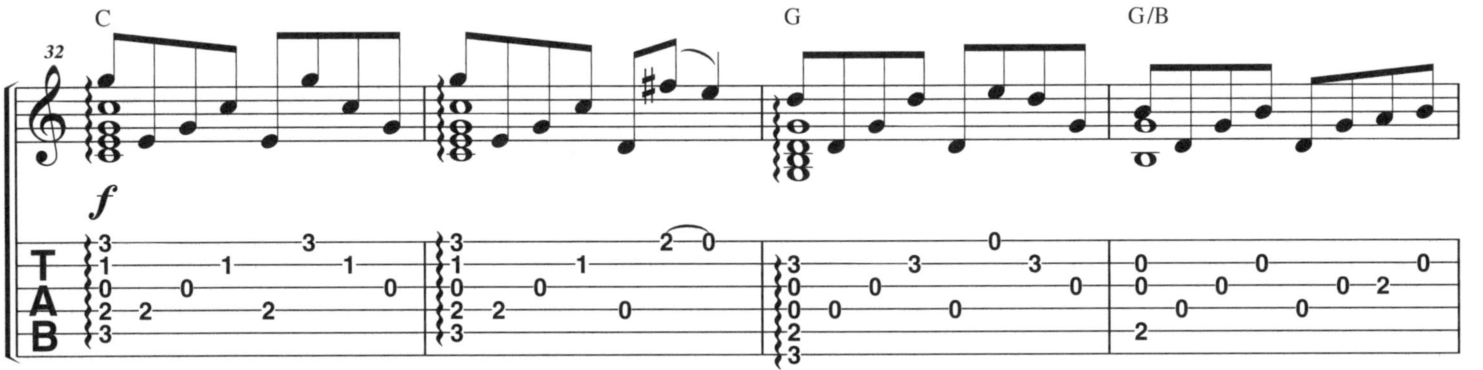
C
G
G/B
32
f

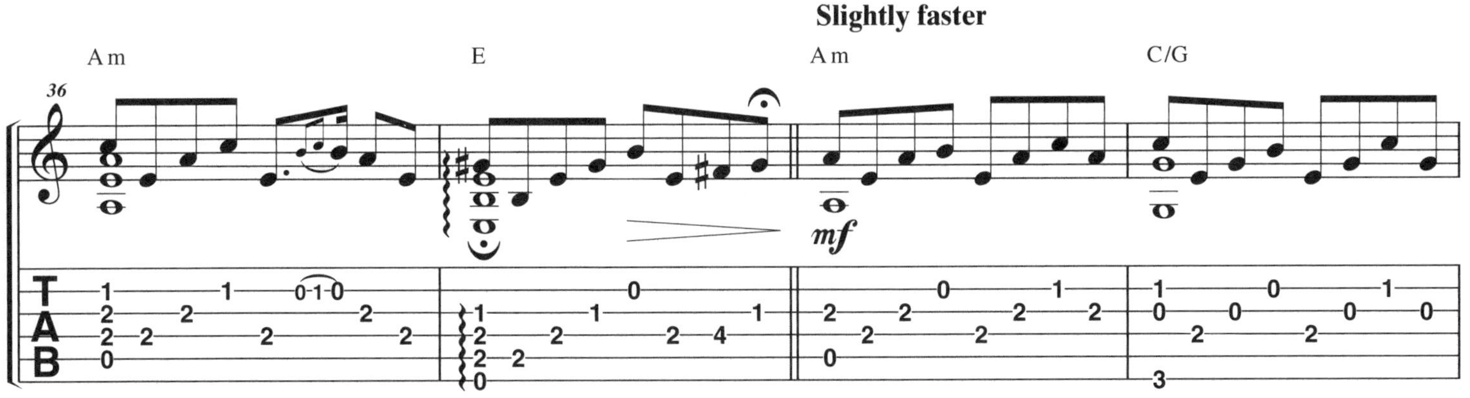
Slightly faster
Am
E
Am
C/G
36
mf

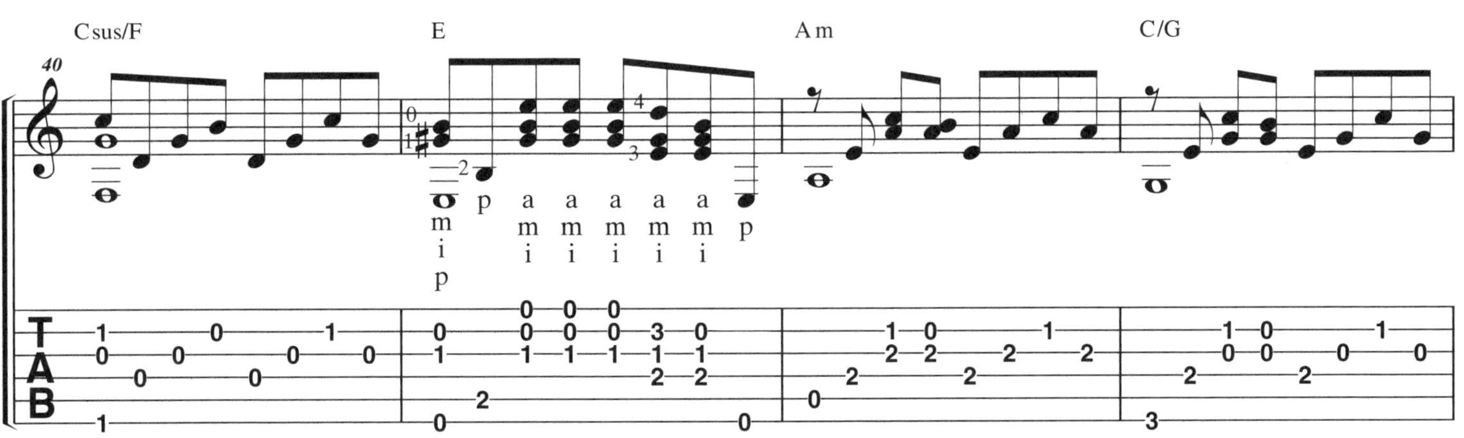
Csus/F
E
Am
C/G
40

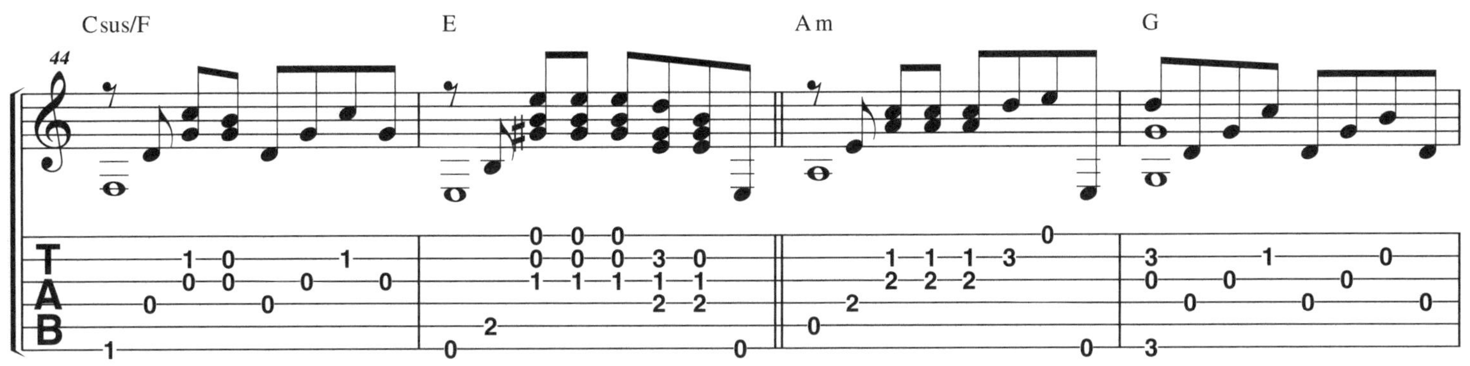
Csus/F
E
Am
G
44

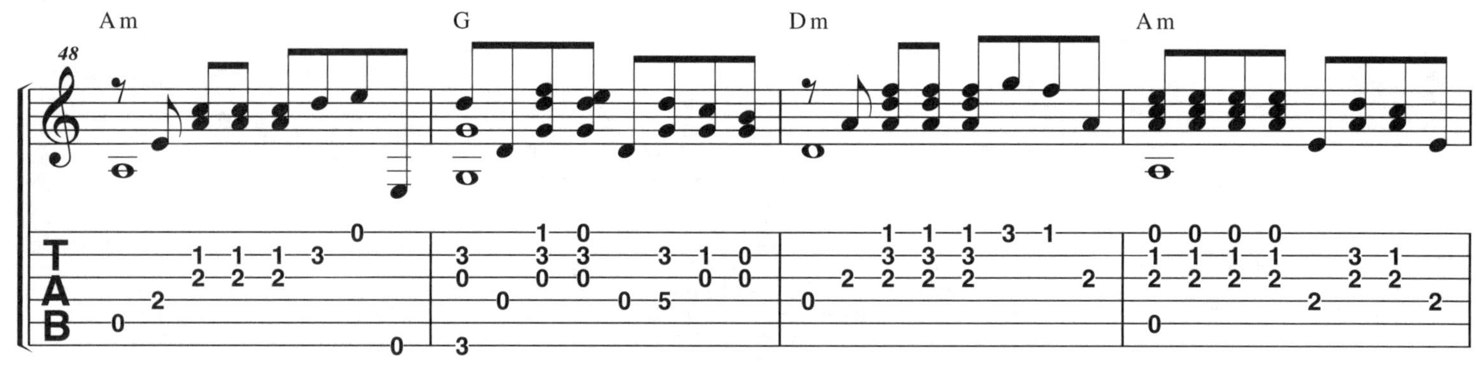
Am
G
Dm
Am
48
TAB

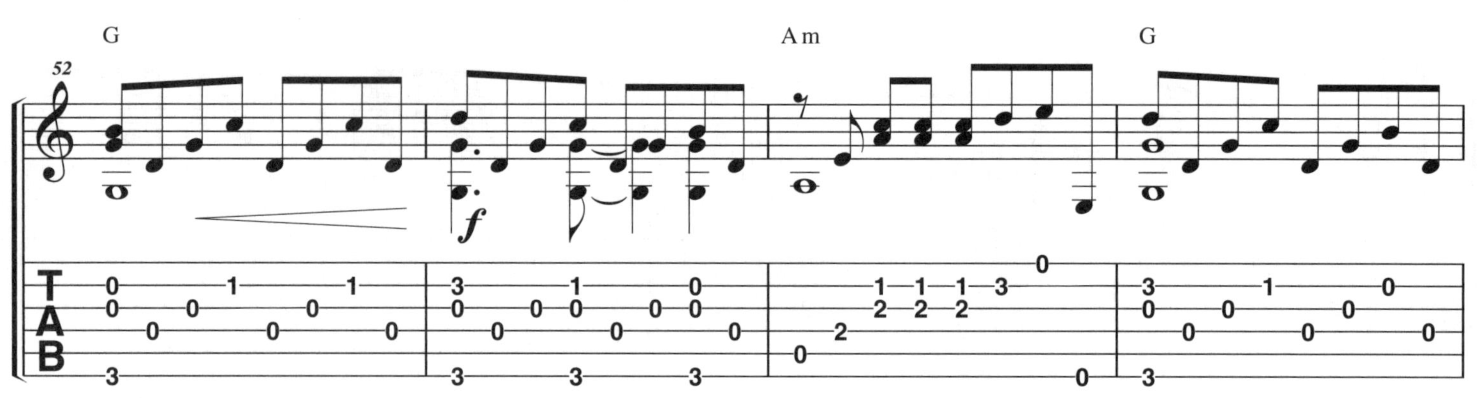
G
Am
G
52
f
TAB

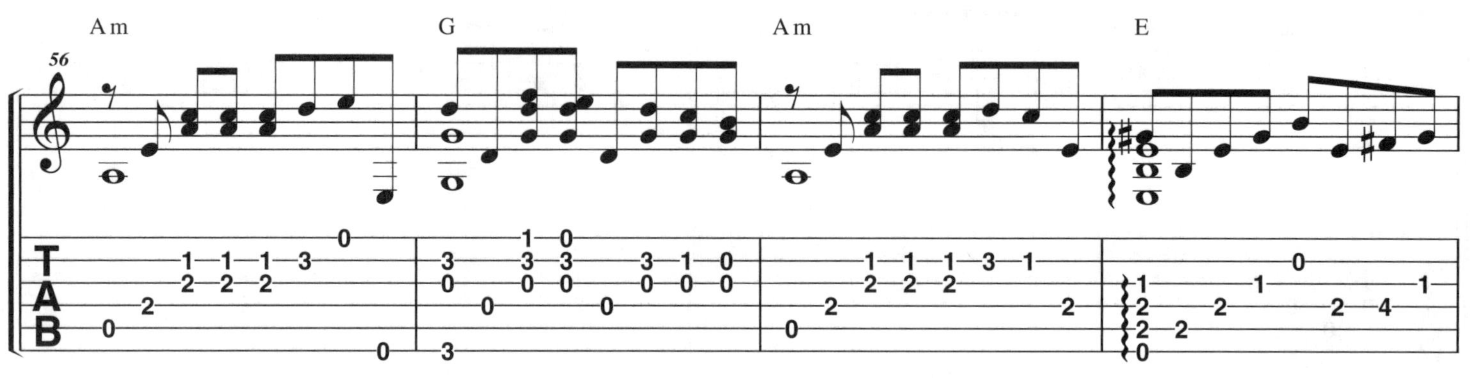
Am
G
Am
E
56
TAB

Am
C
60
TAB

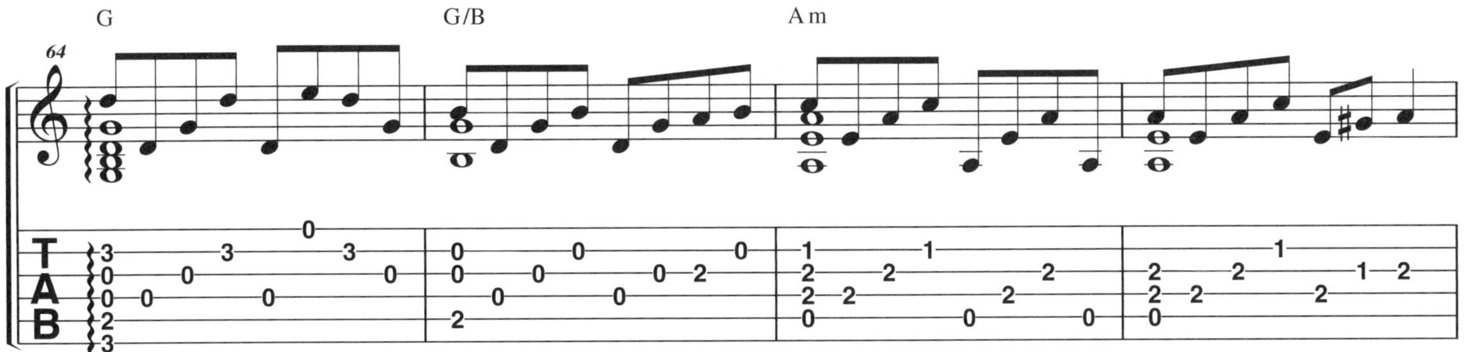
64
G
G/B
Am
T
A
B

68
E
C
mf
f
T
A
B

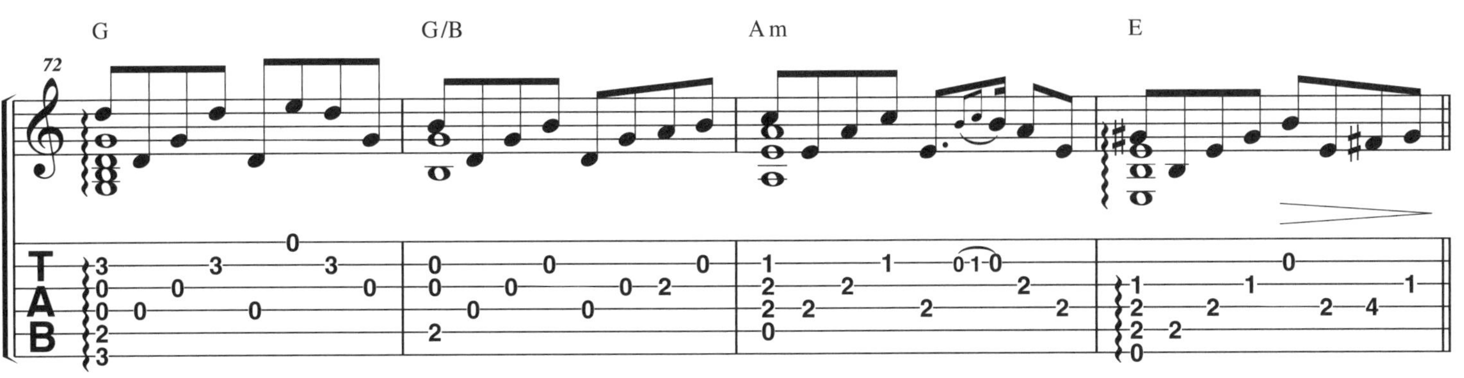
72
G
G/B
Am
E
T
A
B

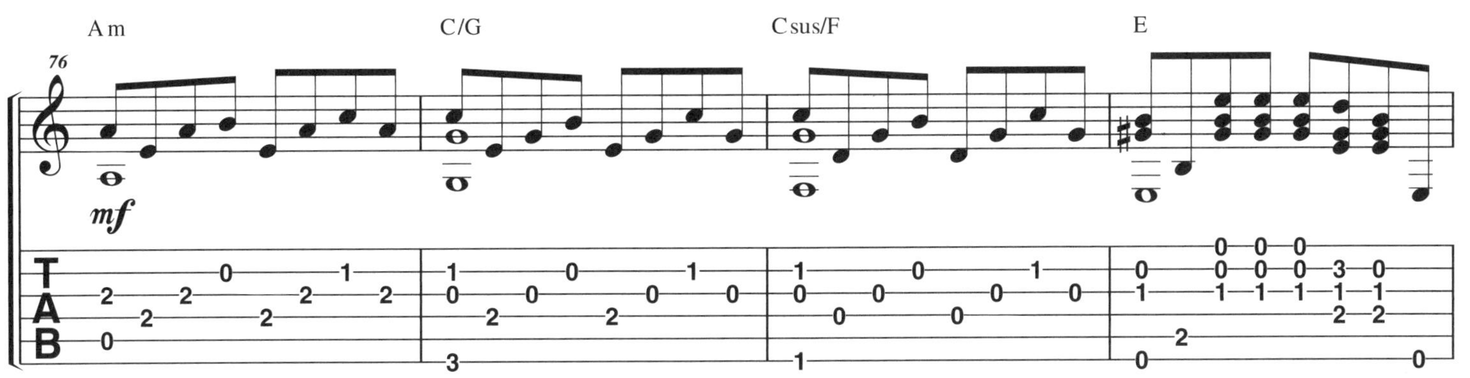
76
Am
C/G
Csus/F
E
mf
T
A
B

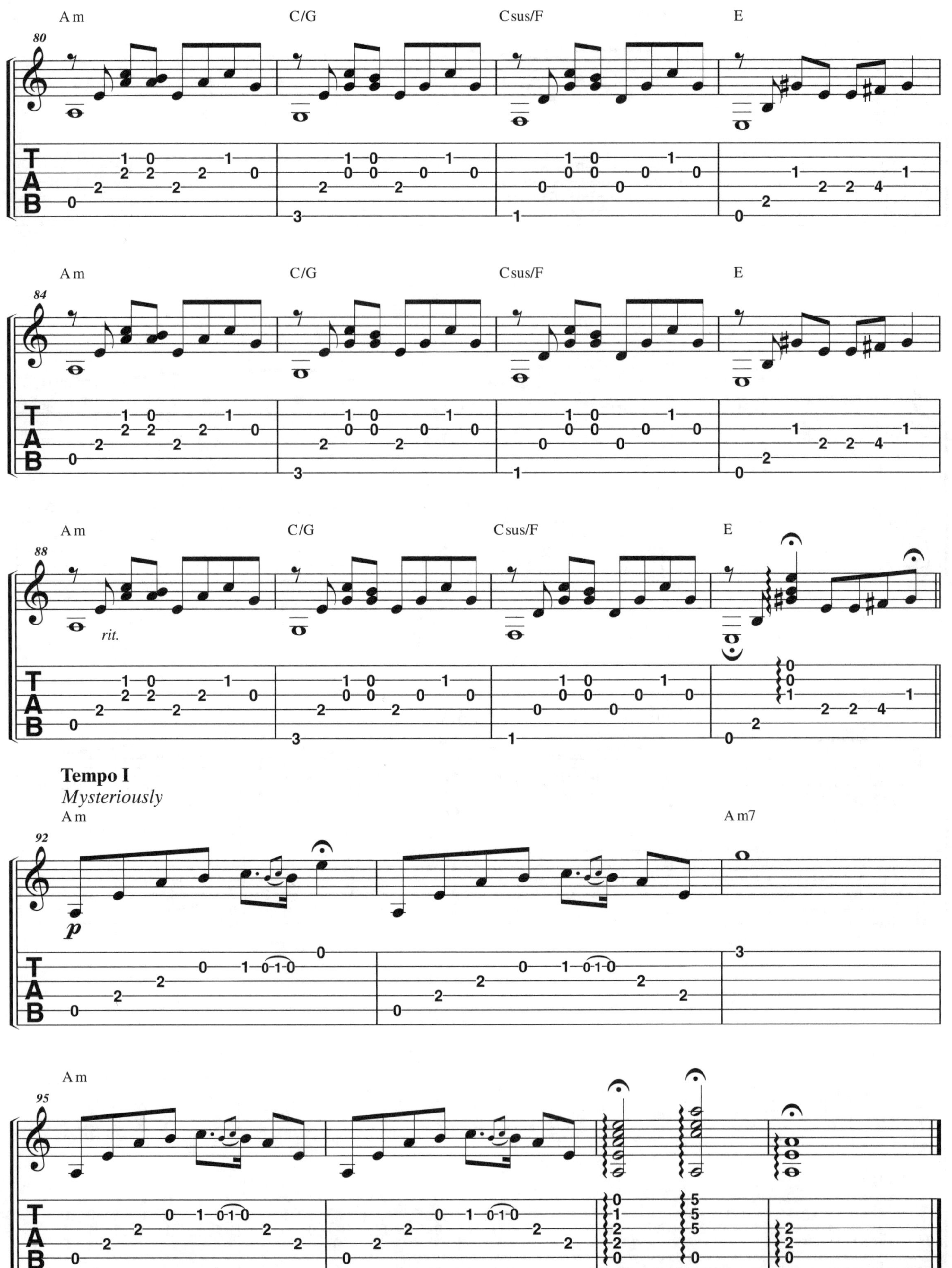
Am
C/G
Csus/F
E
80
84
88
rit.
Tempo I
Mysteriously
Am7
92
95
p